THE ROSENBLUTH CASE: FEDERAL JUSTICE ON TRIAL

THE ROSENBLUTH

JUSTICE

THE IOWA STATE UNIVERSITY PRESS, AMES, IOWA

CASE: FEDERAL ON TRIAL

ROSEMARY REEVES DAVIES

TO MY HUSBAND, PHILLIPS G. DAVIES

ROSEMARY DAVIES, Assistant Professor of English at Iowa State University, is author also of articles about Percy Shelley and Ernest Hemingway. Born in Sibley, Iowa, she received the B.S. and M.A. degrees from Northwestern University.

© 1970 The Iowa State University Press, Ames, Iowa 50010. All rights reserved. Composed and printed by The Iowa State University Press. First edition, 1970. International Standard Book Number: 0–8138–1375–1. Library of Congress Catalog Card Number: 70–116722.

CONTENTS

FOREWORD

THIS CASE of an obscure Jewish army captain who struggled for four years for exoneration from charges of causing the murder of an equally obscure Christian army major during World War I is in the same genre as the Haymarket riot, Dreyfus, Mooney-Billings, Sacco-Vanzetti, and Leo Frank cases, all occurring during the same period of about forty years. It had in it all the ingredients found in some or all of the other cases: anti-Semitism, antiradicalism, military self-protectivism, political ambition, bureaucratic ineptitude, and the all too human urge to vindicate a position hastily espoused.

None of these factors was as prominent in the Rosenbluth case as in the others. Anti-Semitism was there, but far from as dominant as in the Dreyfus and Leo Frank cases. The key to the Haymarket, Mooney-Billings, and Sacco-Vanzetti trials was in each instance antiradicalism; in the Rosenbluth case the Red scare of the early twenties was of minor significance. Militarism, along with anti-Semitism, was the key to the Dreyfus case; in the Rosenbluth case, though coupled with group loyalty to the obsessive General Cronkhite, it was little more than tangential. The political difficulties of Attorney General Daugherty and the presidential ambitions of Henry Ford contributed to Rosenbluth's tribulations, but they were hardly critical to the course of events.

Indeed, one who reads this account of the ordeal of Robert Rosenbluth can well conclude that substantially the same thing could have happened to him if he had been a minor middle-class Christian official in a civil service position during a placid political period, whose superior died from a gunshot while several members of the bureau were out hunting together on a holiday. In a sense it is just this which makes his story so fascinating and at the same time disturbing.

Although it received some degree of public attention at the time, the Rosenbluth case quickly disappeared from history. This was partly because the ordeal was comparatively brief and moderate—Rosenbluth was actually in prison only for a short period, and exoneration came while he was still a young man—and partly because the case lacked the dramatic elements of those mentioned previously. He achieved vindication because although he was a person of modest means he did have influential and wealthy friends who were convinced of his innocence and were willing to stake their political reputations, financial resources, and professional talents on the outcome. Had he been less fortunate in this respect, it seems highly probable that exoneration would not have come at all, or at best after death (as with some of the Haymarket defendants, Frank, and Sacco and Vanzetti) or after long years of imprisonment (as with the other Haymarket defendants and Mooney and Billings).

It is therefore difficult to escape the conclusion that there must be innumerable other Rosenbluths whose ordeals culminated less happily and never escaped from obscurity. It is because this account of what happened to Rosenbluth is essentially a case study in the ordinary rather than in the extraordinary that it merits careful and concerned study.

LEO PFEFFER
Chairman
Political Science Department
Professor of Constitutional Law
Long Island University

PREFACE

MY ACQUAINTANCE with the Rosenbluth case dates back to 1946, when my father and I sat alone in the family living room. He exclaimed suddenly, "Why, I haven't thought of that man in years," and called my attention to a magazine article about a man named Robert Rosenbluth. Then, stimulated by memories of the past, he began to tell me about being at the scene of the death of a Major Cronkhite, and he recalled the part that Rosenbluth and others had played in the subsequent investigation.

During World War I, my father, Lieutenant Fred D. Reeves, was assigned to the 213th Engineers stationed at Camp Lewis, Washington, and served as personnel adjutant of the regiment. The accident occurred during a hike through the wooded country surrounding Camp Lewis. After Major Cronkhite disappeared from view in a patch of brush, several shots rang out, and Captain Rosenbluth, who was in charge of the group, ran forward to see what had happened. He found the Major dying of a gunshot wound. As my father recalled the scene, Rosenbluth was going toward the sound of firing as it ceased, and certainly had been nowhere near when it began. He did not mention—or I have forgotten—the Major's orderly, Sergeant Pothier, who was with him at the time. Privately my father seemed certain the Major had committed suicide in a state of depression following an attack of influenza, but he said the official verdict of accident was generally accepted at the time without question.

Several years later the matter was reopened by the father of the dead officer, Major General Cronkhite, who believed that his son had been murdered. My father stressed the efforts made to show that Rosenbluth had gone forward before the shooting began, and since some years had passed, it proved very easy to confuse the witnesses and to get at least some testimony that tended to suggest murder. He also believed that anti-Semitism, so violent during the early 1920's, had a great deal to do with the case constructed against Rosenbluth.

Rosenbluth was arrested and charged with the murder of Major Cronkhite in 1921, and in 1924 when he was finally scheduled for trial, my father was subpoenaed as a witness for the defense. He and my mother, only recently married, made the trip together and enjoyed a pleasant holiday partly at government expense. The charges against Rosenbluth had been dismissed by the time they arrived in Tacoma, and the witnesses, assembled from all over the United States, were free to return home.

In his account my father stressed his admiration for Rosenbluth's recovery from the ordeal; he was very impressed that the man was able to overcome the handicap of the four-year struggle to clear his name and to establish himself in a worthy professional career. Although I received the impression that my father and Rosenbluth had not been intimate friends, I also am certain he considered Rosenbluth a man of great integrity, totally innocent of the murder of which he was accused.

The conversation was almost forgotten for many years, in fact until 1968 when I had the task of clearing the family home for sale. Amid the debris of seventy years of occupation, I found some records—letters from Rosenbluth to my father, an offprint of a magazine article on the case, and other materials. Out of simple curiosity, I began in the spring of that year to investigate, beginning with the *New York Times*. After setting up some tentative hypotheses on the affair considered purely as history, I discovered through the Yale University alumni office that Rosenbluth was still living. I wrote to him at his home in Chicago and received a most friendly and interested reply. He immediately sent me his unpublished autobiography, which contains an account of his ordeal, and after an exchange of letters we arranged an interview in the summer of 1968.

Robert Rosenbluth is eighty-three years of age, retired, and lives in a comfortable older apartment facing Lincoln Park and Lake Michigan. My husband and I arrived early for our appointment and met him as he walked up the street on his way from the grocery store. He is a short man, stocky and solid looking, and still resembles his photographs taken in 1919. We spent a pleasant afternoon with him, listening to his reminiscences about the case. He stressed throughout his discussion that the important thing to be considered was the travesty of justice that produced the charge in the first place. He believes, and I agree, that anti-Semitism, although it was part of the case, was far less important than the behavior of the U.S. Justice Department, the agency that undertook to investigate the major's death. He was able to supply me with important data, particularly a pamphlet issued by the state prosecuting attorney at Tacoma exonerating him from the murder charge and microprints of important stories that appeared in the New York *World*.

Particularly important to me, however, was the increased sense I received through talking and corresponding with Rosenbluth that the whole confused pattern of events was not merely a puzzle to be solved but an ordeal experienced by a particular human being, who even fifty years later is still vividly aware of what he endured—not only in personal inconvenience and a nearly ruined career but in the shocking discovery that an innocent man *can* be forced into such a position. In my struggles to disentangle the truth of the affair from a welter of newspaper accounts, Justice Department files, and personal letters, it was helpful to recall that the man to whom these things had happened was a real person, not an abstract historical figure. Without Robert Rosenbluth's help, both factual and personal, this book could not have been written.

Others have given me great assistance as well. I wish particularly to thank my colleagues at Iowa State University who through their enthusiastic encouragement and editorial assistance made my task easier: Dr. Keith Huntress who first read the manuscript, Dale Ross, Robert Hoover, Dr. Frank Haggard, Wayne Almquist, and Linda and Aubrey Galyon. In addition, I wish to thank Elizabeth Windsor, Head of the Iowa State University Library Reference Department; Ann Harlow, Chief of the Readers Service Division, United States Military Academy at West Point; Mark G. Eckhoff, Director of Diplomatic, Legal, and Fiscal Records at the National Archives; Major General Kenneth G. Wickham, The Adjutant General; Harold W. Anderson, Clerk of the United States District Court, Western District of Washington; Ernest W. Blue, who kindly lent me a copy of *Liberty* magazine from a private collection; Jacob R. Marcus, Director, and Stanley F. Chyet, Associate Director, of the American Jewish Archives; E. Berkeley Tompkins of the Hoover Institution on War, Revolution, and Peace at Stanford University; and Howard Sokol, formerly Assistant to the Dean of the Law School of the State University of Iowa, for his help in tracing certain legal records.

The greater part of material for this book is contained in National Archives File #211831, the Department of Justice records, 1920–1924, on the Rosenbluth case. While the file is not complete and certain important papers appear to have been removed or lost, it does contain an enormous body of information in the form of letters to and from Justice Department officials, interdepartmental memoranda, analyses of the case written by various people, affidavits, letters from interested private citizens and congressmen, newspaper clippings and other publications, the full transcript of the Rosenbluth hearing held in June 1921, testimony taken at the pre-grand jury conference in April 1922, and the full transcript of the grand jury proceedings. The file contains almost 4,500 pages of material and is divided into seven sections, with materials arranged in rough chronological order. In addition, there is a Special Enclosures Section which contains most of the lengthy documents—legal briefs, court proceedings, and the grand jury transcript, as well as many personal letters.

Other original materials have been useful. Robert Rosenbluth kindly supplied me with two important documents: his unpublished autobiography and a pamphlet "Exoneration of Captain Robert Rosenbluth." This pamphlet is available in the archives file on the case; another copy is in the American Jewish Archives in Cincinnati. The pamphlet reprinted the exoneration as published in the *Tacoma Ledger* in December 1921.

A transcript of the trial proved impossible to trace, although the records in the file show that the full proceedings were actually transcribed at the time. Correspondence with the Clerk of the Court of the United States District Court in Seattle revealed that materials on early cases filed at Tacoma were destroyed by order in 1958. Thus it was necessary to piece the trial together from the various newspapers which covered it extensively.

INTRODUCTION

THE CURRENT INTEREST in what President Harding hailed as
the Age of Normalcy reflects our realization that the twenties,
despite their isolationism and superficial cheerfulness, were in
a variety of ways similar to the sixties.

The short-skirted flapper has metamorphosed into the
miniskirted college girl; the rebellious expatriate of yesterday
has become the shaggy-haired militant on our campuses.

In the twenties youth questioned with ever-increasing
sharpness the values and goals of an earlier America. So it
does today.

The twenties was a period, like our own, of rising prices
and good living for those fortunate enough to enjoy prosperity;
at the same time it was a period of deprivation and hopelessness
for the poor, the minorities, and the underprivileged.

It was a period in which the rapid advance of technology
seemed to promise a vastly improved standard of living, and
simultaneously a time in which the value of such advances was
being questioned.

It was an age of change and of violent resistance to change.
The rapid rise of the Ku Klux Klan, the big Red scare, and
the fear of Bolsheviks and bearded anarchists are paralleled in
the 1960's by fears aroused by student violence, black militants,
Communism, and political assassination.

And it was, above all, a period in which a growing cynicism
and a distrust for those in authority became manifest. When
the great scandals of the Harding administration began to
break, the efforts of those who struggled to unravel the true
story of the graft and corruption were undercut by a general
feeling of disapproval aimed, not at the guilty, but at those
endeavoring to assign responsibility for misconduct. The public seemed to expect corruption in public life and was prepared
to tolerate it in exchange for being left free to develop its
private concerns.

Combined with this cynical attitude toward public life
was a growing tendency to fear and dislike the law and those
charged with its enforcement. Contempt for legal process is
in part a heritage from the frontier. But residual resistance to
formally organized authority was enormously increased by a
series of events in the twenties which placed law enforcement
agencies on all levels in villainous roles. The policeman or

detective from the local to the federal level was associated with the attempt to enforce Prohibition, with strike-breaking activity, with the mass arrests of alleged aliens and their subsequent mistreatment, and with the harassment of private citizens. Groups like the American Protective League in World War I, connected with the Department of Justice, degraded legitimate police investigation to the level of spying and malice.

On the federal level the growing power of the Bureau of Investigation and the steady reports of blackmail, the searching of mail and offices by its agents, and reports of "elaborate files of alleged information about sundry citizens suspected of radical affiliation," increased this uneasiness.[1] In addition, several notorious miscarriages of justice received wide publicity. The trial of Sacco and Vanzetti in 1920 and their eventual execution in 1927 did little to encourage respect for the honesty and integrity of law enforcement officials. Nor did the escape from justice of former Attorney General Harry M. Daugherty, tried in 1925 for fraud. The government failed to convict him because of the stubbornness of a solitary juror, generally assumed to have been bribed.

The case with which this book is concerned has vanished entirely from the history of the period, yet it undoubtedly contributed to the decline of respect for authority and to the growing distrust of federal justice. If Rosenbluth had been hanged for the murder of which he was accused, his story would be as familiar to us as that of Sacco and Vanzetti. But since he was ultimately cleared of the charge, the story of his battle for justice has slipped into oblivion. Yet surely the victories of those falsely accused are as important as the conviction of those probably innocent. The perversion of justice, whatever its outcome, is the concern of every citizen. That Rosenbluth escaped the gallows does not wipe out his four years of struggle and a nearly ruined career. Nor does it remove the conditions that made his ordeal possible.

One would like to believe that the conditions that produced his trial no longer exist, but we, like Rosenbluth, face the same problems: the enormous difficulties of correcting a mistake, once the forces of the prosecution are organized; the unbelievable complications involved in straightening out any error, however simple, when one is dealing with an enormous government department; the ease with which the prejudices and emotions of various groups may influence both prosecution and defense; and the sheer cumbersomeness of legal procedure, which may condemn both innocent and guilty alike to intolerable delays through the glacial slowness of the courts. And to these difficulties may be added another, still uncorrected: the nonexistence of any convenient method of legal redress. Regardless of the magnitude of the mistake and the emotional, financial, and professional damage to the accused, he has little or no recourse in law.

In his introduction to a recent study of the Leo Frank case, Harry Golden asserts that "nothing is so important in this world as an individual's guilt or innocence."[2] Upon this conviction rests the judicial system of every civilized country, and from it follows the legal principle established after centuries of trial and error: the forces of the prosecution must establish the guilt of the accused beyond a reasonable doubt. Ideally the personality, race, ethnic origins, and opinions of the accused are unrelated to his guilt or innocence; in practice they frequently affect the decisions of the investigating officials and the judge and jury. A serious miscarriage of justice ordinarily involves the prejudices, hatreds, and fears of the public and is often explained in these terms. Thus in the popular mind Captain Dreyfus was condemned to life imprisonment on Devil's Island because he was a Jew. Leo Frank was convicted of murder and died at the hands of a lynch mob because he was Jewish. Two Italian immigrants, Sacco and Vanzetti, died in the electric chair because they were anarchists and had avoided the draft in World War I. Much of the interest in these cases certainly was engendered by the emotional responses triggered by the arrests. To belong to an unpopular minority group or to hold unpopular opinions placed the accused in double jeopardy.

But in a very real sense the cry of "prejudice" obscures a more fundamental problem, profoundly dangerous to an effective judicial process and hence to all citizens. It is a problem that affects all police forces, judges, and juries, whether a minority group is in question or not. The three cases mentioned are parallel in this way: in each the forces of the prosecution attempted to construct a case against a man after he was arrested and charged. In theory the requirement that the police produce proof of guilt means that the evidence is followed where it leads, and the arrest is made in terms of objective probability. But occasionally this logical process is inverted. A likely suspect is seized, often on minimal or nonexistent evidence, and the investigation is organized, not to uncover the truth, but to gain evidence against the accused.

When this occurs, the prosecution is concerned not only to build a convincing case but to protect itself from criticism. Once legal processes are set in motion and the officials in charge committed to a particular suspect, there is a strong tendency to overlook evidence favorable to the accused, to encourage damaging testimony, and to exaggerate any available prejudice. A situation has been created in which jobs and reputations are at stake. How much easier it is to remain convinced of the guilt of the accused than to admit publicly (or even to oneself) that factual guilt or innocence is unimportant. No doubt a hatred of Jews, anarchists, and other minority groups assists in this process; but the fundamental error occurs when a case is constructed to fit a particular suspect, arbitrarily selected and charged.

It can be argued also that the routine of police investigation is better suited for dealing with known criminals than with amateur crime. Fictional detectives like Sherlock Holmes, Hercule Poirot, and Lord Peter Wimsey are attractive because of their assumption that the demonstration of innocence is as important as, if not more important than, the identification of the guilty. As W. H. Auden suggests in his essay "The Guilty Vicarage," the traditional detective story is an appealing form of escape fiction for many because the reader identifies with the "suspects" and for a moment at the conclusion is freed from guilt when the identity of the murderer is revealed. But the routine of ordinary police work is a very different thing from a leisurely one-case-at-a-time investigation. In the majority of robberies, murders, and assaults the police are dealing with known criminals and often have detailed information available about habitual patterns peculiar to particular criminals. They have the assistance of tips, inside information, and an understanding of the mentality of probable suspects. No doubt mistakes are made, but they are somewhat less likely to occur when the forces of the law are working within the environment of professional crime.

But when a given or suspected crime is clearly the work of an amateur, the various guidelines disappear. The dependable informer and the police dossier are no longer useful. The private crime can be solved only by a detailed investigation of particular evidence, and this slow and tedious process runs counter to the natural desire to find the guilty person promptly and to secure a tidy and efficient solution. Recent studies of contemporary crime—the Ronald Stump case and Sam Sheppard case in particular—suggest that official routine is liable to error when the crime is a private one and also show the extreme difficulty of reversing an established theory of a crime. Once a suspect has been selected and apparent evidence of his guilt secured, it is enormously difficult to introduce contradictory evidence or to gain a hearing for opposing theories.

The personal prejudices, ambitions, and private purposes of the prosecution can operate to bring about an unfair conviction. The apparent purpose behind the conviction of Captain Dreyfus in 1894 for treason was self-protection of the French high command and the officer who was actually guilty.

The fact that Dreyfus happened to be a Jew was useful in achieving acceptance of the verdict, but had the prosecution not had a Jewish captain handy, they no doubt could have used a non-Jew as a scapegoat. Self-protection, not anti-Semitism, was the primary motivating force behind the trial, the allegedly forged evidence, and the continued refusal to reverse the verdict.[3]

Desire to safeguard oneself or one's associates from blame is not the only reason for such tactics. The trial of Leo Frank in 1913 was complicated not only by the anti-Semitic prejudices of the Georgia community but by the political ambitions of the prosecution. The prosecuting attorney, Hugh Dorsey, had senatorial ambitions and recognized the value of winning a shocking and important case. A politician in decline, Thomas Watson, used the case as a basis for a series of violently anti-Jewish articles in his newspaper, *The Jeffersonian,* and was elected to the U.S. Senate on the strength of them.

Frank's sentence of execution was commuted to life imprisonment by John Slaton who, in his last week as governor of Georgia, acted to save a man he was convinced was innocent. Frank was later dragged from prison and lynched by an enraged mob of citizens; Slaton was forced by the intensity of public fury to leave Georgia and public life as a result of his interference.[4] Slaton shared the usual fate of those who try to interfere in such cases; Colonel Picquard, who attempted to convince his superiors that Captain Dreyfus was innocent, was eventually court-martialed.

In the Sacco and Vanzetti case, motives unrelated to the murder charge operated to cause their arrest. Justice Department agents had been investigating the pair with the hope of deporting them as anarchists, and they cooperated with the prosecution for murder in the hope of finding such evidence. One of these agents, Fred Weynand, later signed a deposition asserting that neither he nor others acquainted with the facts ever believed that Sacco and Vanzetti had committed the payroll robbery and murder and their conviction "was the result of cooperation between the Boston agents of the Department of Justice and the District Attorney."[5] Once under arrest and identified by eye witnesses who previously were unable to agree on their descriptions, the two men faced the violent antagonism of a prejudiced judge, whose hatred of the accused men's opinions shifted the case from a factual to an ideological level. Their eventual execution for a murder they almost certainly did not commit remains a permanent blot on American justice.

Perversion of justice, then, is likely to occur when the investigating authorities make a hasty arrest and then set out to construct their case after charges are filed. The natural reluctance to admit an embarrassing mistake—stronger if the accused is a man of previously good reputation—grows more intense as the case continues. One would suppose that those influential in securing the convictions of Dreyfus, Frank, and Sacco and Vanzetti would have been anxious to correct a possible mistake, but in fact the prosecution officials grew increasingly positive that no error had been made. Hugh Dorsey, the lawyer who conducted the case against Frank, maintained to his dying day that Frank was guilty, and claimed to be in possession of evidence proving his guilt completely. Judge Thayer, whose virulent urge to "get those anarchistic bastards" achieved their conviction, never doubted the complete rightness of his action. The military tribunal that condemned Dreyfus refused him an exoneration.

H. L. Mencken, commenting upon the continuing imprisonment of the Socialist leader Eugene Debs, remarked:

> The plain truth is that the plain people have very little liking for martyrs, and are not actively opposed to the injustices and atrocities which make them. It is one of the hardest things in the world, indeed, to stir up public indignation against legal injustice. . . . The sense of justice, like the sense of honor, is the exclusive possession of a small and usually miserable minority of men.[6]

That Mencken's cynical assertion has a solid basis in fact is shown in the Rosenbluth affair. Although it was called "the American Dreyfus case" in the press, it is in fact parallel with any and all cases involving a miscarriage of justice. Self-protection became more important than an individual's guilt or innocence, and the massed forces of the law were organized to shield themselves from blame and political reprisals. The enormous difficulty of the private citizen opposed to such forces is also pointed out by Mencken:

> The difference between the two gangs is that that of the professionals is supported by an unfair advantage—that it has the law on its side. It controls not only the executive and legislative arms; it also controls the courts, and what that advantage is worth has been shown in the cases of Daugherty and Wheeler. [After Senator Wheeler had successfully begun an investigation of the Justice Department, Attorney General Daugherty arranged to have him indicted in Montana for allegedly using his position illegally on behalf of private clients.] The other gang is almost unarmored. The Government is always able, when so disposed, to single out a few of its ring-leaders and clap them into jail. But the Government gang is well-nigh immune to punishment. Since the first days of the Republic less than a dozen of its members have been impeached, and only a few understrappers have ever been put into jail.[7]

Mencken's observations are applicable to the Rosenbluth affair in several ways, particularly in his remark that the government is immune to punishment. But more generally, both quotations imply that a love of justice is more likely to flourish among individuals. Even Mencken would not have denied that within the "Government gang" were many persons with a love of justice and a strong sense of personal honor. The problem is that a member of a large and complex organization may find it very difficult indeed to use his sense of justice to good effect. His position very probably depends to some degree upon his cooperation with his superiors. A subordinate official, even one quite highly placed, is not always free to do as he might prefer. He may be placed in the ugly position of having to risk his job or his chances of promotion. Or if he is highly enough placed to make interference possible, he is invariably vulnerable to political pressure. As the courageous interventions of Colonel Picquard and Governor Slaton attest, such men do exist; but it would be unrealistic to expect to find them in large numbers. It is also important to remember that these men were absolutely certain of the innocence of the accused man, and a savage sentence had actually been pronounced. A man less sure is correspondingly less willing to interfere; he may have doubts but be unwilling to act on them, particularly if the accused is not in immediate danger.

In any large organization one man seldom knows everything about a particular matter. Responsibilities are delegated; various aspects of research are parceled out to different people. The more people involved and the longer the case is studied, the more difficult it will become for any one person to marshal all the relevant facts. This is especially true of those who have no special responsibility to the case but have merely been assigned to assist. An attorney, for example, who is told to check certain legal questions will research these, without any need to study the case as a whole. A detective who is assigned to interview certain witnesses will do his task and file a report, without any knowledge of the reports of others or of the case as a whole. Furthermore, the employee will be working on many cases at once; his responsibility is divided among several different investigations. Actual responsibility for a decision thus is pushed up the line to senior officials who cannot follow each case in detail. These men must depend upon data assembled by subordinates and, in addition, are more likely to be vulnerable to outside pressures. The sheer size of government departments handicaps fair and efficient investigation and easily makes for deliberate complication of an essentially simple matter.

One of the minor mysteries of the Rosenbluth case is that it vanished utterly from public notice as soon as it was ended.

The leading protagonist, worn out from his four years of struggle and anxious to resume his long-interrupted career, declined various offers to write and talk about his ordeal. The second man accused was poorly educated and slipped inconspicuously back into his own world. Few of the many famous and near-famous people concerned in the affair were writers and of those who did publish autobiographies, Lewis Strauss was the only one to mention this case. Nor is it referred to in the many books published on the Harding administration, the decade of the twenties, and the scandals of the time. Although the case was covered extensively in the major metropolitan papers for more than three years and received detailed study in Henry Ford's *Dearborn Independent* and in the *Chicago Tribune,* no student of the period refers to it.

Several obvious reasons account for this neglect, of course; there were just too many scandals at the time. The intricacies of Teapot Dome quite naturally seemed more worthy of study. In addition, research on the case would have been very difficult until fairly recently, since the records of the Justice Department would not have been available. Just as the passage of time has made recent studies of President Harding possible by making his papers available to scholars, so the extended time has opened files that earlier would have been closed. And, sad to say, a case that has a nonfatal ending tends to attract less attention than a trial that ends in tragedy. The enormous volume of materials on the Sacco-Vanzetti case, for example, or the several studies published recently on the trial of Leo Frank, testify to the sustained interest that the execution or lynching of probably innocent men can create. If Rosenbluth had been hanged, I have no doubt his case would be as familiar to us as these others. But the trial ended with one accused man acquitted and the charges against the other dismissed. True to Mencken's assertion, we are not as interested in justice as in drama; the freeing of the innocent is not as exciting a "show" as the execution of a victim.

Thus it came about that a murder case which lasted from 1918 to 1924 and was for much of that time of national interest and importance vanished from memory. It is worth reviving, if only to partially disprove Mencken's observations. The contemporary distrust of the police and the expressed cynicism for legal processes are profoundly disturbing; they did not just happen. They have been produced over a period of years by cases like the one in question. Respect for the law and its enforcement cannot exist unless every citizen is reasonably safe from capricious arrest and machinery exists to permit efficient correction of the occasional mistake that will occur. It was the latter problem which contributed so heavily to Rosenbluth's growing bitterness under indictment. His initial belief that the affair could be settled quickly and his natural assumption that the Department of Justice was necessarily concerned with justice and truth weakened steadily as the years passed. His personal struggle for vindication became gradually submerged in a struggle on a higher level—to change, as he said, "a private wrong into a public good."

Since the Rosenbluth case is unusually involved and is undoubtedly completely unknown to the reader, a brief chronology should be helpful. The case enjoys the curious distinction of being a murder mystery which may not contain a murder; the mysterious features of the affair center on the behavior of the U.S. Department of Justice and its handling of the matter. On October 25, 1918, Major Alexander Cronkhite was shot and killed in Camp Lewis, Washington, and a board of inquiry decided that the wound was accidental and self-inflicted. Through the efforts of Major General Adelbert Cronkhite and his wife, the parents of the dead officer, the Department of Justice rather casually reopened the case in October 1920. Little was done until the change of administration in March 1921 and the appointment of Harry Daugherty as Attorney General. Then, a Bureau of Investigation agent was assigned to the case, and in March 1921 ex-sergeant Roland Pothier, the major's orderly, was taken into custody and persuaded into a series of confessions, finally alleging he had shot the major deliberately at the order of Captain Robert Rosenbluth. Rosenbluth was arrested at once as a result of this confession, which was retracted within a few days. The Justice Department was formally notified of the retraction in April, and a newspaper interview with Pothier in May publicized the methods by which the confession had been obtained.

Despite this the government did not drop charges against Rosenbluth, nor did it make any serious attempt to investigate the conduct of its agents. Instead, on July 19 Attorney General Daugherty ruled that the federal government had no jurisdiction over the offense, and charges were dropped prior to turning over all the files on the case to the state authorities in Pierce County, Washington. In December the state prosecuting attorney, after waiting for months for additional materials, published a formal exoneration of Rosenbluth, basing his judgment upon a limited number of documents in his possession: Pothier's confused "confessions," the fact that they had been retracted, the methods by which they had been obtained, and many affidavits attesting to Rosenbluth's character and distinguished reputation.

The Justice Department ignored this exoneration, and in January 1922 quietly resumed work on the case without notice to the accused. In October of that year the case was brought before a federal grand jury without explanation or excuse. In spite of the strenuous efforts of U.S. Attorney Revelle, who was totally convinced no case existed, the jury insisted upon indicting the two men for murder. Since Rosenbluth had been privately informed that the government had no intention of trying the case, he believed that the grand jury indictment was a reprisal for his demand for an exoneration from the federal authorities. Therefore, both he and Pothier resisted extradition to Tacoma on the grounds that the government lacked jurisdiction. This action went slowly through the courts and reached the Supreme Court in April 1924. This court held that the jurisdictional issue must be decided in the lower court appointed to try the case.

Six years after the death of Major Cronkhite, the case was finally brought to trial. Pothier was tried first and acquitted, and the charges against Rosenbluth were dismissed, it being obvious to Prosecuting Attorney Osborne (as it had been to most persons who seriously studied the affair) that no case against Rosenbluth ever had existed. Four years of his life had been lost, nonetheless, years for which he received no compensation or apology from those responsible.

ON OCTOBER 25, 1918, A HIKE BEGAN FROM
THESE UNPRETENTIOUS WOODEN BARRACKS
OF CAMP LEWIS, WASHINGTON, WHICH WAS
IN GREATER OR LESSER DEGREE TO AFFECT THE
LIVES OF THE MEN ON THE FOLLOWING
PAGES. . . .

THE LEADING CHARACTERS

Major Alexander P. Cronkhite,
whose death was alleged
to be murder.

**Sergeant-Bugler Roland R.
Pothier,** whose confessions,
elicited by improper
methods, were the basis
for the murder charges.

Captain Robert Rosenbluth,
who was accused of
masterminding the crime.

Colonel Robert S. Thomas, West Point officer in command of the 213th Engineers at the time of Major Cronkhite's death, privately criticized Rosenbluth as being "unmilitary."

Major General Adelbert Cronkhite, the father of the dead officer, who was convinced a sinister murder plot had been perpetrated against his son.

THE BOARD OF INQUIRY

Major Henry Tucker, whose testimony about powder on the dead man's uniform could not be remembered by Lieutenant Colonel Howard.

Major John F. Zajicek, who was accused of influencing witnesses to testify for "the honor of the regiment."

Lieutenant Colonel William J. Howard, who insisted that the fatal wound could not have been self-inflicted.

SOME OFFICERS AND MEN

Lieutenant Arthur Miller,
the intelligence officer who
was aware of speculation
among the men concerning
the accident.

Lieutenant Fred Rustenbach,
who thought there was
something "funny" about the
major's death.

Lieutenant Jay Morrison,
who among others believed
Pothier accidentally fired the
fatal shot.

Lieutenant Fred D. Reeves,
who believed the death was
suicide.

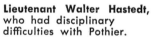

Lieutenant Elmer Seaburg,
who was the young doctor
attending Cronkhite at the
scene.

Lieutenant Walter Hastedt,
who had disciplinary
difficulties with Pothier.

Lieutenant Samuel Haag,
who denied that Cronkhite
and Rosenbluth had
quarreled.

Lieutenant Thomas J. Harron,
the regimental chaplain
who believed "natural
antipathy" and prejudice
were factors in the case
against Rosenbluth.

OF THE 213TH ENGINEERS:

Captain Eugene Caffey, who was a strong believer in Rosenbluth's innocence.

Lieutenant Donald Hannaman, who burned the dead man's uniform.

Sergeant Charles Wuthenow, who administered artificial respiration to the fatally wounded man; **Sergeant George Root,** who loaned his gun to Major Cronkhite and picked up exploded shells at the scene; and **Corporal Edward Tippel,** who testified as to Pothier's unpopularity.

THE ROSENBLUTH CASE: FEDERAL JUSTICE ON TRIAL

CHAPTER ONE
ACCIDENT AND AFTERMATH
OCTOBER 1918

THE THREE MEN whose lives became so fatally entwined at Camp Lewis, Washington, as World War I drew to a close, came from remarkably different backgrounds. The youngest of the group, Roland Roch Pothier, was born to a Roman Catholic family of French-Canadian descent and grew up near Providence, Rhode Island, among lower-middle-class laboring families. In personal appearance he possessed the build associated with the south European: he was very short and stocky, with small hands and feet and a dark complexion. He enlisted in the army in 1913 and served without any special distinction for three years, except for receiving the rating "Musician." His record was marred by a series of court-martials, most of which concerned minor offenses with the exception of one, being found guilty of sleeping while on guard duty. After leaving the army, he enlisted in the navy and in 1918 was given a bad conduct discharge, following a court-martial which found him guilty of "having the property of another in his possession."[1] In the summer of 1918 he was drafted into the army and assigned to Camp Forrest, Georgia, in the 213th Engineers, Headquarters Company. Although his service record does not mention it, he was made a bugler at Camp Forrest and subsequently was promoted to sergeant-bugler by his commanding officer, Major Cronkhite.

Pothier's promotion to noncommissioned officer rank was viewed with considerable disfavor by all the officers and men who were acquainted with him. He was considered untrustworthy and disagreeable by his associates, a reputation supported by his earlier service record. His arrival at Camp Forrest was described by a fellow sergeant, George Root:

> The first time I met Pothier was in Camp Forrest, Georgia. There was a bunch of men came down there from up in the New England states and New York and I had the job, you

know, of helping to round them out, and sort them out and
one thing and another. I took them over to the infirmary to get
their shots, you know, that is the typhoid vaccination and the
prophylactic. I met Pothier. He volunteered the information
that he was a bugler and could blow a bugle. These were just
men that were being conditioned and being selected for the engineer outfits. Pothier was negligent in his speech, really negligent altogether in his habits. He was very disagreeable. Very
disagreeable. He was very mouthy. He was disliked by everybody in the outfit with the exception of Major Cronkhite, because when he was assigned to the 213th he continued as bugler.
He was made sergeant-bugler. How he ever was made sergeant-
bugler has remained a mystery and always will remain a mystery, because as a bugler he was a good salesman. He was always running over to Major Cronkhite's quarters. We put him
down in the Army as what we call a boot-legger, [licker?] that
is he was running after some of the officers for favor or promotion. He was disliked by the rest of the buglers and all of the
men in the company. . . . There were little things missing—
fountain pens, blankets, there were several guns lost, there was
a camera and a few little things. A fellow lost a razor; just
petty—you know—annoying thievery.[2]

Root's comments are echoed by the enlisted men who later
testified before the grand jury. It proved impossible to pin
down the various witnesses to exactly what Pothier did that
was so disagreeable, but the reaction to him was definite and
strong. He is regularly described as "low-down," "rotten," not
the sort that "decent-brought-up young men would care to
spend any time with." Sergeant Tippel explained, "To be plain
no one ever had use for him—for him personally. . . . In the
Headquarters Company there was a little room off in the corner
of the barracks. This room we allotted to him in order to keep
him separate from the rest of us fellows. We allotted that room
to him just for the simple purpose of keeping him away from
our association."[3] Even those who were more charitable in
their comments agreed on the result; another sergeant said tact-
fully that most of the men in the barracks had some college
education and tended to avoid the poorly educated Pothier.

Similar opinions are voiced by the officers who had deal-
ings with him. Lieutenant Walter Hastedt first met Pothier
during a barracks inspection at Camp Forrest.* The other men
were standing at attention, but Pothier

was standing slouching, had his leggings off, and presented an
unmilitary appearance. His bunk was ruffled, while all of the
others were in very good shape. I questioned him . . . I didn't
know the man at all at that time. He said, "I don't have to
stand inspection," just in a surly manner. I said, "Why not?"

---

* The name is spelled Harstedd in the grand jury transcript, apparently an
error of the court reporter.

He said, "Why, I am teaching buglers." That was true enough, but I didn't know who he was at that time.

Hastedt's subsequent meeting with Pothier was even odder. An enlisted man, a "farmer sort of fellow," had come to the lieutenant to ask his help in recovering nine dollars from Pothier. "He said that about a month before he paid his bus fare and the driver handed back his change—he paid ten dollars and he handed nine dollars over the edge of the car, and Pothier grabbed it and ran down the street. He called him, and Pothier said, 'I will see you Monday.' " The man explained that he had tried several times to recover the money and feared that either he or Pothier would be transferred before he managed it. Hastedt talked to Pothier: "I asked Pothier if it was true, and he said it was. He didn't seem to think there was anything wrong. I finally got his signature on a little slip of paper that he would pay."[4]

Other officers had similar experiences. One captain (apparently Rosenbluth) was asked to speak to Pothier for his sullen refusal to salute and later delivered a talk to his company on the subject of such disagreeable behavior. The regimental chaplain, Lieutenant Harron, said he had loaned Pothier ten dollars, and when he threatened to report the matter, after waiting a long time for its return, Pothier paid him promptly. But the same day another sergeant reported having lost twelve dollars.[5]

Since Pothier had a general reputation as a thief, he was regularly assumed to be the culprit if anyone missed anything. The regimental surgeon, Major Henry Tucker, believed that Pothier had taken his .38 automatic pistol. Investigation, however, did not succeed in tracing the lost property to Pothier. His last court-martial found him guilty of a minor charge, that of being found in another part of the camp after being confined to the barracks area. Colonel Robert Thomas used the occasion to reduce him to private "Just on general principles. I had the authority to do it. . . ."[6]

In the opinion of almost all of his service acquaintances, Pothier was an unlikable and untrustworthy man. Thus it is rather odd that he succeeded in impressing one officer favorably, particularly since he and Major Cronkhite could hardly have been more different in background, education, and general temperament. Alexander Pennington Cronkhite stood at the opposite end of the social, educational, and moral ladder.

Cronkhite was an only son and descended on both sides from distinguished forebears. The West Point yearbook, *The Howitzer* for 1915, mentions that he traced his descent back to the early Dutch settlers of New York State. His paternal grandfather was Colonel Henry McLean Cronkhite, U.S. Army; and his maternal grandfather, Major General Alexander C. M. Pennington, was graduated from the U.S. Military Academy at West Point in 1860 and fought in the Army of the Potomac during the Civil War. His great grand uncle, Joseph Swift, was the first graduate of West Point in 1802, and several other relatives had taught there. His father, Adelbert Cronkhite, was graduated from West Point in 1882 and served with Pershing in the last campaigns against the Sioux in 1891. The elder Cronkhite served in various capacities before the First World War, and during the war was given the 80th or Blue Ridge Division, which he commanded with the rank of Major General in the final assault of the war, the battle of the Meuse-Argonne. On his mother's side he had connections who were in politics. William S. and William Pennington served as governors of New Jersey, the latter subsequently being Speaker of the U.S. House of Representatives. General Pennington was also a congressman.

With this sort of family history, Cronkhite's future was probably taken for granted. He attended Brooklyn Polytechnic Preparatory Institute and upon graduation entered the U.S. Military Academy at West Point. Possibly this choice of career represented his family's wishes more than his own, for his yearbook entry mentions that for the first few months he seemed present "in body only" and was markedly withdrawn in spirit from his classmates.[7] Much later a fellow officer who shared a hospital room with the major reported surprise at his suddenly saying he was tired of the military game and thought he would resign his commission after the war and go into business. But clearly, with the upright soldierly figures of both Penningtons and Cronkhites behind him, nothing could have kept him out of the academy except physical deformity or a strongly rebellious temperament.

Neither physical handicaps nor a rebel's nature were his. He soon settled down at West Point and eventually was graduated among the highest in his class, having distinguished himself as a marksman and as an athlete. He was notable as a wrestler and was credited with the ability to "twist himself into knots" while engaged in this sport. His yearbook page is decorated with a comic photograph of him—his feet around his neck, with legs clasped in his arms; apparently he amused his classmates with his unusual flexibility. His rapid advance in rank after graduation was caused both by the war and by his extremely successful military career. He was considered an almost perfect officer by those whose task it was to rate him; three years after leaving West Point, he held the rank of major in the Corps of Engineers and was in full charge of training the 213th Engineers for duty overseas.

Personally, Major Cronkhite was unusually attractive. Tall, blond, rather slender, and handsome in appearance, he was also blessed with an engaging and warmhearted personality. If it is true that almost no one spoke well of Pothier, it is also true that no one could be found who had anything but whole-hearted approval for Major Cronkhite. His fellow officers united in their praise of him as an excellent officer, a talented man in field tactics, and a first-class instructor. The enlisted men and noncommissioned officers were similarly enthusiastic; he was considered an ideal officer in every possible way. Even his friendship with Pothier was excused; most of the men explained it by saying the major did not realize the sort of man Pothier was. His popularity with the men and junior officers is probably best explained by his informality and complete lack of the autocratic severity sometimes found in academy officers. He could make criticisms of performance in a way that never caused any hard feeling, although he was also considered a strict disciplinarian and a model soldier.

His strictness, however, was never employed unless the occasion demanded it. The intelligence officer, Lieutenant Arthur Miller, said of him:

> We were a little unmilitary in our company. The Major and I used to have wrestling matches in the woods. He was a playful sort of a fellow. I got to be pretty familiar with him, as I did with about everybody else in that office. It so happened that every time he wanted anything he would say, "Jim, get this." That is a funny way to address a junior officer, but he did it.[8]

Cronkhite was young—twenty-five when he died—and would naturally have associated with the junior officers. He was apparently youthful in temperament also. He was regularly spoken of as a boy, not only by men older than he but by his contemporaries. But his boyishness was never criticized; no one suggested he was immature, but rather that he had the joyous spirit and openheartedness of a younger man. His nickname, Buddy, was used by his parents and intimates in preference to the formal Alexander.

There is really no way to explain such a man's friendship with Pothier except in terms of the major's genuinely friendly personality and interest in his regiment. He was said to know each and every one of his noncoms, and this interest very likely drew out an aspect of Pothier's personality which was never seen by the rest of the regiment. A possible link between the two was music. Cronkhite sponsored the regimental quartet and quite probably admired anyone lucky enough to have as good a singing voice as Pothier. Although the men seemed convinced that Pothier's attention to the major was inspired only by his desire for promotion, there is reason to believe that Pothier was really attached to Cronkhite. Several of the men reported that Pothier seemed much more withdrawn and quiet after the major's death; he saved the field notebook in which the major had been writing and carefully recorded on the final page, "The last handwriting of Major Cronkhite."[9]

The third member of the trio was Captain Robert Rosenbluth, who represented yet a third sort of background and education. His parents emigrated from Russia to this country in the 1880s, having been forced to leave their homeland for political reasons.[10] With Russian friends they worked for five years on a communal farm near Grant's Pass, Oregon. When the community was disbanded, the Rosenbluths moved to New York City, where their second son, Robert Owen—named for the British Socialist—was born. Robert Rosenbluth was precocious, and his family clearly a remarkably intelligent one. His mother studied for and received a medical degree after her children were born. When Robert was eight, the family moved to Philadelphia, where his father was employed as a hospital superintendent and his mother as a doctor. He attended a demanding high school, and although delayed by a year's illness, was graduated at sixteen. He then entered Pennsylvania State Agricultural College, majoring in forestry. This rather unusual major was his personal choice; he had been inspired by the example of conservation leaders like Gifford Pinchot to enter what was at that time a very new field of endeavor. He transferred to the Yale Forest College for his junior year and was graduated in 1907 with a degree of Master of Forestry.

Thus Rosenbluth had ten years before the war to establish himself professionally. He entered the U.S. Forestry Service and volunteered for duty in the Philippine Islands, where he and three other foresters trail-surveyed the unknown interior. When he returned to the States in 1910, he was put in charge of the original surveys of rugged country in Utah, Nevada, and northern Arizona, working under the most primitive and adventuresome conditions.

He then joined the New York State Forest Service as director of forest investigation and drifted into what was to be a lifetime career in social service work through a scheme of his to use the land around state penal institutions as a means of rehabilitating prisoners. He was allowed to try his plan at Dannemora, a security prison for repeating offenders, after a riot there destroyed what few work facilities the prison possessed.

Assisted by one civilian, Rosenbluth worked with twenty convicts and was extremely successful in training them in forestry techniques. His plan expanded to include more men and attracted nationwide attention. Just as he had been inspired to become a forester when this was a relatively new profession, he moved into prison reform when there was a growing feeling that prisoners should be helped to adjust to future life by learning suitable trades rather than idly waiting out their sentences for years.

While he was engaged with his convict gang, he stumbled on another enterprise by discovering the original survey marks of the area. From these marks, which determine legal boundaries (if they can be found), he realized that the recorded surveys were seriously in error. He was unable to interest state officials in his discovery and went ahead on his own, tracing records and exploring statehouse documents. Finally his case was complete, and the courts awarded thousands of acres of timberland to the state of New York as well as a substantial cash payment from the Delaware and Hudson Railroad, whose subsidiary, the Chateaugay Ore and Iron Company, had been cutting timber on state land. The *New York Times* reported in March 1923 that a court of appeals had just upheld the original decision and credited Rosenbluth personally for the recovery of the land. He reports in his unpublished autobiography that during his original researches he was offered a sizable bribe to persuade him to drop the matter.

His successes at Dannemora led a noted sociologist, Dr. Katherine Bement Davis, to persuade him to leave forestry temporarily to become the head of the New York City Reformatory. This departure from his original career turned out to be permanent; Rosenbluth's career—which did not end until age eighty when he retired from the position of assistant commissioner of public aid in Cook County, Illinois—was concerned with various kinds of social and institutional work. After resigning his position with the New York Reformatory, he joined the staff of the Institute of Public Service, a New York foundation devoted to assisting in city planning and the spending of public moneys and to promoting and improving good government. Again he was instrumental in preventing a costly mistake. An exchange of land between the city and the New York Central Railroad was proposed for the purpose of permitting the railroad to relocate its tracks. Rosenbluth and an assistant investigated the arrangement and found that the trade was not an even one; the railroad would make a profit of about $15 million on the exchange. This information was presented by Rosenbluth at a meeting of the Board of Estimate which was attended by Mayor Mitchell. The mayor demanded to know if

Rosenbluth's figures were correct, and the city comptroller admitted that a mistake might have been made. The trade was called off as a result of this session.

Rosenbluth on the eve of World War I was a man of very great physical and mental energy, considerable intelligence, and enormous determination. He enjoyed the very real hardships of life in dangerous places and was indifferent to physical danger and pressure. He could not be turned aside from a job by apathy or by antagonism. His impulse when he saw a mistake was to correct it, and he was stubborn enough to refuse any suggestion of compromise in a matter involving right and wrong. His work had brought him to the attention of prominent men and women, who were impressed by his capabilities. In addition he very likely had made some enemies; his determination to rectify mistakes undoubtedly offended those who lost by his correction.

These qualities were displayed by his behavior when the United States entered the war. He volunteered for service at once, trained at Plattsburg, New York, and was informed he was to be assigned to the Port of New York with the rank of major, having made a reputation as an authority on terminal and loading problems. However, he wanted to go to France; and when his superior officer refused to release him, he asked for the help of the Assistant Secretary of the Navy, Franklin Roosevelt. Roosevelt, much amused at the spectacle of a man trying to avoid a major's commission, discussed this problem with the Assistant Secretary of the Army and explained that the only way to manage was to leave for France at once. Commissioned as a first lieutenant, Rosenbluth sailed for the front that night. Roosevelt persisted for the rest of his life in addressing his friend as Major Rosenbluth, ignoring protests that he had never risen higher than captain.

Rosenbluth was trained overseas and saw active duty with the First Division, First Engineers, in the spring of 1918. A superior officer, Ross H. Boas, later described the way he had reported Rosenbluth's work:

> Your services had been of the best and I emphasized several duties which you had executed in exceptional manner, for example, the general handling of the regimental prisoners; the manner in which you got ammunition quickly to our alert position on the night that a boche attack was expected; and the exceptional manner in which you handled your platoon the night we worked on a communication trench to the 18th infantry, P. C. and during which we were severely bombarded.[11]

Another officer, Colonel A. D. Akin (Reserves) said, "I will say that your energy, 'pep,' and habit of getting things done and your absolute subordination to authority gave me a very fine regard for you and it was on these grounds that I recommended your promotion from the rank of first lieutenant to that of captain. . . ."[12]

Rosenbluth's war record, then, parallels his civilian one. Apparently he was at his best in circumstances which demanded prompt action, when delivering the ammunition or getting the trench dug were far more important than following the rule book or paying strict attention to the correct procedure. As a result he was more highly regarded as a soldier by those who knew him in France than by those who worked with him in the United States. The commanding officer of the 213th Engineers, Colonel Robert Thomas, supported Rosenbluth in public statements very vigorously but in private tended to criticize him as "unmilitary." He was not, in other words, a parade-ground soldier; in the army as in private life he was always more concerned with results than with the rules.

An anecdote from his civilian career illustrates this well. When he was in charge of a reform school for older male teenagers, he was regularly challenged by the authorities for permitting the boys to smoke. In fact, he issued three cigarettes a day to those who wished them, convinced that the bad effects, if any, were far outweighed by the elimination of smuggling and secret smoking—a major problem with young men who had been smoking for years. State law forbade smoking by inmates of juvenile schools, but to Rosenbluth the law was less important than the correction of a disciplinary problem.

Rosenbluth was sent home from France after undergoing a major gas attack and artillery bombardment that placed him in the hospital for a time. He requested permission to remain in France, but his request was refused because of the great demand for instructors with combat experience. After his promotion to captain, he was assigned to Camp Forrest and joined Pothier and Cronkhite in the 213th Engineers. Although Rosenbluth had almost no contact with Pothier then or later, he and Major Cronkhite became friends at once. Lieutenant Hastedt recalled that Cronkhite on several occasions asked Rosenbluth to talk to the noncommissioned officers school, to share valuable information gained from his combat experience. Lieutenant Miller—although he, like several other men and officers, considered Rosenbluth a poor drillmaster—asserted that Cronkhite thought him a "damn good man to have around" and was willing to overlook his limitations "because of other things that offset that."[13] As a result, when the regiment was skeletonized to go to Camp Lewis, Rosenbluth, who had at first been assigned elsewhere, was included in the group at the last moment at the suggestion of Major Cronkhite.

The slow train moved west, stopping daily for exercise marches and guard problems; the officers in the compartment section—Colonel Thomas, Major John Zajicek, Major Cronkhite, and Lieutenant Donald Hannaman—whiled away the time playing bridge; the men gossiped, smoked, and endured the journey. The dreaded influenza was beginning to appear, and one man after another, including Major Cronkhite, became ill on the way. The sullen, poorly educated Pothier, who had spent his entire adult life as an enlisted man; the boyish, brilliant Cronkhite, who seemed headed for a distinguished military career; and the equally brilliant Rosenbluth, who had already established himself in several professions, were linked fatally together. It is possible to wonder at the chain of circumstance that brought these three to the same place at the same time. What if Pothier had not received a bad conduct discharge and had remained in the navy? What if Cronkhite had not succumbed to influenza during the trip west? What if Rosenbluth had not been suddenly assigned to the regiment? The tiny bits of the mosaic were in place, nonetheless, as the train crawled westward.

II

UPON ITS ARRIVAL at Camp Lewis on October 8, 1918, the regiment was very small, consisting of only 20 officers and 178 enlisted men with an additional 3 officers and 24 enlisted men in the sanitary detachment. Six hundred men were to have been added to the group at once, but the plans for enlargement and immediate last-minute training quickly collapsed. Colonel Thomas described the arrival:

> We were immediately put in quarantine. . . . The Flu was raging there. Immediately we were put in quarantine and not allowed to leave the camp area. A guard was put around the camp. The scheme was to push them through with quick training. That scheme was knocked in the head. So we had these 175 men with the possibility of an indefinite stay of two or three weeks or a month.[11]

In addition to the disruption of plans for training, the regiment was severely handicapped by its tiny size and by the flu. Many of the men were ill; among the officers, Major Cronkhite and Lieutenant Saunders went from the train to the base hospital and spent almost two weeks there, sharing a room for a time.

The regiment was struggling with a series of difficulties at a time when the war itself was at a crucial stage. American, French, and British forces were massing in France for what turned out to be the final assault on the German line. The influenza epidemic and a delay in the draft had held down the number of overseas sailings of troops, and constant pressure was applied to ready the 13th Division for embarkation to France. In this atmosphere of pressure and tension the senior officers decided a few days before official lifting of the quarantine to take a battalion on hike into the wooded country surrounding the camp.

As most of the officers remember it, the hike of October 25 was planned primarily as exercise to give some relief to men who had been confined to the camp area for more than two weeks. The colonel explained it was his custom to order such exercises for a particular day but to leave specific plans and destinations to Major Zajicek. Colonel Thomas was uncertain if he had talked over possible destinations with any of his officers: "If I did so it is that they came up to me and asked me where they ought to go. We talked over these things very informally and discussed them freely.[15] He did recall a discussion the previous evening about plans during which he told Major Cronkhite, just out of the hospital, that he did not have to go if he did not feel like it. According to the hospital records Cronkhite was released on October 21, his record marked "Duty," but his hesitation in deciding to accompany the battalion suggests he was not feeling entirely fit. During the evening discussion Major Zajicek tried to persuade him to go along, offering him the loan of a horse for the trip, but Cronkhite replied jokingly, "You go straight to hell."[16] Other officers remembered his saying he would wait until morning and see how he felt; there was universal agreement he was uncertain about going until the very last minute.

The morning of the hike several other changes were made. Captain Eugene Caffey, pressed with paper work, decided not to accompany the battalion; and Major Zajicek and Lieutenant Milo Orr rode out toward Lake Nisqually by a different route, with the plan of meeting the battalion for the noon field-cooking exercise. Zajicek and Orr left somewhat later than the hikers, delayed by Zajicek's being thrown from his horse and by various accidents en route. The battalion was formed at 7:30 a.m., and due to last-minute changes of plan Captain Rosenbluth found himself unexpectedly in command, heading the column rather than marching back with his own outfit, Company D. The only other officers accompanying the group were lieutenants Miller, Rustenbach, Reeves, Morrison, Haag, and Seaburg, who was a doctor.

Just as the battalion was ready to leave, Major Cronkhite decided to accompany it. He told Captain Caffey "it was a good day and he wanted to go out and take a walk, and stretch his legs."[17] Sergeant Root, who was a member of the group, seemed certain that Cronkhite was not in command of the column. "Captain Rosenbluth was really in charge of it. That is, Major Cronkhite took more or less the attitude of going along for the fun of it to get the air or exercise."[18] The major borrowed a .45 Colt revolver from Root at the last minute, his own gun being out of commission. Lieutenant Hannaman, the regimental adjutant, remembered Cronkhite going through his office on his way to the woods, "like a boy going off on a lark."[19] Major Cronkhite took a companion with him to act as his orderly, Sergeant-Bugler Roland Pothier. Despite his high spirits as he left, many of the men recalled he seemed white and tired later. They believed that the long walk had been too much for him after his recent illness.

The major and his orderly eventually overtook the column, but did not join it. Cronkhite strolled along at his leisure, leaving Captain Rosenbluth in charge. He assisted with some advance guard problems designed to simulate traveling through enemy country and went ahead of the group to send back orders as an advance scout. Several of the men recalled that one of the captain's responses did not satisfy Cronkhite, and he came back to notify the captain he should have found out first how many "enemy" had been sighted before issuing his order. Although there is some conflicting testimony on this point, most of the men in a position to hear did not recall any heated argument or serious disagreement between the two officers. Sergeant Charles Wuthenow reported that Major Cronkhite said to the captain, "What the hell are you trying to do—kill all your men?"[20] but there is no reason to suppose the remark was made harshly or even that it was an accurate quotation. All of Wuthenow's testimony before the grand jury is studded with profanity; quite possibly he rephrased the criticism in his own language. He also said Captain Rosenbluth made no reply, and another sergeant remembered that the captain took the rebuke very good-naturedly.* Since, of the fourteen men and officers who were later interrogated about the hike and were in a position to see and hear, only one—ex-sergeant Samuel Moore—asserted that Captain Rosenbluth replied with anger and insubordination to his superior officer,[21] his testimony could be discarded as malicious or mistaken. Other sergeants standing near the scene did not remember the major speaking critically to Captain Rosenbluth at all.

After the guard problems were finished, the column was ordered to fall out for a rest in a field near an abandoned

---

* Rosenbluth assured me in July 1969 that Wuthenow's testimony about the Major's supposed remark was entirely a figment of his imagination.

schoolhouse; while the men rested, Rosenbluth and Cronkhite, maps in hand, discussed which of two routes to take. The intended road led to the left, but a machine gun installation in the vicinity created some possibility that the road might be dangerous. A great effort was made during the grand jury hearing to show that the road was not guarded, in order to suggest that the change in route was not necessary, but part of a deliberate plot. Some of the men recalled seeing a guard or at least a warning sign, and a few thought they remembered hearing firing. Others did not recall either a guard or the sound of guns. There was, of course, very little reason for most of the men to remember one way or the other, since most of the column did not know either the planned route or the destination and attached no importance to the final order to turn to the right.

In a conversation with Rosenbluth in July 1969, he assured me of his certain conviction that the road was both posted and guarded and his decision to turn to the right resulted from a conversation with the guard. The correctness of this memory is borne out by an affidavit made before the trial in 1924, in which Rosenbluth requested that ex-major Samuel Royse and other members of the machine gun battalion be subpoenaed, since they could testify Rosenbluth had learned from consultation with them that the route of march would have to be changed to avoid the artillery range.

Despite his certainty on this point I think it possible his memory might be inaccurate. Lieutenant Chambliss testified before the grand jury that he was working that day on the target range with a number of men digging trenches and no firing was permitted. Chambliss remembered the day in question because the runner came to his group to request an ambulance after the shooting.[22] Chambliss had no other connection with the case and would not have had any reason for giving misleading information. In addition, in Rosenbluth's testimony before the board of inquiry he made no mention of fears that he had led his men into a target area; instead he spoke as if he feared an accident to Major Cronkhite as soon as he heard the shots. Perhaps on a later hike he encountered the guarded road, and subsequently confused these two occasions.

Another detail suggesting some confusion is that Rosenbluth cannot now recall seeing or talking with Major Cronkhite during this halt; his present recollection is that he did not see Cronkhite at all until just before the tragedy. However, the memories of many others contradict this. Many of the men recalled the two officers discussing the road in a friendly way, and several were sure Major Cronkhite was determined to turn

to the right. One sergeant made the sensible suggestion that
Rosenbluth could not have ordered the change against Major
Cronkhite's wishes; if the major had not wished to turn right,
he could have countermanded the captain's order. Lieutenant
Seaburg, although not too dependable as a witness, recalled
the major saying jokingly of the rejected road, "We won't go
that way—I am not ready to die yet."[23]

In any event, the column turned right and entered a section of dense forest, proceeding single file down a narrow trail.
After a half-hour or so the column received the order to
halt, and either before or immediately after this order several
pistol shots rang out. Although again there is some contradiction in testimony, the majority of the men recalled that Captain Rosenbluth ran forward after the shots began and was
disappearing as the second or third shot was fired. Some recalled he halted the battalion because of the shots. As Rosenbluth now recalls the scene, the men were halted for a prescribed rest stop when the shots rang out. Since the country
was unknown to him except from maps and they had just been
warned away from an artillery range, he supposed the alternate
road had swung back into the danger zone and ran forward
at once to investigate.

Before the halt occurred, Major Cronkhite and Sergeant
Pothier were seen strolling forward about fifty yards ahead of
the column, and they disappeared into a dense patch of brush.
A slight hill, a curve in the road, and the thickness of the underbrush made it impossible for anyone to see them. When Rosenbluth reached the scene, he found Major Cronkhite engaged
in target shooting, aiming at a tobacco can set on a post. He
was standing on the road at the entrance to an abandoned
farm, and since he was well ahead of the battalion and the farm
buildings were clearly uninhabited, apparently had decided that
informal shooting was safe. Captain Rosenbluth commented
jokingly that the major had made a clean miss, and Cronkhite,
challenged by the remark, turned again and fired at the can,
hitting it. He turned to his friend and called out, "I got it
that time, Rosie," and the revolver somehow slipped backward
in his hand. As his fingers automatically tightened to straighten
the twisted revolver, the gun, which had a lighter pull than
most, discharged, aimed back at the major's body. He fell to
the ground, calling out, "My God, I'm shot," and Rosenbluth
rushed forward to his assistance.[24]

Despite the major's choked cry as he fell, Captain Rosenbluth was unable to see any sign of a wound or bleeding in his
first hurried examination. He quickly looked at the heart and
the neck, and seeing no sign of injury, concluded that the major
had had a heart attack—his recent hospitalization and apparent

weakness lending credence to this idea. Rosenbluth rushed back to the road, called for the doctor, Lieutenant Seaburg, and returned to the major. Seaburg double-timed forward accompanied by two medical orderlies and found Major Cronkhite on the ground, his head held by Captain Rosenbluth; Pothier was standing nearby. Unaware that the major had been shot, Rosenbluth urged the doctor to give him a stimulant, and Seaburg, with trembling hands, began to prepare an injection of strychnine. In the meantime two sergeants, Root and Wuthenow, came forward in response to a call for men with knowledge of artificial respiration. Assisted by the orderlies, these two attempted to revive the major, although it was evident he was dead or dying. The injection was given, and shortly thereafter one of the assistants—Wuthenow and Medical Orderly Croy both claimed the honor—opened the major's shirt fully and discovered a bullet hole high in the right chest. As Wuthenow reported it, he cried out, "Why the man's been shot!" and the doctor replied, "Why so he has."[25]

Those who studied the case later found it very difficult to believe that witnesses to the accident would have been unaware the major had been shot or that the doctor would not have looked carefully for a wound. But the nature of the wound made its delayed discovery perfectly possible. According to the autopsy performed shortly after death, the bullet entered the body about three inches above the right nipple, passed slightly upward and backward through the torso, smashing the aorta and lungs, and lodged in the left shoulder muscle. There was almost no external bleeding, the shirt and uniform blouse were unmarked, and the undershirt was only slightly stained.[26] Only a tiny hole in the right flap of the blouse marked the bullet's entrance. Given the sudden emergency and the major's recent illness, the mistake in judgment was not surprising. The doctor's failure to check seems more unusual, but Dr. Seaburg was very young and just out of medical school. There is little doubt that he panicked and did not function as efficiently as a more experienced doctor would have. In a later affidavit he carefully avoided mentioning that it was not he who discovered the wound, nor did he admit this to the grand jury until specifically asked. He also admitted his intense relief when the autopsy showed that no treatment could have saved Major Cronkhite.

After the wound was found and the major clearly dead, the body was straightened, covered with a raincoat, and placed under guard to await the ambulance. During the confused attempts to assist Cronkhite, Rosenbluth sent his fastest runner to the nearby artillery range for help; later he sent two other men, Lieutenant Morrison and Sergeant Rooney, back to headquarters. While they waited for the ambulance, the cause of the accident was discussed. The tobacco can and four empty shells were collected, and the revolver and the major's haversack and hat set aside. The artillery range ambulance arrived within a short time, and the body and equipment were loaded in it. Some disagreement arose later about who rode back in the ambulance, but apparently Rosenbluth, Seaburg, and Pothier accompanied the body and were with it when it was delivered to the base hospital. The men in the column had been taken earlier into a nearby field where they could rest, and they were eventually marched back to camp by a lieutenant, stopping en route for lunch. A second ambulance sent from headquarters passed the men as it was going toward the scene but arrived some time after the major's body had been removed.

At the base hospital Major Cronkhite's body and his possessions were turned over to the officer of the day, Lieutenant Wallace, who placed the gun and holster and the major's watch in his safe, where they remained for several days before being turned over to the board of inquiry. The shells and the tobacco can were given to Lieutenant Colonel Howard by Captain Rosenbluth. Wallace asked the three men to write out separate statements of the accident, and they did so. He read them as he received them and sealed each in an envelope before turning them over to the commanding officer of the base hospital. These statements, oddly enough, completely disappeared. As far as is known, no one but Wallace ever read them, and they were never traced later. Wallace also caused some confusion by his insistence that the gun turned over to him was a .38 caliber automatic with three shells in the clip. The gun Major Cronkhite had borrowed from Sergeant Root was a .45 Colt revolver, and the introduction of a different type of gun later appeared sinister.[27]

No one thought of it at the time, but it is possible that a simple explanation exists. Lieutenant Morrison, who was sent several miles to headquarters as a runner, left his gun, holster, and haversack near the body when he left on his errand, returning with the ambulance to reclaim his property. At the grand jury hearing he did not remember whether or not he had found his equipment on the ground at the scene or whether it had been returned in the first ambulance. Quite possibly it was dumped in with the other equipment, and Lieutenant Wallace was given Morrison's gun, apparently a .38 automatic. Lieutenant Rustenbach seemed certain that Morrison carried this type of weapon, and during Morrison's testimony the same thing was implied. When Morrison spoke of the major's "pistol," he was asked if he used the word exactly; he at once denied it, saying he was sure the major was carrying a revolver. Later, while explaining about leaving his own weapon at the scene, he consistently called it a pistol.[28]

It is possible, then, that the officer of the day was given the wrong gun. Presumably it was eventually returned to its owner, but no one attached importance to the incident or recalled it. Wallace, of course, would never have known that the gun in his custody turned out to be another's property. Another minor confusion was the loss, unnoticed at the time, of the major's campaign hat. Lieutenant Saunders remembered seeing it near the open door of the ambulance, and in all probability it simply fell out and was never missed.[29]

Later in the afternoon an autopsy—really a postmortem— was performed by Dr. Ernest Sommer, who was in the morgue doing routine autopsy work. He opened the chest, traced the course of the wound, and extracted the bullet, dictating his findings to a nurse as he did so. Apparently Rosenbluth, Seaburg, and Major Tucker were present at the autopsy; Sommer testified to the grand jury with the greatest assurance that he had no doubts at all about the sincerity of those who witnessed the tragedy. He admitted surprise at the angle of the wound but assured the jury he had had considerable experience with sudden death—he had served for many years as a coroner— and was completely convinced of the naturalness and genuine grief of those who explained the accident. Dr. Sommer did not, however, sign the postmortem report and later said he never saw it in written form. It was signed routinely by the chief of laboratory service, Major Staniford. When shown the report several years later, Sommer agreed it appeared to be somewhat inaccurate; he explained, for example, that he always indicated the presence or absence of powder burns in a shooting case, and this information was not included. He thought, however, that the nurse taking down the information in longhand had not been able to keep up with him.[30] There had been, in fact, no sign of powder burns on the skin around the bullet hole; witness after witness reported it was the cleanest wound he had ever seen—small, neat, relatively bloodless, and in no way burned from powder.

Later that day or early the next the summary court officer, Lieutenant Colonel William Howard, held a preliminary hearing roughly equivalent to an inquest in civilian life. His hearing was quite informal; he talked the matter over with the principal witnesses, interrogated a few other men briefly, and reported his findings orally to Colonel Thomas. Greatly grieved at the major's death, Thomas did not wish to be personally involved in any investigation of it and appointed a board of inquiry to make the necessary investigation. But as it was subsequently discovered that this board must be appointed by the commanding officer of the base, the final order came from him.

Since the board of inquiry that investigated Major Cronkhite's death was later criticized severely for the perfunctory nature of its proceedings, the questionable legality of its procedures, and the probable motivations of its members, the various factors which operated to produce a demonstrably casual investigation should be explained. The board was directed by Major General Leitch, the base commander, to inquire into the death of Major Cronkhite and to investigate the possibility that the officer had met his death through willful misconduct. The three members of the board—Lieutenant Colonel Howard, Major Zajicek, and Major Tucker—met for perhaps an hour, questioned the three principal witnesses—Rosenbluth, Seaburg, and Pothier—and concluded that the cause of death was an accidental, self-inflicted wound and the major had not been guilty of misconduct.

It is quite apparent that the board had already substantially decided upon its verdict and the inquiry was a mere formality. The first question asked, "You were present when the Major shot himself?" clearly implies that the interrogator assumed the wound was self-inflicted. Similarly, discrepancies in testimony were ignored. Pothier said first that he did not see Rosenbluth until after the major was shot; a moment later he asserted that Rosenbluth came up just before he was shot; a few questions later, he said "Rosenbluth come up while Major Cronkhite was shooting." But apparently no one considered it necessary to ask him which of these three conflicting statements was correct. There is little doubt that the board had decided upon the essentials of the situation in advance, through conversation with Rosenbluth and Seaburg the day of the accident.

Captain Rosenbluth's description of the tragedy before the board of inquiry is the fullest available account of testimony taken at the time.* This record ends with a brief statement by Major Tucker, the regimental surgeon.[31]

The board of inquiry report was viewed by the grief-stricken father, General Cronkhite, as an effort to cover up a sinister story, or at the very least, as criminally careless or inefficient. But the causes for this can be explained more naturally. First of all, military custom permits a group to investigate itself without many of the controls which operate in civil law. One has only to imagine what would happen if the senior executives of a corporation or the senior professors of a university were empowered by law and custom to

---

* For the full text of the board of inquiry report, see the Appendix.

sit in judgment upon their colleagues and themselves. A major principle of civil law—a man shall not be the judge in his own cause—may be vitiated in military judicial procedure. For example, at the grand jury proceedings an effort was made to find out if Major Zajicek had been talking to other witnesses about the "honor of the regiment." What he had said and exactly what he meant was uncertain, but the fact remains that the honor of the regiment (or the reputation and standing of a corporation or a university) must be a consideration to those who are members of it. Thus in the Cronkhite case the order to investigate the possibility that the major had died disobeying orders was unlikely to receive any serious attention. There would be the greatest possible reluctance to record officially that a beloved young officer had died as a result of willful misconduct, even though casual target practice was against regulations. Not only was the subject not raised, as shown by the recorded testimony, but the official place of death in the press releases, the *Divisional History,* and the *West Point Biographical Register* was recorded as the target range in camp.[32] It is impossible to avoid the conclusion that the senior officers made the change to remove any possible "misconduct" from the record. A military acquaintance of mine assures me that such a change is not unusual; he suggested that it might have been done for insurance purposes to avoid the claim that the officer had not died in the line of duty.

General Cronkhite and others who later investigated the case argued that the major, a highly conscientious young officer, would never under any circumstances have fired casually at a can while in command of a battalion, and they dismissed the target shooting story as an obvious and clumsy fabrication. However, the actual circumstances may have permitted it. Captain Francis Boynton remarked in his testimony that such shooting was common and no one thought anything about it. Major General Leitch, also a graduate of West Point, denied in answer to specific questions that Cronkhite's actions were in any way unmilitary or improper; Leitch, of course, had previously approved the findings of the board and may have felt obliged to defend his action. Perhaps the real explanation was that Cronkhite did not consider himself to be on duty with the battalion. He had gone "like a boy out for a lark"; he had not taken command, but had strolled along casually with the group and was well ahead of the column when he fired. The group was in a very remote section of the military reservation; the clearing where the major stood was the entrance to the old Shubert farm, an abandoned property with the house and outbuildings clearly uninhabited. Cronkhite may well have considered that the circumstances made casual shooting acceptable.

Only two other witnesses reported seeing the major in the act of shooting. One of them claimed to have seen him fire several times as the battalion hiked along. This may be a false memory; in his testimony before the board, Rosenbluth mentioned that the major had pointed his revolver on several occasions and had clicked the trigger without discharging the gun. Another witness, Sergeant Elmer Kieffer, stated in an affidavit made voluntarily after Rosenbluth's arrest that he had gone across the road to urinate and had been in a position where he could see the major in the act of firing at a target.[33] Kieffer's statement seems to me doubtful for two reasons. First, since many other men reported going to the fence and trying without success to see beyond the heavy underbrush, it is difficult to believe that Kieffer could have seen anything. Second, in a statement to the *New York Times* made about the same time as his affidavit, Kieffer stated that he had actually seen the fatal shot, and many details are clearly incorrect. He said, for instance, that the major fell, blood spurting from his neck, and Pothier was standing nearby holding his bugle.[34] Since everyone else agreed that there was no external bleeding at all and Pothier would not have taken his bugle on the hike, Sergeant Kieffer would appear to be a man with a vivid imagination. His sincerity seems unquestionable, but his story doubtful. That the major was in fact shooting at a target when he died rests upon the testimony of the actual witnesses, Rosenbluth and Pothier.

In addition to the natural reluctance of the board to inquire too closely into possible misconduct, other factors tended to undercut a genuine investigation. The board members were not only friends of Major Cronkhite but also of Captain Rosenbluth, whom they had not the slightest reason to distrust. This fact, I think, explains why many questions were not asked and no formal identification of the various exhibits was made. If a man known and trusted hands over a can and some exploded shells with the statement that these objects were collected at the scene, this statement is not likely to be challenged unless there is strong reason for suspicion. Similarly, if a trusted colleague describes how an event occurred and no serious conflict in testimony exists, why should those investigating doubt the accuracy of the report? This circumstance also seems to explain the failure of the board to call for the statements filed with the officer of the day at the base hospital. Since Rosenbluth was there to be questioned, why should his statement made a few days before be consulted? Again we meet the weakness in procedure that military judicial method permits. The board trusted Captain Rosenbluth and had a low opinion of Pothier's reliability; they quite honestly did not see any need to challenge the captain's testimony or to clear up the variations in the sergeant's statements. A more objective group would probably have reached the same verdict eventually but would have been far more careful to eliminate alternate possibilities.

Even if questions had arisen in the minds of the board members, they would have been reluctant to ask them. Lieutenant Colonel Howard later admitted in several formal statements that he was extremely uneasy at the time and found it impossible to believe that anyone could have shot himself as the major was presumed to have done;[35] but he found it even more impossible to suppose that Captain Rosenbluth was lying. Tucker and Zajicek accepted the story without questioning it; Howard, reluctant to raise doubts of Rosenbluth's accuracy and to criticize his fellow members, kept his reservations to himself and signed the report without making objections.

Another circumstance that tended to eliminate obvious questions was the presence on the board of a physician of considerable reputation and standing, Major Tucker. The other two were engineers; quite naturally Tucker's analysis of the medical details would be taken as final. The autopsy report apparently was not entered in evidence, nor was Dr. Sommer, who had performed the autopsy, called to testify. He had expected to be called and had carefully preserved the bullet taken from the body, supposing it would be wanted as evidence. He later pointed out that his report had not made any judgment about the cause of death, but merely had reported that death was caused by a gunshot wound "said to be accidental."[36] Since Tucker had been at the autopsy, however, Sommer's testimony was not considered necessary. Tucker was also accepted as an authority on other aspects of the case. Major Zajicek, when asked at the grand jury proceedings if he thought an injection of strychnine and artificial respiration were appropriate treatment for a bullet wound, replied irritably that he didn't know a damn thing about medicine. If Dr. Tucker didn't find anything to complain about, why should he, an engineer, have objected?[37]

It was relatively obvious that young Lieutenant Seaburg's behavior was unprofessional, particularly his failure to examine Cronkhite before he applied restoratives. Dr. Tucker no doubt realized that Seaburg's attempts to revive the major were deserving of at least mild criticism, but he also knew that no treatment, no matter how skillful, could have saved Cronkhite's life. He probably felt no useful purpose would be served by holding the young doctor up to official criticism for his action.

And finally, the failure of Colonel Thomas to advise the board or to intervene in the investigation completed the results.

Not only was the colonel in considerable distress at his friend's tragic death but he does not appear to have been the man to handle such a matter with complete efficiency. He was quite young, in his early thirties, and before the war his service career had been concerned with engineering assignments in the Philippines and the United States. At any rate he showed some confusion about military judicial procedures. He originally appointed the board of inquiry himself, only to learn that it must be appointed by the base commander, and he apparently was unaware that the initial hearing or inquest held by the summary court officer should have been taken down in writing. When asked about this later, Lieutenant Colonel Howard replied that his army experience had led him to believe that if anything was done wrong, you were told about it at once. Since his informal hearing was not questioned, he supposed it was adequate. The implication is that Colonel Thomas was not aware of the correct procedure, since he did not protest.

In addition, Thomas appears to have been an "academy" officer, not a brilliant man, but one determined to behave appropriately with due consideration for his rank and his position as commanding officer of the regiment. In describing the arrangements for the hike, he stated, "It was customary for me to communicate generally anything that I wanted them to do to my subordinate. I never did anything anybody below me could do for me." Several times in his testimony he indicated considerable uncertainty about the correct procedure. When first approached by his "advisers" with the suggestion that the uniform not be sent to the major's mother, Thomas refused to withhold it, saying he was absolutely without authority to destroy property belonging to Mrs. Cronkhite. But he quickly changed his mind: "Thinking the matter over, I said to myself, 'you are a Colonel. If you can't assume enough responsibility to save that mother that pain by holding out those clothes,' I said, 'I am going to do that.' "[38] He subsequently took full responsibility for the decision to withhold the uniform; his erroneous impression that the coat was bloodstained perhaps arose from his unconscious wish to justify his action.

The *Regimental History*'s final comment on Colonel Thomas suggests something of the quality of the man: "Colonel Thomas has always been active in outdoor sports, being a horseman of marked ability, a leading polo player, and always prominent in anything pertaining to the welfare of the horse."[39] The total picture of the man produced by his own testimony and that of others suggests a man at his best when engaged in active practical affairs and less effective when dealing with delicate issues of policy and human relationships.

At any rate the colonel's reluctance to interfere with the board of inquiry report produced the final touch of confusion. Thomas admitted later he was disturbed when he received the report because he felt that it was too perfunctory. He did not question its findings, he made clear, but did think that more witnesses should have been examined and more "negative evidence" gathered. But he was disinclined to criticize the board, two members of which were considerably his senior in age. After debating the matter with himself, he decided against returning the report for further investigation and sent it along to Major General Leitch.

Thomas explained that his decision was based on his recognition of the facts that the young man was dead and nothing could bring him back to life, that the regiment was struggling in great difficulties to get ready to go overseas, and that nothing would be accomplished by continuing an investigation upsetting to both the men and the officers. He did not say but no doubt realized that to return the report would be to imply some doubt of its accuracy. Since he accepted the findings without question, he hesitated to take official steps that would seem, however slightly, to call those findings into question. As a result of Colonel Thomas's decision, General Cronkhite, when asked at the grand jury proceedings if he would venture the opinion that Thomas had been remiss in his duty, replied roundly, "I would not venture it, sir, I would assert it with the utmost positiveness."[40]

Official approval of the findings of the board of inquiry ended the case as far as the senior officers were concerned. Since the verdict established that Major Cronkhite's death was a tragic accident, little care was taken to preserve or record the various exhibits. The bullet that Dr. Sommer had taken from the body remained in his desk for some time and eventually disappeared; the doctor said in a press interview later he believed, without being sure, that he had given it to a nurse who wanted it as a curio.[41] The autopsy report recorded it as a .45 jacketed revolver bullet, but apparently no one but Dr. Sommer and Major Tucker ever inspected it. The gun the major was using was not preserved as evidence, nor was it positively identified. Sergeant Root, whose gun it was according to many witnesses, testified he was anxious to get his revolver back since it fit his hand. He believed that Lieutenant Rustenbach had finally been issued the revolver, but the lieutenant could not remember this. Lieutenant Hannaman thought the gun had been left on a shelf in headquarters for a time, but he had never examined it or known what had ultimately become of it. At any rate it could not be subsequently found or identified.

The tobacco can and the shells were given to Lieutenant

Colonel Howard and remained in his desk for several months; when he was discharged he turned them over to Colonel Thomas, who in turn passed them on to the adjutant, then Captain Whiting, with orders to send them along with other regimental records to the War Department. Captain Whiting was later unable to recall being given the shells and can. Although four shells and a can with a bullet hole in it subsequently were filed at the War Department, there was much uncertainty later concerning their authenticity. The major's uniform was left hanging in Lieutenant Hannaman's quarters and was later burned by him on Howard's order.[42] The uniform was not destroyed, however, until February, a month after Captain Rosenbluth had been discharged.

The documents of the case were somewhat disordered also. The statements taken down at the hospital were lost and never afterwards traced. The inquest had not been recorded in writing, and the autopsy was not signed by the doctor who actually performed it. There is some question also about the board of inquiry record itself. General Cronkhite was disturbed by the fact that the copy he inspected at the War Department was marked "Duplicate" and no original copy seemed to exist. He also complained that the report was not signed.[43] It seems only fair to admit there is considerable truth in the General's charges that the investigation was improperly conducted.

But his suspicions of a complicated plot involving the senior officers do not necessarily follow. The particular set of circumstances, the relationship of those concerned, the state of tension and emergency that existed, and the inexperience of the officers who handled the affair combined quite naturally to produce a casual investigation. That a plot existed and evidence of murder was deliberately concealed can be dismissed with the simple reflection that any group of men intent upon falsifying evidence could have done much better. A plot, in other words, might be suggested if a coherent chain of evidence were contradicted by one or two forgotten details. But in this case almost all the evidence is confused, and carelessness rather than deliberate concealment seems the most reasonable explanation. It would have been a simple matter to assemble false evidence that told a coherent and convincing story, had anyone wished to do so. Rosenbluth remarked in a letter written several years later that if there had been collusion, the stories told would have matched. That testimony gathered later was contradictory and confusing tended to show that no official "cover story" had been constructed.

Once the report of the board of inquiry was approved and filed, the officers dismissed the matter from their minds and went back to the work of readying the regiment for overseas.

As far as they knew, the men accepted the accidental, self-inflicted nature of the wound without question. But, as subsequent interrogation made clear, there was considerable discussion of the accident and considerable doubt expressed about the verdict. Major Cronkhite's death was debated and discussed among the enlisted men and the junior officers. Much depended upon whether or not a given group of men had any specific information. Those men who reported little concern were usually those who had never known exactly where the major had been wounded. Those who had seen the wound or talked to eye-witnesses were puzzled about the oddness of the angle. Men in one barracks experimented with their own revolvers, trying to hold the guns in a position that would explain the placement of the wound.

At least one sergeant reported to Lieutenant Miller his conviction that Pothier had fired the shot by accident. He did not think it was deliberate, since as he put it, Major Cronkhite was the only friend Pothier had in the regiment. Lieutenant Miller reported this statement to Major Tucker, but neither officer seemed to think the sergeant's doubts were anything more than one of the many theories being discussed.[44] Miller, who as intelligence officer received all sorts of information, described the interest in the case as "tremendous." In his testimony to the grand jury Lieutenant Morrison denied that no suspicion existed at the time; as he recalled the week that followed the tragedy, there was much discussion of alternate possibilities. Morrison himself recalled arguing the matter with his sister while visiting her shortly after the accident.[45] Insofar as the men believed someone else was responsible for the major's death, their suspicions were directed either at Sergeant Pothier or at some unknown person. No one appeared to believe that Captain Rosenbluth was involved in the tragedy. A few men reported having heard or suspected that the death was suicide; this theory was encouraged by the quietness of the investigation, which suggested to some that something was being hushed up.

No doubt this speculation was inevitable. Major Cronkhite was a very popular officer, and some aspects of his death were a trifle odd. Curiosity and interest in a sudden death which takes place in a concealed spot is a natural human reaction, but it is not to be wondered at that those closely connected with the death neither heard this speculation nor were aware of its existence. After the case had been reopened, Rosenbluth protested in several personal letters, reiterating the questions: "Why did these men not report their suspicions at the time? What prevented them? If they suspected foul play, why did they not say so—if not at once, then in January after I left the regiment?" But Rosenbluth, struggling under the enormous pressure of an unjust charge, failed to realize two things. First, none of the men had anything to report to anyone. Like Colonel Howard they were simply puzzled. A noncommissioned officer is not likely to report nebulous "feelings" to a superior, particularly to a senior officer involved in the matter. Second, the suspicions did not involve Captain Rosenbluth, but were directed at the highly unpopular and much distrusted Pothier. Rosenbluth, who did not know the sergeant at this time, could not have foreseen that Pothier's extreme unpopularity was likely to give rise to suspicion.

The ultimate result of these speculations was disastrous. When General and Mrs. Cronkhite began to write to various members of the regiment asking for confidential details of their son's death, they inevitably received replies that tended to confirm their suspicions. Thus two lines of circumstance coalesced in the Cronkhites. The officers' belief in Captain Rosenbluth's integrity permitted them to accept his statements without hesitation. The enlisted men, not knowing of Rosenbluth's exact testimony, allowed their doubts to reach the Cronkhites. It should be emphasized again that no one concerned in this case who was acquainted with Rosenbluth voiced the slightest suspicion of him at the time or later, but the Cronkhites did not know Rosenbluth. Assured by a variety of sources that there was something "funny" about the death and equipped with the board of inquiry report and Rosenbluth's testimony, they reached an obvious conclusion. If something was "funny," then Rosenbluth must be involved. He claimed to have seen the accident. If the tragedy was not in fact an accident at all, he had lied and must be implicated in the death.

CHAPTER TWO
BUILD-UP
JANUARY 1919- MARCH 1921

THE CRONKHITE CASE was reopened almost at once by the major's mother, who was reported to have said upon receiving the details of the accident, "I don't believe it. He was too much of a man to kill himself and too expert with arms to accidentally shoot himself in that way."[1] It is easy to sympathize with Mrs. Cronkhite's distress. Her husband, Major General Cronkhite, was in France exposed to heavy fighting on the Meuse-Argonne, and her remaining child, a daughter, was seriously ill with pneumonia. Nor was Mrs. Cronkhite herself in good health. General Cronkhite remarked on several occasions that she was an invalid, and he often used her ill health as an explanation for his failure to appear for appointments. The nature of her illness is not known, but it is possible she was experiencing the physical and emotional strains that often occur in women in their late forties and early fifties. Certainly her emotional stability, like the general's, appeared to be increasingly in doubt as the years went by. Besieged with family trouble and sickness, Mrs. Cronkhite could easily interpret the events that followed her son's death to support her personal suspicions.

Already somewhat bewildered by the contradiction between the newspaper reports of her son's death (which stated that he had been killed on the target range) and the information she had received from Camp Lewis, Mrs. Cronkhite traveled alone to West Point for her son's burial there. She had expected to talk with Lieutenant Saunders, the officer who had accompanied the body, but discovered he had arrived a day earlier than he had planned, had turned the casket over to the authorities, and had left the city. Saunders subsequently explained he had misread the train schedules and his arrival twenty-four hours early was simply a mistake. He had been given a five-day leave to begin as soon as his military duties were performed, and understandably anxious not to lose one of those days and perhaps reluctant to undergo a painful interview with the mother of the dead officer, he had slipped away. Saunders had not been on the hike and probably justified his abrupt departure with the reflection that he could not give Mrs. Cronkhite any new information. The mother, however, interpreted his absence as sinister and believed he had deliberately wired incorrect information about his arrival time to avoid meeting her.

Mrs. Cronkhite was further distressed by small cuts and scratches on her son's face and later made an effort to find out what had caused them. No one ever explained their presence nor had anyone seemed to notice them at Camp Lewis. Dr. Tucker later suggested they occurred somehow en route to West Point, although this seems unlikely. They may have been caused by careless handling in the morgue, where attendants were struggling to keep up with the endless stream of bodies produced by the flu epidemic. It is even more likely that the scratches were made while the men were attempting to revive the major with artificial respiration. Lieutenant Morrison testified that when he was called to the scene the body was lying face down; minor abrasions could easily have resulted if his face had been pressed against the roadway. Nevertheless these scratches, carefully described by witnesses, became part of the evidence in the Cronkhite file.[2]

Mrs. Cronkhite almost at once began writing letters to members of the regiment requesting any information they could give about the death of her son. She also corresponded with several officers concerning the failure of those in charge to return his uniform. After his effects had been returned to her in January 1919, she protested that several pieces of property were missing—his watch, campaign hat, revolver, and high school fraternity pins, as well as the uniform and insignia. Correspondence with Captain Boynton produced the information that the uniform had been burned by orders of Colonel Thomas and the regimental adjutant. In a letter to the colonel written in August 1919 she strongly protested this decision, and demanded to know why the uniform had been destroyed without consulting her.

The missing blouse was important because of the failure of the Camp Lewis authorities to examine it for powder marks. Neither the autopsy surgeon nor Dr. Seaburg recalled having looked carefully at the blouse, and none of the men at the scene noticed any scorching. At the board of inquiry Dr. Tucker testified that the inner right sleeve was burned by powder, but his statement was unfortunately unsupported by convincing confirmatory testimony. Major Zajicek did not examine the blouse at all; Colonel Howard maintained steadily that he had examined it and had seen no powder marks.[3] He did not recall Dr. Tucker's testimony at the board of inquiry, and was unable to explain why, if he had heard it, he did not re-examine the coat. He rejected a suggestion that unknown to him Tucker's testimony was added to the transcript later. The only support for Dr. Tucker's statement came from Lieutenant Hannaman, in whose room the uniform hung for several months before it was destroyed. He believed there was a mark on the inside of the right sleeve as Tucker claimed.[4] It seems to be at least possible that Colonel Howard's failure to see a powder mark was caused by his examining the front of the coat where the bullet entered rather than the sleeve. Also possible is that Tucker's testimony was added to the report later, probably at the suggestion of Colonel Thomas. Thomas was uneasy about the brevity of the investigation and may have felt it advisable to include a formal statement on the subject. From a purely practical point of view the testimony could have been added; the pagination of the report leaves almost all the last page blank, while the signatures of the board members and the base commander appear on a cover sheet beneath the statement of the board's findings.

In February 1919 Mrs. Cronkhite received a phone call from Captain Rosenbluth, by then discharged from the service. A voluntary call of condolence does not suggest a guilty man; it is difficult to see why Rosenbluth should have called Mrs. Cronkhite if he had indeed been involved in her son's death. The Cronkhites however, managed to read a great deal into his call and subsequent visit. At the grand jury session General Cronkhite described the event as Mrs. Cronkhite had reported it to him and to the Department of Justice:

> When Capt. Rosenbluth came in from the West in February of 1919 she was living at the Brighton. I was over on the other side in command of the Sixth Corps. It was there that somebody called her on the telephone and stated that he was Capt. Rosenbluth; and at that time my daughter was there and recovering from an attack of pneumonia. She had been very, very sick and the boy lost his life. . . . As soon as Mrs. Cronkhite learned who was on the phone she motioned to my daughter, Dorothy, to go to the phone extension so she could hear exactly what was going on or what conversation took place. And as a result of Mrs. Cronkhite's conversation with Capt. Rosenbluth she induced him to come up and see her so he could talk with her in person, and he did come up and talked to her for a matter of—oh I think two or three hours—being continuously anxious to get away and yet they held him there and plied him with question after question.
>
> During the course of these questions though he went so far as to illustrate the way in which—that is his relative position as regards the boy at the time he was shot. He illustrated by taking

pieces of furniture and placing them in the living room, so as
to show just exactly what had happened at this time; when he
did make this illustration he changed his position in regard to
Maj. Cronkhite and placed himself at Maj. Cronkhite's right
instead of his left as he had stated before the so-called board of
inquiry; I call it "so-called" because it bears no signatures.
He was very indefinite; did not know how many shots had been
fired at the time the boy lost his life; but he said that the pistol
upset—or the revolver or the gun—upset in his hand and he
shot himself through the windpipe, and that the reason he died
so quickly was on account of his extreme weakness; that he had
been greatly reduced by his illness and had further over-
strained himself by this long march which he had not expected
to make, because Zajicek had been expecting to come out and
assume command of the troops. . . .

He said that he had a gun with no safety catch, and a hair-
trigger—just exactly what that means I have never been able to
discover—there is no such thing as a safety catch on a revolver—
there is on a pistol—but I have never been able to learn positively whether he was shot with a revolver or a pistol. . . . He
also stated that at this time Pothier was nowhere around there
when the boy shot himself; that Pothier was twenty paces up
in the woods, and that he did not believe it was possible for
Pothier to see what took place.[5]

Several points emerge from this description. Since the
visit was hardly the act of a guilty man, it is more probable
that Rosenbluth, the first of the officers in the regiment to
be discharged, phoned as an act of kindness to offer his sympathy to the bereaved family. Mrs. Cronkhite was already
highly suspicious of Rosenbluth, as waving her daughter to the
phone extension indicates. The description of Rosenbluth "anxious to get away" is a matter of interpretation. Almost any
man, however sorry he felt for the family, might be made uneasy by three hours of steady and persistent questions; he could
hardly have been unaware of their antagonism and suspicion.

Allowing for the fact that these remarks are filtered
through both parents' memories, they do not seem to be seriously at variance with the original testimony. The confusion
about the make of gun is a constant one and reflects the tendency of the nonexpert to use the terms "pistol" and "revolver"
interchangeably. The gun Rosenbluth apparently meant was
Sergeant Root's Colt—a revolver known to have an easy action.
The only real change (granting that the Cronkhites recalled and
reported the conversation accurately) is the statement that
Pothier was a short distance away when the accident occurred
and could not have seen it. In all probability Rosenbluth, who
had paid very little attention to Pothier during the emergency,
was not entirely sure of the sergeant's position and perhaps
placed him at a slight distance with the vague idea of discour-
aging Mrs. Cronkhite from continuing her futile researches.
Even more likely, the general, repeating a conversation three

years in the past, may have modified it in terms of his own obsessive need to believe that his son had been murdered.

Major General Cronkhite was not verbally told the conversation until the summer of 1919, when he returned from France. By this time his wife had collected an assortment of data in support of her belief that the major had been murdered; the general, broken-hearted at the loss of a beloved and thoroughly satisfactory son, joined her at once in her suspicions. His inspection of War Department records confirmed an already positive conviction that the whole affair had been mishandled to conceal a sinister plot. Discovering that the board of inquiry report was an unsigned "Duplicate," that no inquest was held, that the autopsy report was not signed by the physician who performed it, and that the written statements taken down at the hospital had vanished, the general was further outraged to find that the exhibits in the case had been carelessly preserved. The missing hat, uniform, and revolver were matched by the confusion about the can and the shells.

Without doubt something is very curious about these exhibits. It will be recalled that the can and shells remained in the desk of Colonel Howard for a time, then were transferred to the desk of Colonel Thomas. They were not kept locked up and could easily have been tampered with, had anyone wished to do so. I cannot help suspecting this may have happened but occurred *after* the shells and can left Camp Lewis and arrived in Washington. In an analysis of the case written in 1922 the general claimed that the can and shells he was shown at the War Department were clean and shiny; the can, supposedly picked up casually from the road for use as a target (neither Rosenbluth, Pothier, nor Cronkhite used chewing tobacco), was without a single mark of dirt, rust, or weather damage; the shells, which supposedly had rolled around in desk drawers for several months, were as bright and clean as if they had just come from the box.[6] In contrast to this, a government expert who was asked to inspect the shells and make certain judgments about them for the grand jury in 1922 complained that their corroded condition made certainty impossible.[7]

In addition, these exhibits traveled around a good deal. They were sent in 1921 from the War Department to the Justice Department at the request of Assistant Attorney General Herron. Late in that year they were sent to the U.S. attorney in Seattle. They were presented as evidence, under seal of the War Department, to the grand jury in 1922. When the trial was being prepared in 1924, they had been mislaid, and after a series of desperate wires to various cities, were rediscovered in Seattle. Obviously their authenticity could never be fully established.

To add to the confusion, frequent references are made to

two cans. Various witnesses recalled that the can was a Piper Heidsieck tobacco can, a Prince Albert tobacco can, and a tomato soup can. In the Justice Department files on the case, a single page of testimony, undated, unpaginated, and unidentified, begins with the assertion that the speaker had sent, at the request of the U.S. attorney in Providence, two tobacco cans— one shot through against a post, the other as it lay on the ground. These were apparently sample cans designed to show how the angle of the shot would vary depending on the can's position.[8] The matter was further confused at the trial, when Colonel Thomas insisted he had been shown two cans at the grand jury session and had been asked to identify the one he remembered having had in his possession. Two attorneys denied he had been shown more than one can; he retorted that his testimony had been tampered with. Here, the colonel is correct. The grand jury transcript, a copy marked "Original," makes it clear he was asked to choose the can that fit his memory; he rejected the first one as utterly unlike what he remembered and agreed that the second matched his recollections.[9] Subsequent witnesses were shown only one can, presumably the one identified by Thomas.

What this was all about can only be conjectured. It is very likely that in an effort to construct some kind of a case, someone had the bright idea of trying to tell from the bullet hole whether the can had been shot at on a post or on the ground. That an attempt was being made to show that the can was on the ground when shot at is reported in the *Chicago Tribune* in 1923; the reporter explained that Justice Department experts were convinced that the can they had examined was not standing upright when it was hit.[10] This analysis was important because it tended to support Pothier's later allegation (drawn out by Agent Lee) that Rosenbluth had deliberately shot at the can as it lay on the ground to provide faked evidence of target shooting after the major's death.

Mrs. Cronkhite's collection of letters from members of the regiment and the general's examination of the official records combined to create what was for them, in their distress, a convincing case. Their obsession was given further impetus by the persistent rumor that the young man's death had been suicide. How widespread these whispers were is impossible to establish, but several members of the regiment gave testimony later that the possibility was at least discussed. The personnel adjutant, Lieutenant Reeves, from whom I first heard the story of Cronkhite's death, personally believed it was suicide. He based his conviction on the reply he received when he inquired how the major was feeling. Cronkhite replied, "Fred, I feel so bad I'd like to go out and shoot myself!" Reeves stressed the fact that influenza usually left its victims in an abnormal state of depression and honestly believed that the major had taken his own life.

A study of the case makes suicide extremely unlikely; the many reports of his cheerfulness that morning and the peculiar angle of the wound both testify against it. But inevitably Reeves would have talked about the remark at the time and thus encouraged this rumor. Also in the files on the case is a curious bit of testimony taken from a nurse at Camp Lee, Virginia, who claimed to have overheard three officers talking about suicide, one asserting that Cronkhite had been told to go west and kill himself.[11] This and similar reports would seem products of lurid imaginations, but the Cronkhites were naturally concerned. Some whispers reaching them asserted that the young man feared overseas duty and shot himself to avoid the battlefield. General Cronkhite explained in a newspaper account published in 1923 that he had been falsely reported in the press to have been convicted of treason in France and that his name, vaguely Germanic in sound, gave some color to this report.[12] He said it was being whispered his son killed himself because of the disgrace of his father's reported treason—thus the suicide rumors reflected upon the general as well as his son.

The Cronkhites' suspicions followed a distinguishable pattern. Pothier's bad service record combined with the hints from the men in the regiment made him a primary candidate for the role of murderer. The board of inquiry testimony established Captain Rosenbluth as an eyewitness and thus involved him. But the general could not believe that the various confusions in the records had been deliberately arranged to protect either man. No regular army officer would have falsified records to protect Pothier. It was also doubtful that such protection would have been extended to Rosenbluth, who says in his autobiography, "By no conceivable stretch of the imagination would any of these men serving on the official bodies which reported these findings, or any of the officers and men of the regiment, have done anything to 'protect' me or to 'cover-up' any details about the death of Major Cronkhite. . . ."

Here undoubtedly Rosenbluth is correct. It is impossible to believe that a group of regular army officers with West Point backgrounds would combine to protect a temporary army captain from the suspicion of murder of his superior officer, particularly when the dead man was universally beloved. It is additionally unlikely when we consider there was apparently a distinct prejudice during World War I against Jewish officers. A noted lawyer, Louis Marshall, protested during the war the phrasing of an official officer's manual which stated "the ideal officer is a Christian gentleman." His objections effected a change from "Christian" to "courteous" in the wording. Similarly, in a statement in the *Daily News,* April 18, 1921, Rosenbluth was quoted as saying Pothier must be the "willing tool of the dying war-time system responsible for the so-called [anti-Jewish] round robin and its contingent suicides." An additional example of such feeling appears in the *Congressional Record.* A protest was filed against the continued harassment of a Jewish cadet at West Point, who endured the hatred of his classmates for four years. This antagonism culminated in the yearbook; the cadet's picture was printed on a perforated page so that it could be removed by anyone who wished.

The feeling in the 213th Engineers against Jewish officers does not appear to have been severe, but it did exist. The chaplain, Lieutenant Harron, later stated in an affidavit that he believed the charges against Rosenbluth were helped by the "natural antipathy" some persons had for those of the Hebrew race.[13] Asked at the grand jury session if he had requested that Rosenbluth be assigned to the regiment, Colonel Thomas made emphatic denial, saying that he would never have voluntarily chosen a Jewish officer to serve under him. Several other witnesses before the grand jury showed a tendency to stereotyping; Captain Rosenbluth's behavior in emergencies was described as "excitable," the speakers clearly implying this was an ethnic trait. Nevertheless, the degree of prejudice existing within the regiment did not lead to suspicion of Rosenbluth, then or later. With one exception, both officers and men strenuously denied a belief in his involvement, despite the fact that all the officers and almost all the men who testified were Gentiles.

The likelihood is much greater that Rosenbluth's superiors would *not* have covered up for him. But this consideration did not lead General Cronkhite to conclude that his suspicions were false. Instead he decided that the plot against his son, put into operation by Rosenbluth and Pothier, had originated with several senior officers who had combined in a secret and sinister plan to bring about the young major's death.

II

General Cronkhite thus began a deliberate investigation into his son's "murder." He invited correspondence from many members of the regiment, urging them to report anything, however small, they recalled about the fatal day. By combining partial sentences and phrases from their letters, he was able to construct a case which convinced him and his wife and eventu-

ally others. Witnesses were found who were willing, at least in
private letters, to encourage the general's suspicions. One man
was asked at the grand jury proceedings if he had heard a groan
from the clearing where the major died, a detail substantiating
the general's belief that Rosenbluth had physically attacked
his son. The witness sheepishly admitted he had invented this
groan; the general's repeated demands for anything he could
recall had led to exaggeration and false stories.[14] At least one
correspondent claimed that the two men were enemies and
Major Cronkhite's criticisms of Rosenbluth's field performance
were steady and severe.

An examination of Rosenbluth's efficiency rating sheet
showed he was not placed very high, and in the general's opinion even this somewhat low rating had been altered by Colonel
Thomas or Major Zajicek to raise it to passing level. He explained Rosenbluth's return from France as an instructor as
being a penalty for inefficiency. He became convinced Major
Zajicek was untrustworthy and secretly in league with Rosenbluth. Believing that Zajicek was in the plot, he discovered
all sorts of sinister implications in Zajicek's decision not to
accompany the hike and in the later confusion about exactly
when he had returned to camp.

The depths of the general's obsession can be seen from
his mental quirks. Lieutenant Morrison, for example, had told
him in a letter of condolence that Major Cronkhite was much
beloved by the junior officers. General Cronkhite immediately
concluded that the sentence implied his son was not popular
with the senior officers, and although he did not succeed in
getting Morrison to explain the remark further, used it as partial evidence of a plot.[15] Similarly to reassure the bereaved parents, the chaplain said the boy's death was not suicide; this,
the Cronkhites felt, hinted strongly that it was murder.

There seems little doubt the general's mind was not entirely sound as his investigations proceeded; although he expressed himself rationally and vigorously both in speech and
in writing, his judgment was clearly faulty. In 1921 for example, Rosenbluth sent a quotation to Colonel Thomas from
a letter written by the general to ex-sergeant Frank Turner,
apparently in response to previous correspondence. General
Cronkhite demanded that Turner answer a series of questions:

> For instance, you say that my son was put in command but was
> advised not to go. Who put him in command, and who advised
> him not to go and why? Kindly tell me whose battalion was
> out for this march, and what the regular battalion commander
> was doing which prevented him from being present. Did he
> join the command later, and did Colonel Thomas finally join
> the column as was expected? And again I have never been able

to learn whether my son accompanied the command when it left camp or whether he joined it later, and if so, where. There seems to have been some doubt as to whether he would go or not, and I have never been able to learn why he finally decided to go, whether voluntarily or under orders.[16]

Rosenbluth called Thomas's attention to the fact that it was unusual for generals to ask such questions of ex-sergeants; no one in a reasonable frame of mind could have supposed that Turner would have known the answers. Rosenbluth also reported in his letter to Thomas that he had been asked repeatedly by government agents why he was covering up for Zajicek and Thomas; in another letter to his former colonel, Rosenbluth suggested quite seriously that Thomas keep an eye on Cronkhite's investigations in order to protect himself.

The letter to Turner demonstrates how the general managed to collect his information. A man receiving such a request might attempt to answer the questions by making guesses or by actual invention designed to discourage further frantic correspondence. Or if the correspondent insisted he did not know the answers or did not recall them, the general had more "evidence" that something was being deliberately concealed. Either a cooperative reply or a refusal would confirm what he already believed true. But insofar as evidence is available, no sign of any nervousness or concealment existed in the men General Cronkhite particularly suspected.

For example, in March 1920 Colonel Thomas received a letter from the commanding officer at Camp Lewis, asking for information. General Cronkhite, the officer explained, wanted to know for sentimental reasons exactly where his son had died and what the line of march on the hike had been. Thomas obligingly wrote to Rosenbluth, Seaburg, and Rustenbach, asking them if they would assist. Several letters were exchanged between Thomas and his former officers—friendly, chatty letters giving news of Lieutenant Hannaman's marriage, Dr. Seaburg's new baby girl, and the business partnership of captains Boynton and Whiting. The colonel asked them to report anything they could recall which might be of interest to the general, and all three traced on maps the course of the hike as they recalled it. Rosenbluth's map, marked in his handwriting, later became for a time an important exhibit in the case against him. But at the time, as the tone and contents of these letters make clear, none of the men felt the slightest nervousness at the request. That the general merely wanted the details to satisfy his need to know all about the tragedy was accepted as a sufficient reason for the inquiry.[17]

The same obliviousness to danger is shown in a personal letter written by Dr. Tucker to a friend after Pothier's first confession. Tucker was much surprised to learn that Pothier had confessed to firing the fatal shot accidentally, but the tone of the letter does not suggest alarm. He commented lightly, "All this shows a mother's intuition is better than evidence, circumstantial or direct."[18] Tucker was apparently aware that the Cronkhites had been investigating, but had not expected their researches to lead anywhere.

After he began his investigation, General Cronkhite acquired a private detective, William Jones, a former captain in the New York City Homicide Squad and a licensed pistol expert. The exact nature of Jones' connection with the case is a trifle mysterious. At the grand jury proceedings, Jones said he had not known Major Cronkhite but was told of his death by an acquaintance. "Yes, it was through Major [A.H.] Strauss—that is Major Strauss that is going back and forth on the flying ship. He was in the Intelligence Office in New York City, and he is the one that called my attention to it. He brought me the autopsy report." Strauss's "flying ship" was a C-2 dirigible, which made a slow transcontinental flight in September 1922 from New York to Los Angeles. Probably more significant is his connection with military intelligence; that he had this report in his possession suggests that interest in the Cronkhite case was fairly widespread. Interestingly, according to one newspaper account the special agent who produced Pothier's confessions had worked for military intelligence also, before he joined the staff of the Bureau of Investigation.

In any case, Jones's immediate reaction to the report was that a self-inflicted wound was impossible, and he later went to Washington and so informed General Cronkhite. Why Strauss showed the report to Jones and why Jones went to visit the general is not explained. When asked at the grand jury proceedings if he was employed by the general, he denied it. "He requested me to get a doctor. I never put in a bill to him for that." Asked if the general had ever paid him anything, Jones replied, "No, sir." He denied also that he was employed by the Bureau of Investigation. "I got a communication from the Government telling me to go on to Providence when Pothier was picked up that time, but I never even received my car fare for the trip. . . . because I would not work for the salary they gave me. . . . I never put in a bill for it."[19] Oddly enough, Jones testified at the trial in 1924 that he was employed by General Cronkhite as a private detective and had been made a special agent by the bureau during his investigations; it is possible, however, that his actual employment followed his testimony to the grand jury.

His position in the case is thus somewhat strange. Jones

ran a private detective agency, and as his comment on government salaries implied, was making money at it. Why should he go, apparently voluntarily, to visit General Cronkhite in Washington? Or if the general, notified by Major Strauss of Jones's opinion, invited him to visit, why did Jones neglect to submit a bill for his travel and time, either for the trip to Washington or the 1920 trip to West Point for a second autopsy? He accompanied Mrs. Cronkhite frequently; in February 1921 he visited Pothier with her, and later in New York he was with her when Pothier was brought to a New York hotel to be interviewed.

In addition to his services to the Cronkhites, Jones was called to Washington for a conference in the spring of 1922, receiving on this occasion only the regulation four dollars a day the government offered those whose appearance it requested. Another visitor at this conference, ex-marshal John Richards, refused to come for the minimum fee and firmly informed the Department of Justice he would submit a bill for his actual expenses. In other words, why should an apparently successful professional detective contribute substantial amounts of time and effort on behalf of an apparent stranger? His cooperation with the Bureau of Investigation is easier to understand. Agents of the bureau and the local police authorities worked closely together on occasion and assisted each other informally. For example, when Pothier was later brought to New York to appear at Rosenbluth's hearing, he was locked up in the police station under the name of Joseph Brown and spent his nights there for about a week. If the city authorities were prepared to do favors for the bureau, it is likely that a private detective would also be willing to oblige.

Captain Jones arranged for a second autopsy, performed by Dr. Otto Schultze, a surgeon employed as medical assistant to the district attorney of New York County and a professor of medical jurisprudence in Cornell University Medical College. Schultze, who was not acquainted with General Cronkhite, had performed thousands of similar examinations of exhumed bodies in cases of homicide, suspected homicide, or deaths where the cause was unknown. On July 9, 1920, the body of Major Cronkhite was removed from its casket, identified by the general as that of his son, and reexamined by Schultze in Jones's presence. This examination was far more detailed than the original, although Schultze's findings did not differ materially from those previously reported by Dr. Sommer. The second examination produced a more precise description of the exact path of the bullet and a more accurate measurement of the dimension of the wound. More important, however, Schultze gave his professional opinion, with Jones concurring, that the wound could not have been caused by a revolver held in the hand of the major. As both Schultze and Jones explained the matter, once the gun was twisted back into a position which would allow for the angle of the wound and the path of the bullet through the body, the hand would be in a position which would make contracting the finger on the trigger a complete impossibility.[20] In Schultze's opinion the diameter of the wound suggested a .38 caliber bullet rather than a .45, although Jones disagreed with him on this last point. The .38 caliber bullet, however, matched Lieutenant Wallace's story that the gun he was given at the hospital was a .38 automatic. It also fit with the rumor that Pothier had stolen Major Tucker's .38 automatic pistol, as well as with the general's assertion that this weapon was commonly carried by former A.E.F. officers like Rosenbluth.

General Cronkhite, armed with the expert testimony of professional witnesses and his own theories, now descended on the War Department demanding that a complete investigation of the case be undertaken. The department was reluctant to act in the matter—no doubt the general's suspicions of the senior officers promised an embarrassing investigation. It is not unlikely also that the other officers were aware the general's mental balance was somewhat disturbed. He was encouraged to present his case to the Department of Justice, and in late September or early October 1920 he had an interview with Attorney General A. Mitchell Palmer. The department agreed to open the investigation, and John Suter, then assistant head of the Bureau of Investigation, was placed in charge.

It is difficult to ascertain why the department decided to look into the case. The general did not have at this point much to show beyond his subjective suspicions and the report of Dr. Schultze. But, as with so many other aspects of the case, coincidence may have been at work. In September 1920 a bomb was hurled at the New York Stock Exchange, killing 30 people and injuring many more. The bomber was believed to be a Bolshevik and anarchist, and an immediate search was begun by the Department of Justice. Nineteen twenty was the year of the big Red scare, a state of panic produced by a widespread belief that a Communist revolution was about to begin in the United States. German Jews were popularly credited with spreading Bolshevik doctrines in this country and in Europe. In January of that year a massive raid was carried out in several eastern cities, and thousands of alleged aliens were arrested and examined to determine if they planned to overthrow the government by force. This raid was much criticized after it was learned that most of the arrests and seizures of property had been made without warrants, that many of the arrested men had been mistreated, and that many more were confined for extended periods under very primitive conditions. A few hundred of the more than 10,000 arrested were eventually deported as undesirable aliens, but no evidence of a revolutionary plot emerged.

But given a department trained to think in terms of spies, aliens, and radical movements, it is perfectly possible and even likely that a suspect named Rosenbluth would be investigated simply because of his name, which is obviously Jewish and sounds German. In addition, Rosenbluth was at this time actually in Russia. This combination would have been enough, given the bombing scare and the intense fear of radicals, to begin an investigation. Considered in this light, there are certain parallels with the more famous case of Sacco and Vanzetti. Under arrest on a murder charge, which according to later statements by a former agent no one in the bureau took seriously, they could be investigated for their political beliefs at leisure. It is certainly possible the bureau at first supposed the Rosenbluth affair would turn out to be the same sort of case. Major Cronkhite's death provided a convenient excuse for investigating a man whose name and whereabouts were suspicious in themselves. The various newspaper stories issued later, in which Rosenbluth was labeled a "dirty German Jew spy," suggest that this completely absurd charge was the original impetus of the investigation.

The Department of Justice was unable, however, to connect Rosenbluth either with the Wall Street bombing (if this was in fact its interest) or with a murderous assault on Major Cronkhite. In fact, the perfunctory nature of the researches into the Cronkhite aspect of the affair suggests that the department was not greatly interested. A detective named Conley interviewed Pothier and attempted to get him to admit the "truth" about the case by pretending to be an insurance agent interested in proving the suicide theory. He did not succeed in getting any new information, although he offered to split with Pothier the imaginary bonus he would receive. Pothier was also interviewed by Police Chief McMahon in Providence, apparently without result. The army records of Rosenbluth and Zajicek were examined in November, and a couple alleged to be acquaintances of Rosenbluth were interviewed concerning him. Somewhat earlier in 1919 Captain Edwin Ross, General Cronkhite's aide, had interviewed Pothier at Mrs. Cronkhite's request without obtaining any new information. Rosenbluth's whereabouts were known, since Chief Baley, assistant head of the Bureau of Investigation, later announced that his arrest had been delayed while they searched for him through

Europe and Asia. In any event, the initial investigation of the
case turned up no evidence worth acting upon, and it seemed
destined for oblivion. The failure of the Justice Department
under the regime of A. Mitchell Palmer to push the case suggests that the original interest was in Rosenbluth as a possible
anarchist, not as a possible murderer. When the radical theory
proved a blind alley, the matter was quietly dropped.

III

IN THE MEANTIME Rosenbluth, unaware he was being tracked
by generals, private detectives, and special agents, had taken up
his life as a civilian again. He was discharged from his regiment in January 1919 and took a position as consultant to an
Ohio legislative commission concerned with improving state
penal institutions. Sometime in 1919 he was asked to investigate food and grain resources in Europe and Asia, as part of
the American Relief Administration (ARA) then under the
direction of Herbert Hoover. As junior member of the team
Rosenbluth was assigned the least attractive area of study, the
Balkans and southern Russia. He toured there for several
months in 1919, observed conditions in a revolution-torn country, and returned to the United States in November. Since it
was later alleged by certain periodicals like the *Dearborn Independent* that his connection with the ARA was a cover-up designed to conceal his real, presumably sinister, purposes, it is
important to add that he is listed among the personnel of the
organization in Volume III of Hoover's *American Epic*. In addition he wrote two reports concerning political, economic, and
agricultural problems in Russia as he observed them. These
were submitted to Julius Barnes, head of the United States
Grain Corporation. At the time of his arrest he was being interviewed by the *New York Times* about conditions in Russia
and her relations with Japan. In the summer of 1920 Rosenbluth was once more preparing to settle down to civilian life
and his own career and was considering an advantageous offer
from the *New York Globe* to write a daily column on public
affairs, when he was again solicited for an important charity.
Felix Warburg, one of the partners of the banking house of
Kuhn, Loeb, and Company, and his employee, Lewis Strauss,
asked Rosenbluth to undertake a venture to rescue some Hun-
garian prisoners of war who were interned in Siberia and unable to reach their homes. The Joint Distribution Committee,
established by American Jews for war relief, was one of the
sponsors of the project. Rosenbluth somewhat reluctantly
agreed and returned to Europe. During the next six months

he traveled between Shanghai and Siberia, arranging ships to transport the refugees home by sea. His accomplishments were real; almost 8,000 men were shipped back to Budapest at a cost of less than $60 a man—a figure much below what had been anticipated. Lewis Strauss in his recent biography *Men and Decisions* pays high tribute to Rosenbluth's energy and efficiency in this project.[21]

Rosenbluth returned home in March 1921, visited Hoover in Washington where he also reported his observations of the Japanese buildup in Manchuria to military intelligence, and returned to New York. Here he heard for the first time, from Lewis Strauss, that the Cronkhite case had been reopened and serious investigations were in progress.

Rosenbluth does not seem to have been particularly disturbed at the report at first. He had no way of knowing just what General Cronkhite had discovered and, more than anything, felt sympathy for parents so tragically obsessed by the loss of their son. That he would spend the next four years fighting to clear his name could not possibly have occurred to him. Secure in his knowledge of his own innocence, aware of his established reputation in his profession, on friendly terms with a large number of prominent people, he would naturally pay little attention to this obsession of a grief-stricken couple. The death of Major Cronkhite had been under investigation for several months without any alarming developments. No doubt Rosenbluth assumed that the entire matter would be forgotten quickly and the tortured suspicions of the Cronkhites could not cause serious trouble.

Early in 1921 the War Department was not interested in the investigation, and the Justice Department had not discovered any reason for taking action. But in March 1921 the situation changed dramatically: in that month Harding was sworn in as President of the United States, and on March 4 he officially announced his Cabinet, naming Harry M. Daugherty as his Attorney General.

Little doubt exists that the Cronkhite case was reopened and pressed on Daugherty's personal order. On March 3 James Lee, a special agent for the Bureau of Investigation, was sent by the Washington office of the Department of Justice to inquire into the affair. On March 10 the *New York Times* carried the information that agents were investigating in the Seattle-Tacoma area. J. F. McAuley, chief of the Bureau of Investigation in Seattle, was quoted as expressing surprise at news dispatches saying Cronkhite had been killed on the target range in camp, since his office had always understood that the major had died in the woods.[22] In other words, under the preceding Attorney General the case was not pressed; desultory inquiries made since October 1920 had led nowhere. It cannot be simply coincidence that the decision to push investigation appeared simultaneously with Daugherty's appointment to this office. The question of why Daugherty agreed to press the charges unfortunately remains obscure now and probably will remain so forever.

An examination of Daugherty's political career, however, may provide some suggestive possibilities. Historians and political analysts agree he was probably the worst Attorney General ever to hold that office; his selection—along with Senator Fall as Secretary of the Interior, Edward Denby as Secretary of the Navy, and Charles Forbes as head of the Veterans Bureau—is usually seen as dramatic proof of the unfitness for high office of Warren Harding, who made the appointments.

The general impression of Daugherty is of a man whose mind and character were on a small scale; he is not a flamboyant villain to be admired for the scope and daring of his schemes. From his early career in the Ohio legislature to his later career in Washington, he remained a small-town shyster. He is often described by both his friends and enemies as a fighter, but an examination of his tactics shows that his bravery was characteristic of a certain type of politician. His instinct, when attacked, was to refuse to admit fault, to blame the previous incumbent or the Bolsheviks, to conceal, to muddy the waters, and to attack the character and reputation of his op-

Attorney General Harry M. Daugherty (left), whose personality and politics were influential in continuing the investigation and prosecution of the murder case, is shown here with his friend, Secretary of the Interior Albert Fall of Teapot Dome fame.

ponent. He knew, as that sort of man always knows, that sooner or later almost everyone will become weary of an increasingly confused and drawn-out struggle. He was apparently incapable of considering any situation in terms of abstract justice; he moved instead within the narrow confines of protection for himself and his circle of intimates and supporters. Like Iago, he would have replied to Cassio's despair at having lost his reputation with the sensible remark: "I had thought you had received some bodily wound."

Daugherty's pre-Washington career was inauspicious and was used by the New York *World* before his appointment as Attorney General to protest his probable selection. James M. Cox, the governor of Ohio who ran against Harding in 1920, relates a story of Daugherty's early tendencies: ". . . he was early caught in a cheap trick to best the local gamblers. He and his brother, Mal Daugherty, had set up, a few miles from Washington Court House, an equipment under a culvert to tap telegraph wires and get sporting news in advance to be used in sure thing bets." Cox went on to say that had Daugherty changed as he grew older, such youthful tricks could be forgotten, but unfortunately "Mr. Daugherty did not respect the ethics of public life."[23] After taking a law degree at the University of Michigan, he drifted into Ohio politics and only rarely practiced law. Karl Schriftgiesser in his book *This Was Normalcy*, sketches Daugherty's early career:

> he had been found guilty of unethical practices by the grievance committee of the Ohio Bar Association, but he was saved from disbarment by intervention of a friendly judge whose son was later associated with Daugherty in questionable activities around the Ohio State House. There Daugherty was known as "paymaster for the boys." In 1900 he solicited $1500 each from several insurance companies, telling them that the legislature was controlled in both houses by his friends and that it would pay them to have him around Columbus working in their interests. He engineered a number of what were then called "milker bills," a legal way of extorting money from interests threatened by legislation introduced for that purpose. . . . He was involved in the failure of a Columbus bank and only escaped prosecution because Governor James M. Cox was convinced that he could not be convicted and that prosecution might be perverted into charges of political persecution. . . . He had close connections with, if not membership in, the Ku Klux Klan, and these were of estimable value when Warren Harding ran for the United States Senate in 1914.[24]

Another scandal of Daugherty's early career was the Morse pardon case, used in 1922 by Senator Thaddeus Caraway of Arkansas and Senator Thomas Watson of Georgia as ammunition against the Attorney General. Morse had been convicted of fraud before World War I and sentenced to a long term in the federal penitentiary at Atlanta. Thomas Felder, a lawyer of dubious reputation, and Harry Daugherty managed to procure a pardon from President Taft, producing medical evidence to show that Morse was dying of Bright's disease. However, after being released from prison, Morse recovered his health completely, and the evidence of his illness was generally believed to have been faked. Daugherty's friends denied he had been involved in this affair, but his friendship with Felder—later in practice in New York City—continued.[25]

At the time of Daugherty's appointment to the Cabinet, he was not particularly well known outside Ohio politics. Oswald Villard, then editor of *The Nation,* described a visit to a friend who had served in the Ohio legislature with Daugherty and the "Ohio gang." The friend, after carefully closing the door, asked Villard his opinion of Harding's Cabinet, and when the editor replied he knew only Hoover, Hughes, and Weeks, began a hysterical denunciation of some of the other appointees. He described them as a "set of third-rate, small-time grafters" and said "Washington had never fallen so low." Villard was inclined at the time to dismiss this as exaggeration but later realized that his friend was entirely correct.[26] Daugherty did not come to Washington alone. He was accompanied by a horde of political hangers-on—the Ohio gang, "as unsavory a gang of psychopaths and thieves as ever invaded a national capitol this side of the Balkans."[27]

Daugherty was perfectly capable of reopening the Cronkhite case as a favor if requested by an important business or political interest. He apparently did not know General Cronkhite; the general's military career and Daugherty's political one do not intersect at any point. Secretary of War Weeks mentioned having arranged an interview between Daugherty and Cronkhite, which implies that the two men were strangers. Nor does Rosenbluth know who or what was behind the reopening of the case. When I asked him if he knew anything of Daugherty's motives, he replied in substance: "Daugherty was showing off! An important military man had asked a favor; he would show him what he could do." This was probably not the only motive, but it seems to fit well with the man. He had been vigorously attacked as unsuitable for this position previous to his appointment; even those who were willing to give him the benefit of the doubt in matters of honesty expressed concern for his lack of experience as a lawyer. Daugherty very likely saw in the Cronkhite case an opportunity to prove his critics wrong. The case was certain to be much discussed, negligence could be imputed to the previous administration, and the present Attorney General could claim credit for exposing the truth of a long-concealed major crime and coming to the rescue of a military hero fresh from his victory on the Meuse-Argonne. In addition, the case was attractive because it seemed to be a private one, unrelated to any political or business interests. It is perhaps significant that Rosenbluth's arrest was the first important act of Daugherty's administration. Certainly the reopening of the case and the way it was handled served as immediate evidence that the doubts of the Attorney General's fitness for high office were well founded.

CHAPTER THREE
CONFESSION
MARCH 17, 1921-
APRIL 1, 1921

SPECIAL AGENT JAMES LEE went promptly into action. Ex-sergeant Roland Pothier, who was now married and working as a train brakeman for the New York, New Haven, and Hartford line, agreed on March 17 to come to the Federal Building in Providence, Rhode Island, to discuss the death of Major Cronkhite. Under the pressure of interrogation he confessed almost at once to having shot the major by accident and signed a statement to that effect on March 19. Several days later he agreed to sign a statement alleging that Captain Rosenbluth had ordered him to shoot the major during the hike. Then, after several variant versions of his story, he signed his last confession on March 25, charging that the murder had been planned in advance by Rosenbluth, who had explained to Pothier what he wanted done, told him to borrow a pistol, and to be prepared to kill the major in a particular secluded clearing. After being taken to New York to appear at Rosenbluth's arraignment, he told officers he would not testify against Rosenbluth and returned to his accident confession once more. Later in Providence he alternated between claiming that the shot was accidentally fired by himself and hinting at a mysterious "shot from the bushes" from which Rosenbluth emerged.

The questionable methods used to produce these various statements are available for inspection in several reliable documents. Agent Lee's reports concerning his interrogations of Pothier were reproduced extensively in an exoneration later published by the Washington state prosecuting attorney, James Selden. Selden was given these records by the U.S. attorney at Seattle, acting under orders of the Attorney General. Pothier himself described his ordeal in a lengthy newspaper article. At the grand jury session very detailed testimony was taken from Agent Lee; Peter Cannon, the U.S. attorney at Providence; John Richards, the U.S. marshal at Providence; and David Jordan, the deputy marshal. From these various statements several prefatory generalizations can be made. Cannon, Richards, and Jordan appear to have been honest and competent officials who were by no means anxious to involve Rosenbluth in the case and do not seem to have heard of him until Pothier's later confessions were obtained. But the preliminary interrogation of Pothier was handled by the Bureau of Investigation agents assigned to the case, James Lee and Billups Harris, and by the Providence agent in charge, Thomas Callaghan. The Bureau of Investigation at this time has been described by a recent historian as "an odd-job detective agency with fuzzy lines of authority and responsibility."[1] It had participated in the Red raids of 1920, and had a well-deserved reputation for using extralegal methods of investigation and a readiness to find spies and Bolsheviks everywhere. In addition Lee worked on orders issued directly from Washington and thus was independent of any local authority.

According to the official biography of the Federal Bureau of Investigation, one of the important changes that J. Edgar Hoover made when named head of the bureau in 1924 was to place special agents under the authority of agents in charge, so that field work was handled locally.[2] But in 1921 agents sent from Washington were not under the authority of anyone at the scene of the actual investigation. In a letter written in 1924 to Assistant Attorney General Earl Davis, Hoover reported: ". . . it appears that this investigation was directed and handled exclusively by Mr. Herron up to the time of his death and that agents working on this case worked directly under his instructions."[3] As a result Special Agent Lee, a minor employee who had worked for the bureau for less than a year, was free to conduct his researches as he saw fit, without being required to submit reports or gain the permission of the authorities in Providence.

Furthermore, it appears almost certain that Lee was specifically chosen for this investigation. As he himself described his appointment in a letter to Assistant Attorney General Crim:

> Early in 1921 I was called to Washington, D.C., and given an important part in the Cronkhite investigation, in fact the Chief's office had reached the stage where some one had to be assigned to the Cronkhite case, who, in addition to understanding the military game, must be possessed of a nature that was not afraid to face an almost unlimited amount of propaganda. Whether I possessed these qualities or not I do not know, but nevertheless I was informed that my work in the field had attracted the attention of the Powers in Washington, hence my assignment to the Cronkhite case. My personal investigation resulted in the arrests of both Rosenbluth and Pothier. That is, the confession I obtained from Pothier was directly the cause of the arrests and the indictments which followed.[4]

There is reason to believe that Lee was appointed at the request of General Cronkhite himself. Many changes in Pothier's story from one interview to the next seem to reflect suggestions of Lee's which must have been obtained from the general's personal theories on the case. Lee had served in the A.E.F. as a lieutenant and was briefly connected with military intelligence after the war; thus it is possible he may have known the general. After the trial in 1924 they seemed to have been on intimate terms and mutually concerned about the case, in spite of the fact that Lee was discharged from the bureau in the fall of 1921.

Lee's status as an independent agent created a situation in which the authorities in Providence were not entirely sure who was in charge. A hint of this is shown in the conclusion of an article later published in the New York *World*:

> When agents in Providence learned that Lee had visited Pothier alone in the jail and obtained a confession involving Rosenbluth they were indignant. There was some thought of going to the jail without letting Lee know and getting Pothier's story first hand. After some discussion, it was decided that since Lee had been assigned to the case such a step as that would be exceeding authority.[5]

That the authorities in Providence had some definite suspicions of Lee's methods was shown by Attorney Cannon's and Marshal Richards' reluctance to permit Pothier to go to New York to appear against Rosenbluth and by Cannon's statement to the grand jury: "Deputy Marshal Jordan went with him to New York. I did not want to trust him with the Department of Justice agents. I wanted to be sure that Jordan would be with him at all times, so there would be no threats or intimidations used."[6] Cannon's doubts about Lee's methods are also suggested by the fact that, after receiving the confession involving Rosenbluth, he went to a jail to question a prisoner directly for the only time during his term as U.S. attorney. Although Richards and Cannon testified before the grand jury that they believed there was something to Pothier's story and were unable to shake him seriously in it, Cannon's testimony also showed they were somewhat uneasy about the way it had been obtained.

That government agents at this time were in the habit of taking suspects into custody and interrogating them privately is demonstrated by a variety of sources. William Preston, Jr., in his book, *Aliens and Dissenters,* argues that the increasing tendency to ignore due process began in the Bureau of Immigration. A Supreme Court decision of 1893 held that deportation was not punishment for a crime, but a right of the federal gov-

ernment in appropriate circumstances; the usual legal safeguards extended to accused criminals did not apply. Thus it
became the custom in deportation cases to make arrests without
warrant, to hold preliminary hearings without counsel, and to
delay the presence of counsel until the prisoner had provided
sufficient evidence of his guilt.[7] These procedures were adopted
during the mass arrests of alleged aliens during the big Red
scare in 1920. In his study of the Federal Bureau of Investigation Max Lowenthal shows that these practices were used by
the men in charge of the mass arrests: "The detectives' orders
read that 'persons taken into custody [are] not to be permitted
to communicate with any outside person until after examination by this office and *until permission is given by this office.*' "[8]

Although the Red raids were sharply criticized by many
prominent lawyers, there is no reason to believe that the ordinary special agent saw anything wrong with this accepted way
of doing things. Special Agent Stone, questioned before a Senate committee about his interrogation of an arrested alien said,
"No, sir, I did not feel that he was entitled to more than any
person arrested under the criminal statutes, whom it is the
practice of we law-enforcement officers to obtain admissions
from him [sic] without counsel being present." A lawyer at
this hearing pointed out that this was contrary to American
legal statutes, but Senator King replied that the right to counsel
before interrogation was constantly disregarded by all police
forces.[9]

Coupled with Lee's unquestioning acceptance of pre-
counsel interrogation was the mentality of the detective. Lowenthal quotes a discussion between Secretary of the Interior
James A. Garfield and several congressmen concerning the po-
tential dangers of a yet-to-be-formed Bureau of Investigation:

> GARFIELD: Without in any way reflecting upon the work of
>   good detectives, I find that the moment a man has perfected
>   himself as a detective, he approaches nearly every case with
>   a desire to prove that the person against whom a charge is
>   made is guilty.
> BOWERS (Mississippi): He is a partisan, in other words?
> GARFIELD: Yes.
> OLMSTED (Pennsylvania): It redounds more to his credit to dis-
>   cover a criminal than it does to discover an honest man?
> GARFIELD: Exactly.[10]

Later, Lowenthal quotes Burton K. Wheeler, junior senator
from Montana, in a similar comment:

> As a prosecuting attorney I came in contact with the Depart-
> ment of Justice men during the war, and most of the men . . .
> were high-class men, but nevertheless they had the detective

mind. . . . I do not care how good a man is, how able he is, he
cannot be placed in a detective service without being affected
mentally, and becoming of the snooping detective type.[11]

That Agent Lee possessed this type of mind to an extraordinary
degree can be demonstrated by his own words.

Admittedly Pothier confessed rather readily under the
questioning of Lee, Callaghan, and Jones to having shot Cronkhite by accident. He had been interrogated about the case on
at least two earlier occasions and must have been aware for
more than a year that the case had been reopened. As Lee described the scene: "With the assistance of Mr. Callaghan I was
able to get Pothier twisted in his story, and after about an hour
of cross-examination Pothier broke down and began to cry and
requested us to give him a few minutes to get his composure,
and he would tell us the truth about the whole affair." Pothier
then denied the story he had told before the board of inquiry
and had repeated to Captain Ross in 1919 and to Agent Conley
in 1920. Instead he asserted that he and Major Cronkhite had
both been shooting at the can and that after the major hit it,
Pothier started to unload his gun and in the process somehow
fired it, fatally wounding the major.[12]

Superficially considered, there is nothing obviously unreasonable about this story. As shown later Pothier had borrowed a gun from Sergeant Kreutz the day of the hike and admitted he had taken, without Kreutz's knowledge, three bullets
from the saddlebag in which the revolver was kept. As many
of the men later agreed, Pothier and the major were friendly;
it is not unlikely that Cronkhite, a young and informal person,
would have suggested some competitive shooting to his orderly.
In addition, Pothier was inexperienced with handguns and was
not an expert shot. But in spite of the seeming simplicity of
this explanation none of the men concerned in Pothier's interrogation believed his statement.

Callaghan and Lee, assisted by Captain Jones, General
Cronkhite's agent,

> gave Pothier a .45-calibre revolver and had him demonstrate
> just how the bullet was fired. Pothier's demonstration of the
> accident was so ridiculous that even had Pothier's gun dis-
> charged it would have been a physical impossibility owing to
> Pothier's height, for Pothier to hold the gun high enough to hit
> the major in the breast. As Pothier demonstrated loading the
> gun, the bullet could not have hit the major above the waist
> line, as the major was 70½ inches tall. After working on Pothier
> for hours endeavoring to get him to tell the truth, he would not
> stir from his story, admitted that perhaps it was impossible to
> have killed the major by accident, but that he had told every-
> thing as it happened. Pothier said that he would not implicate

anyone and that if we could prove that he shot the major intentionally that he was ready to take all the blame and go to the electric chair if he had to. Following the most rigid questioning we could not get Pothier to say a word about Rosenbluth; says that Rosenbluth and the major were good friends and he never heard them quarrel. Also claims that Rosenbluth and the major were very friendly on the morning of the shooting.[13]

Several things are obvious at this point. The men interrogating Pothier were prepared to disregard the accident confession at once. It was barely spoken before they were at work to prove that the shot could not have been accidental. Pothier clearly was being asked leading questions about Rosenbluth from the first, and might never have thought of bringing Rosenbluth into the affair had it not been steadily suggested to him. Various details added to his story later seem to have been given to him by Lee. For example, in an extended talk with Marshal Richards several days later, Pothier changed his statement about the friendliness of Cronkhite and Rosenbluth and made a vague reference to their having had "words" on the hike. This reversal of his original testimony strongly suggests he had been informed of the testimony of a few others who did remember, or thought they did, an argument between the two officers.

In his testimony before the grand jury Marshal Richards described his several interviews with Pothier. Pothier appeared before him on March 19 and, having been duly cautioned and read a warrant charging him with accidental homicide, pleaded guilty to that charge. Richards talked with Pothier—"we were naturally interested in his story. I felt kind of sorry for him"—and in the course of the conversation realized that his story could not be correct. Pothier said he was using an automatic pistol and

> he pulled the slide back and it slipped on his wrist and turned sideways and the bullet hit the Major . . . and he said he pulled the slide back in order to take out an empty shell. . . . It dawned upon me that that thing would be impossible because there is never an empty shell in an automatic. . . . So I called his attention to that, and he sort of got confused and shut up.

Some days later, Richards reported, Pothier changed his story and claimed he had been shooting with a revolver, and in unloading it, "I started the cylinder to the left out of the frame [and] the pistol exploded." This, Richards asserted with the greatest positiveness, was impossible. "The slightest movement of this cylinder in that direction will make it impossible to discharge that gun. . . . I own one myself."[14] Richards, it should be noted, was experienced with handguns and was paid as an expert witness on the subject before the grand jury.

The incorrectness of the accident confession was then agreed to by the men concerned in the case at this time. Pothier had indeed signed a confession and was charged with accidental homicide, but regardless of this the story appeared to be false. If he had seen a lawyer at this point and bail had been arranged, this probably would have been the end of the matter. Men have in the past (and will in the future) confessed for a variety of reasons to crimes they have not committed—a neurotic desire for punishment being the most obvious, combined often with a desire for attention, for being in the spotlight. A reasonably competent lawyer probably could have arranged to have the matter dropped with some cooperation from Pothier. But matters were not allowed to rest there. Pothier, still without legal advice, was returned to his cell—his family was not prosperous, and there was some difficulty about posting bail—and was left to the guardianship of special agents Lee and Harris for the next three days. Not only did these men disbelieve the accident story but they were also certain that Rosenbluth was involved.

Although Agent Lee denied in an interview with the New York *World* that he had had any knowledge of Rosenbluth prior to Pothier's confession of his involvement, this was clearly not quite true. He had studied the board of inquiry testimony and must have had access to General Cronkhite's files from the beginning. His interview with Rosenbluth in New York as he described it for the grand jury makes clear that he was certain of his quarry's guilt before Pothier had been persuaded to implicate him. After Pothier had confessed to accidental homicide, Lee went to New York and invited Rosenbluth to come for an interview. Rosenbluth, unaware that anyone had confessed anything, agreed to come voluntarily to the offices of the Justice Department and discuss the case. The interview was taken down by Agent William Dunn in the presence of another agent, George Starr; these men were later able to testify that the interview had been given freely without duress. Rosenbluth later stated, however, in an interview with Donald Ewing of the *Chicago Tribune* (April 4, 1923) that the transcript of this meeting had been grossly tampered with.

> "What I really said," he explained, "was that I thought that the bullet wound was in the neck, but that they had better consult the autopsy. The man questioning me turned to the stenographer and said, "Don't put that part in about the autopsy. Just record the answer 'in the neck.' Any other discrepancies in my statements were due entirely to the fact that Cronkhite's death took place two and a half years before and that my

memory was naturally hazy. In many places in this hearing where I said 'I think' they changed my answer to a positive answer."[15]

The formal transcript did not, however, include the entire conversation. Before the grand jury Lee explained: "After we got through with the interview which is reported, I had a personal talk with him in the room. I asked him a few questions. I told him I would like to get his personal idea of just how he stood on the matter. He absolutely refused to answer." Asked by a member of the jury just exactly what questions Rosenbluth had refused to answer, Lee continued:

> After I had talked with Washington on the wire previously, I had obtained some admission from Pothier, and as a matter of making a character study of the man I started to talk casually with him. I told him that he was pretty lucky—just as a matter of satisfying my own mind. He says, "How is that?" as I recall it. I says, "Well, one of the men that was up near the scene of the shooting has admitted killing Major Cronkhite." He says, "Well, that is news to me." I again asked him if he could account for the story told by this sergeant which I did not tell him in any way what it was—but there had been some conditions that looked as though the Captain had told a rather peculiar story. He told me, "I refuse to say anything along that line without consulting my attorney." . . . It was nothing that went into the record. It was something that I wanted to know personally, just how he stood on the matter.

Later recalled before the grand jury, Lee amplified his report of this conversation:

> I remember telling him before I left him, I said to him something along this line: "Captain, I think you have got an awful nerve to try to convince me of some things you have been saying. Being a captain in the army I am surprised at you. I was only a junior officer and I know better than to make some statements you have made." He said, "You mean to say you don't believe me?" I said, "No, I don't believe you unless you can tell a better story than you have." I said, "I think you have put yourself in a pretty bad predicament."

Rosenbluth, clearly astonished by this direct attack upon his honesty and seeking some explanation for it, said, according to Lee, "I appreciate your stand. Your point is to try to draw me out. I know you haven't anything against me; it is just part of your work."[16]

Lee's own testimony clarifies that the official report of the interview by no means included the whole conversation and was in fact misleading, since it seemed to show that no pressure

or duress had been used. The private conversation following
the formal interview was calculated deliberately to surprise
some admission from Rosenbluth. He was told abruptly that
Pothier had confessed to shooting the major, although no details of the confession were given. Rosenbluth's immediate and
perfectly legitimate request for a lawyer was ignored and not
put into the record. Lee's insistence that Rosenbluth was not
telling the truth was doubly offensive because at this time
Pothier had confessed only that he had shot the major by accident, and Lee himself rejected this as impossible. Thus if Lee
did not believe Pothier's confession of accidental shooting he
had no actual reason for accusing Rosenbluth of lying.

Rosenbluth's version of this interview in his unpublished
autobiography is somewhat more highly colored. "Attempted
third degree methods were used, but as I told the agents, 'You
know I was the head of a reformatory, and I know third degree
methods—yours are very stupid.'" In a personal interview
Rosenbluth said that during his interrogation the officer in
charge reminded him of the "suicide" about a year before of a
man named Salsedo, who had been confined in those very offices for some weeks and was found one morning dead on the
pavement fifteen floors below. The agent apparently hoped to
frighten Rosenbluth by the implication that the fall had not
been suicide and Salsedo had been deliberately disposed of.
Rosenbluth, however, did not respond to this attempt to alarm
him, and he was released the next morning with the guarantee
that the agents would "get him."

Agent Lee followed up his interview with Rosenbluth by
an investigation of his victim's "associations" in New York City.
His references to his visit to the Civic Club and to Rosenbluth's
occupation establish the strong probability the various stories
about Rosenbluth as a spy and Bolshevik emanated from him.
Asked before the grand jury what business Rosenbluth was in,
he replied:

> That is a rather hard question to answer. When arrested he
> had a secret code in his possession, which is supposed to repre-
> sent some firm he was in touch with in Lavinski. I was told
> . . . that code was sent to Washington to be deciphered. . . .
> He told me he was gathering grain data to send to Russia.

Asked about Rosenbluth's nationality, Lee replied, ". . . I
would say he was a Russian Jew. I would not say he was an
anarchist." Lee appeared to believe that Rosenbluth was not
a native-born citizen; he mentioned Rosenbluth's flashing his
"citizenship papers" when challenged about his loyalty. What
these papers were is uncertain, but they could not have been

what Lee supposed; Rosenbluth had been born in New York
City in 1887 and was not a naturalized citizen.

After telling the jury *The Nation* was "a magazine that
will go the limit in supporting a man whether right or wrong,"*
he volunteered information about his visit to the Civic Club:

> A. I might tell where I found Rosenbluth in New York. The
> morning I went out to look over his quarters,—he was stay-
> ing at the Civic Club—the first thing I saw as we entered
> the door was pictures of two radicals who were sentenced
> to death up there in Massachusetts. There was other propa-
> ganda on the wall. There was no American flags or any-
> thing of that sort hanging around. I looked over the regis-
> ter and found Rosenbluth's name—R. Rosenbluth—regis-
> tered on three consecutive days. . . . There was a woman
> in there and a man, a foreigner.
> Q. Did you get the possible impresssion that it was Russian
> Soviet propaganda in there?
> A. I would not be very far wrong if I said so.[17]

Lee's reports of this visit show a great deal about the way
his mind worked. Clearly, he was prepared to find at the Civic
Club dramatic evidence of Rosenbluth's political unreliability.
His description of the club suggests an atmosphere of foreign
spies and secret agents, as does his careful investigation of the
register to find Rosenbluth's name—at a club of which he was
quite openly a member! The many later stories in the press
concerning Rosenbluth's alleged shady past, his undercover
work in Russia, and his connection with German and Bolshevik
spy networks appear to have originated entirely within the mind
of a man bedazzled with dreams of tracking down foreign
agents. A man capable of believing that any and all members
of a club sponsoring the cause of Sacco and Vanzetti must be
in sympathy with the Soviets was not to be restrained by any of
the ordinary rules of logic and evidence.

Certain in his own mind of Rosenbluth's guilt, Lee raced
back to Providence where he and his colleague Billups Harris
set out to persuade Pothier, as they phrased it, "to tell the
truth." On March 19,

> Mr. Harris kept under cover while I took Pothier to a room and
> talked to him for about two hours, but to no avail. However, I
> satisfied myself about a number of things I was not sure of and
> although Pothier refused to change his story, I feel confident
> that we are making headway. Mr. Harris then went to him, as
> one of Rosenbluth's agents, but Pothier would have nothing to
> do with him. In the morning . . . I also talked to Pothier
> again, and tried to get from him just what his motive was in
> sticking to such a ridiculous story.[18]

---

* This magazine had published two articles before the grand jury hearings
in defense of Rosenbluth.

Pothier insisted that Lee be summoned after Harris's visit, and gave him a full description of a man he believed was sent by Rosenbluth. Other methods besides this attempt to trap Pothier into admitting a conspiracy were resorted to:

> Pothier being a Catholic, I decided that it would be a good idea to have him consult his own spiritual adviser and Pothier told me that he would be greatly obliged if I would bring Rev. Father La Liberte of Central Falls to him. This I did, and the priest worked on Pothier for three hours, urging him to tell the truth, no matter what it might be, but even this did not avail.[19]

In Pothier's own description of his stay in the Providence jail, he told of the visits of his priest and his family:

> I told Father Liberte again that my gun went off accidentally, but he just seemed to be convinced that I was keeping something back, and he told me again to tell everything I knew about it.
>
> The next day Lee went out to see my wife and he filled her full of a lot of stuff about how I was shielding somebody and how the best thing I could do for myself was to come clean. That afternoon she came to see me in jail and she started after me the same way that Father Liberte did. . . .
>
> The next day Lee came in to see me, and he insisted that I was shielding Rosenbluth. I told him I didn't know anything at all against Rosenbluth. But he said, "He's a dirty, German Jew spy. . . ."
>
> Then my wife came with my uncle . . . and my brother and father. They all kept begging me to tell the truth, and saying it wasn't right for me to shield another man. They just about drove me crazy, and I didn't know what to do.[20]

Pothier weakened steadily under these combined assaults.

> I am certain that he shows signs of weakening every time I visit him. My chief motive now is to gain his confidence and he has got to a point where he actually asks my advice on some things. . . . Little admissions at a time are helping wonderfully to bring Pothier to the truth and I cannot see how Pothier can stick it out much longer especially when his wife is in such a condition. [Mrs. Pothier was pregnant and in a hysterical state.] . . . He talks with me very frankly now and I feel sure he will tell me everything as he realizes now that he must tell the truth for his own interest and as I am about the only person who goes to see him at the jail he is especially friendly toward me and asks me each time to come the following day and help him to get this story off his mind.[21]

In addition to these methods of persuasion, there is considerable reason to suspect that Agent Lee employed another device to engage Pothier's cooperation. His comments on Pothier's growing dependence on him and his increasing willingness to cooperate raise the question of how this goal was achieved. If Pothier gradually came to see himself as working with Lee (as his report of Agent Harris's visit implies) and if he was willing to deny the relatively minor crime of accidental homicide and lay himself open to a charge of murder, he must have been offered something in return.

Apparently Pothier was encouraged to believe that he would be protected from prosecution if he consented to involve Rosenbluth; press releases following the arrests stated "the police sought to hold Pothier only until the man high up was taken." But in addition to this, we have the fact that Lee led Pothier to believe that Rosenbluth was an enemy of the country. There is little reason to doubt the truth of Pothier's assertion that Lee repeatedly called Rosenbluth a "dirty German Jew spy." Lee's remarks to the grand jury showed that he suspected Rosenbluth of some connection with foreign agents. There can be no reason for such a claim being made except to persuade Pothier that his confession would assist in the successful prosecution of an enemy agent.

Exactly what Lee told Pothier is not known, but later newspaper stories are suggestive. Allegedly Rosenbluth was a member of a German spy ring which had planned Cronkhite's murder in order to render his father, Major General Cronkhite, incapable of functioning well in the Allied offensive just beginning overseas. If Pothier believed that Rosenbluth was a spy and his "confession" would merely clinch an already impressive case, his behavior is understandable. It is probable that Lee not only used the pressure of priest, family, and hours of steady interrogation on his victim but offered him a "reward" as well. If Pothier would cooperate, he could go to New York and appear as a star witness in an important spy trial. This interpretation is borne out by two things. First, Pothier's excited report to Lee when visited by Agent Harris pretending to represent Rosenbluth strongly suggests that Pothier was acting almost like an agent himself, reporting to a superior about an attempted contact by the "enemy." Second, Pothier's willingness to go to New York, although advised and even urged by Cannon and Richards against it, suggests he really wanted to make the trip. Certainly his expressed anger when no hearing was held and he had no opportunity to appear in public implies that he had looked forward to the notoriety.

A comment of Lee's refers to this aspect of Pothier's personality:

> Pothier is an expert at telling untruths and is the type of fellow that likes to talk about himself and is very forward about bringing himself into notice. I do not believe that he has much courage. He impresses me as a cowardly sort of man that would do about anything to help his own cause along.[22]

That Pothier discovered during his New York visit that he had been misled is implied in Lee's statement, "Asked as to why he had gone back on his story, Pothier said that he was being tricked. . . ."[23]

Whatever combination of methods was employed, on March 22 Lee got the results he sought:

> agent . . . spent three hours with Pothier, bringing every pressure to bear on this man to induce him to tell the truth. By using his wife's delicate condition and a newspaper story which told of Pothier's intended removal by the government to the state of Washington, I was able for the first time to break him away from his accident story and he finally admitted to me frankly that Capt. Rosenbluth got him into this mess, that there was no target practice at all, and that he shot the major intentionally but was put up to do it by Rosenbluth.[24]

II

LATER THAT DAY, Pothier's basic admission was put into written form and he signed a confession charging that during the hike Rosenbluth had ordered him to go forward and shoot Major Cronkhite, "and being in the army at the time, I did not stop to think what I was doing." After the major fell, Pothier alleged, Rosenbluth came forward, shot a hole through a tobacco can on the ground, and told Pothier to back up the target-shooting story. "I continued to do everything that Capt. Rosenbluth told me to do and I do not understand why I done these things, it seemed that Capt. Rosenbluth had some influence over me, which I could not understand."[25] This confession was handed to the U.S. attorney that day, and his reaction was immediate:

> as a result of receiving that statement—an astonishing statement as I thought at that time,—I said to Callaghan, "I will go out to the jail myself this afternoon and I will question this man. If it is true, it is a damnable thing; if it is not true, the sooner we know it the better." We went out a little after two and I was there till seven.[26]

Cannon's interrogation of Pothier is quoted at length in the Selden pamphlet and shows, I believe, that he was really trying to get at the truth of the story. The questions asked are aimed at showing the weaknesses of this confession. Particularly he probed for motive, for any sort of association or communication between the two men. Pothier was asked if he had ever seen Rosenbluth or corresponded with him after the war, and Pothier replied, "No, I have never heard from him at all."

Questioned about the written statements he and the others made at the base hospital, he explained that they were all asked to write out statements and did so in separate rooms. "I wrote mine myself." Asked to whom he gave the statement, he did not remember but was sure he neither gave it to Rosenbluth nor saw the captain's statement. After several questions about talking with the captain, he replied, "I don't remember speaking to him at all after the accident." Questioned about the board of inquiry, Pothier said the three witnesses testified separately and he passed Rosenbluth going out as he went in. "He said nothing to me."

Attorney Cannon was also disturbed at the unlikelihood that the killing had not been planned ahead of time. After Pothier continued to insist there was no advance meeting and Rosenbluth had approached him during the hike, Cannon exploded: "Now listen, Mr. Pothier, no sane person would believe that story. There must have been some previous arrangements and plans made for this thing."[27]

As a result of Cannon's incredulity Pothier, with Lee's assistance, revised and altered his story in an attempt to align it with General Cronkhite's supposed evidence and theories about the case, as well as to overcome Cannon's objections. In a later interview with Marshal Richards, Pothier claimed that his first statement written out after the tragedy was torn up because it was "not right" and he was asked to make another "correct" one. This is clearly a fabrication, probably suggested by Lee. No mention is made of a second statement in the interview with Cannon. Furthermore, since these statements were never found and were apparently accidentally misfiled or destroyed, it is unlikely that Pothier was asked to make a second "correct" one.

Other remarks made by Pothier in various interviews suggest Lee's help, particularly the pointless mystery of the major's missing campaign hat. The only actual clue is a statement made by Lieutenant Saunders to the effect that he noticed the hat lying on the floor of the ambulance near the open door as the vehicle passed him on the way to the hospital and thought at the time it might fall out. Mrs. Cronkhite, in her concern for her son's possessions, listed the hat as one of the missing items. Lee reported asking about the hat and being told by Pothier that he had no idea what happened to it and did not remember it at all. Later, however, both Richards and Cannon reported that Pothier mentioned the hat to them as a solution to the mystery of the major's death: "Produce the hat; that will tell the story." Neither man was able to influence Pothier to explain what he meant, but Richards interpreted the hint to mean that the hat contained a bullet hole. He suggested that the major had been shot at twice and the first shot had pierced the hat. Its destruction was vital, therefore, to maintain the false story that the major had been shooting and had accidentally killed himself.[28]

There is a startling discrepancy between Pothier's first statements and his later ones. Given the general picture of the case and Lee's steady visits to Pothier, Lee's questions no doubt provided Pothier with a series of red herrings to toss out to his questioners as he wished. Lee was also clearly in communication with the Cronkhites, or at least had access to their reports to the Justice Department, since no other source would have indicated that the hat was a possible clue.

Apparently then, by the time Cannon and Richards were questioning Pothier, he had already been exposed to several days of interrogation by Agent Lee, whose questions had not only produced a series of confessions but had provided Pothier with many clues to allegedly mysterious features of the case. After the interview with Cannon, Pothier agreed to sign a final confession which incorporated Cannon's insistence that Pothier and Rosenbluth must have met to plan the murder beforehand. Pothier's version of that confession follows:

> Well, when I got thinking about it that night I didn't know what to do. They had me so damned mixed up that I couldn't remember what I'd said and what I hadn't said, and I knew I couldn't stand it much longer. I was almost crazy with Lee pestering me all the time. It was terrible. He came in to see me the next night and started after me again and I knew I'd just have to say whatever he wanted me to say. And so when he asked me a question I'd tell him whatever he wanted to hear. He'd ask me a question like this: "Didn't you have a talk with Rosenbluth three days before the shooting? You know damn well you did! Come through with it." And I answered, "Yes." That was all I had to do—just say "yes" and "no."[29]

The confession produced by this question and answer technique was an extended document incorporating all the details Lee and others could invent or imagine. In spite of this, it is a curiously unconvincing document:

> I, Roland R. Pothier, on oath, depose and say that about four or five days before the shooting of Major Cronkhite, Captain Rosenbluth called me over to a space behind headquarters company and asked me if I was any kind of a shot, and if I ever handled a pistol before; that I answered that the only time I ever handled a pistol was at target practice, and he asked me where, and I said at Panama; that he then said, "You don't have to be an expert for what I want you to do"; that I did not ask him what that was; that he then said, "All right, I will see you later"; that I then left him and went to my quarters.

That on the next night or the night after, I again met
Captain Rosenbluth at the same place; that he asked me if I was
going out with the school of reconnaisance, and I said that I
had heard nothing about it; he told me that it was for all noncommissioned officers and he didn't see any reason why I
should not go; that I said, "If that is so, I guess I am included
with them"; he then asked me if I remembered what he said to
me the other night about firing a pistol; I answered "Yes," and
he then asked me if I had any idea what it was for and I
answered, "No"; that he then said, "I want to get Major Cronkhite": that I asked him what he meant, and he said, "I want
you to kill him"; that I asked him what his reasons were for
wanting me to kill the Major, and he said, "Because we want
to get him out of the way"; that I asked him why he wanted to
get the Major out of the way; and he said, "You never mind,
you will find out later"; then I asked him who he meant by
"we" and if I was included in it, he said, "No, you are not included in it"; and that I then said, "How am I going to get out
of this thing if they put the blame on me," and he said, "Never
mind, I will see that everything would be all right"; that I then
asked him how would he see that everything would be all right;
he answered, "If you get sent to jail, I will get the best lawyers
I can to get you out of it."

That I then asked him about the disgrace on my father and
mother and he said that he could not say anything about that;
when I told him I was the one who would suffer, he told me that
he would see to that and I need not worry about it; that I then
asked him how I was to do the job, and he then asked me if I
had ever been to this place before (meaning Camp Lewis) and
I told him that I had not; he then said, "I have looked over the
maps, and from what I could see I think I have found a good
location for it, (meaning the killing of the Major), and when
we get there I will tell you." Be sure that you get him in a good
place so he won't have a chance to say anything"; that I asked
him where he wanted me to shoot him and he said, "Of course,
you will be standing on his right side and it won't be a bad idea
to get him about here (pointing to a spot about even with his
heart); that I asked him what I was going to do after I shot him,
and he said, "You never mind, I will be somewhere around and
when I see him fall, I will run up and grab him"; that he said
further, "Then I will yell for a doctor and get him down there
and we will go about it just as if he shot himself accidentally
and that I was to say nothing"; that I said, "Suppose they ask
me how it happened," and he said, "You tell them it was target
practice and that the Major shot himself accidentally and everything will be all right"; that he then said, "That is all, I will
see you on the day of the march, which will be on the day after
tomorrow."

That on the morning of October 25, 1918, after the company had been dismissed on the way back to my quarters, Captain Rosenbluth stopped me and asked me if I had forgotten
what he told me the night before; that I said no; that he then
asked me if I had a gun, and I told him that I did not; that he
then said, "You want to borrow one then, and get ammunition
too. The person from whom you borrow the gun must not be
told what you want it for, and when you get the ammunition
put it in your pocket, and when the company falls in you know

where your place in line is, and after we get on the march I think we will have some advance guard problems, and I will talk this over with you when we have these problems. That is all for now."

That we then started on the march and had proceeded about two or three miles from the camp and started doing advance guard problems. In the meantime, Major Cronkhite showed up, and apparently assumed command; that I asked Captain Rosenbluth if it would be all right to go with the Major now, and he said, "Go ahead," which I did; that while engaged in advance guard problems Captain Rosenbluth said to me, "If anything comes up after the shooting, you explain that he was engaged in target practice, and that he shot himself accidentally. If they ask how it happened, you say that the Major was holding his gun barrel up a little inclined to the rear and that his gun twisted in his hand and as he went to catch it, he accidentally shot himself." That the Captain then told me to go with the Major and stay with him; that we came to a place where a trail led off the right of the road and the company was assembled, and the Major and the Captain went in front of the company and I was about six paces behind both of them, and the head of the column was about 50 yards behind me; that we had proceeded to a point about four miles from camp by this time, and while going down a slope, Captain Rosenbluth dropped back and told me to go back and halt the company, which I did; that I told Lieutenant Rustenbach to halt the company.

In the meantime Major Cronkhite kept on walking until he arrived at this little open space behind some bushes and stood there with his back to the road; that I met Captain Rosenbluth as I was on my way back to join the Major and the Captain; that the Captain told me to get him now; that I then joined the Major in this open space and when about two feet behind him, I loaded my revolver with the three shells; that I fired one shot into the open field, and as the Major was turning around in my direction I fired my second shot at the Major, hitting him in the right breast; that about that time I heard another shot from behind where I was standing; that Captain Rosenbluth came rushing upon the scene and picked up the Major and dragged his body so that it lay in a position parallel with the road.

That Captain Rosenbluth then drew his gun from his holster, the cap of which was unbuttoned, and shot a hole through a Piper Heidsiek tobacco can, and said, "Do not forget about this being a target practice and that the Major shot himself accidentally, and if any questions are asked about this let me do the talking and you keep still"; that I did this; that Captain Rosenbluth then looked over Major Cronkhite and said, "I think he is dead," that he then called for Dr. Seaburg, and about ten minutes had elapsed between this time and when the Major was shot; that Dr. Seaburg arrived a few minutes later, and Captain Rosenbluth asked him if he had any strychnine, and Seaburg said, "Yes"; and he injected a dose of strychnine into Major Cronkhite's body; that Captain Rosenbluth then asked for someone who knew anything about artificial respiration; that Dr. Seaburg had already pronounced the Major dead; that Sergeants Root and Wuthenow came up and worked on the

Major for about 20 minutes; that Lieutenant Seaburg called for a fast runner to go to camp and get an ambulance, which later arrived; that I accompanied the body to headquarters in the ambulance and then to the hospital where I was ordered by the officer of the day to make a statement concerning the shooting; that Captain Rosenbluth and Dr. Seaburg were also requested to write out statements; that these statements were each written in a separate room and handed to the officer of the day after they had been written; that before leaving the hospital Captain Rosenbluth stopped me on the way out, after I had made the statement, and told me to meet him the night after the following night after tattoo in the same place where I had met him on several occasions previous to the shooting; that on this night I met Captain Rosenbluth as requested; that he told me not to forget about explaining the shooting as the result of target practice and that the Major shot himself accidentally, and for me not to fear as everything would be all right; that I later went before the Board of Inquiry when it met and testified the way I had been told by Captain Rosenbluth.

/signed/ ROLAND R. POTHIER.[30]

Disregarding the methods used to achieve this confession and considering only the results, it is easy to see that the case against Rosenbluth is extremely hard to believe. We have to suppose that an intelligent man of thirty decides to murder his superior officer with the assistance of a sergeant, a man he does not know, a man whose very name he had apparently forgotten at the time of his arrest two and a half years later. He plans the crime for a particular day when his intended victim is still recovering from a serious illness, not knowing whether he will be well enough to go on the hike. He selects a particular spot for the murder from a map, without any way to tell if the place is actually screened from view and will be safe He offers Pothier no reward and no guarantees except the promise of a good lawyer. To increase his risk of discovery, he directs his accomplice to borrow a weapon—a dangerous proceeding, since the owner of the revolver cannot be depended upon to keep silent. He plans the crime for a time when he will be accompanied by a hundred men and officers and arranges a "target practice" explanation, despite the fact that casual shooting is against regulations. After the deed is done, he suddenly decides to pretend the major has had a heart attack, risking serious confusion of his accomplice with no apparent object.*

---

* That this confession was concocted by Lee using the board of inquiry testimony, and did not represent Pothier's memory is shown by the fact that the testimony taken by the board contains no reference of any kind to the initial belief that Major Cronkhite had had a heart attack, and that strychnine and artificial respiration were given before the bullet wound was discovered. There is overwhelming testimony that the doctor and Captain Rosenbluth were at first misled by the inconspicuous nature of the wound.

The total improbability of this arrangement is clear. As a friend of Rosenbluth's remarked in a letter after his arrest, "If you had been willing to [make] such an arrangement, I think you have too much sense to have made it with a non-commissioned officer of a detachment other than your own."[31]

III

DESPITE these manifest incongruities, Cannon and Richards appeared to be convinced by Pothier's story. They did not think it was entirely told, but they seemed certain a crime was somehow involved. Richards, for example, asked by a juror for his personal opinion of the case, had this to say:

> My opinion based entirely upon what Pothier said and his manner and the confidential way he talked about it and the relief he seemed to experience after having told—he said he was awfully glad to get it off his chest; the fact that his people had been with him; the fact that his clergyman had seen him—the fact that there was no interval between the time Mr. Cannon got his story and the time he told it to me; all these things lead me to believe that he was telling the absolute truth except what he was getting out of it. I think he purposely kept that back, because he thought it might hurt his case.

Richards then described the way he thought the shooting had occurred: Pothier had fired once, hitting the major's hat, and when his victim swung around at the shot, fired twice more, finally fatally wounding him. He was then asked by a juror if the story should be given credence considering Pothier's attitude and his reputation. Richards replied, "He did not change his story, you know, other than the natural change that a man would make trying to save himself, trying to look around for something to stand on."[32] The marshal, in other words, seemed to believe that if Pothier's accident story had been accepted, he would have stayed with it, but upon being shown that it was an impossibility, he had no choice except to proceed to another more credible story.

In a somewhat similar statement Cannon also testified to the grand jury that he had been convinced by Pothier's manner, which seemed to him sincere, and by his sustained insistence that he was speaking the truth. Cannon also stressed the fact that Pothier had stolen ammunition when he took the borrowed revolver and did not load the gun until he entered the clearing.[33] Both these men seem honest in their testimony; the

---

Since this confession does not make reference to this, it is clear that Lee did not know about it.

only question is the degree to which they were influenced by extraneous factors. Pothier could make a good impression on people when he wished. The situation of his family, poor laboring people struggling to raise bail (his original bail of $10,000 was finally reduced to $7,500) and the condition of his young wife (described by Cannon as a beautiful girl) also were influential in the impression he created.

But more important is the fact that Cannon and Richards were employees of the Department of Justice and took their orders ultimately from Washington. Obviously Washington was interested in the case and seemed to be backing Agent Lee. I do not for a moment suppose that either man would have agreed to framing Pothier or Rosenbluth deliberately. But perhaps their positions made it easier to accept Pothier's story than to raise questions and split hairs. Cannon clearly had doubts about the methods used in obtaining the confessions, but Pothier had stuck to his story when questioned by him. Why raise doubts about Lee's methods and in so doing annoy his superiors in Washington, who had assigned Lee to the job? Taking their testimony before the grand jury as a guide, I believe that Richards genuinely believed Pothier's final confession was basically correct. Cannon had at least some doubts—not strong enough, however, to impel him to any action other than continuing to protect Pothier from further interviews with Agent Lee.

Allowing for the fact that Attorney Cannon's interference in the case would have been difficult, the real problem appears to have been his inability to shake the accused man from his story in any significant way. This raises the problem of why Pothier did not retract his story after he was in Cannon's hands. According to his own statement, he had no complaints about his treatment: "Callaghan and Cannon were all right. They treated me fine and they were always trying to be sure that I was telling the truth." The reporter taking this interview inquired why he had not told the real truth, and Pothier replied, "Because I was sick of being pestered all the time. And so then Lee came with the confession for me to sign. I felt like killing him."[34] For the purposes of a press interview, then, Pothier implied he would be simply turned back to Lee for more interrogation if he retracted his story.

I cannot help but suspect, however, that another factor was operating as well. Pothier seems to have made a decidedly bad impression on most of those who knew him intimately, but he was clearly capable of impressing and gaining the trust and friendship of certain people. The only thread I can discern to explain this conflicting reaction is this: Pothier made a favorable impression on those whom he wished to impress, particularly if their friendship or interest ran parallel with his own deep-seated need to be treated with respect and attention. With those who betrayed their contempt or lack of interest in him, he was sullen, uncooperative, and apparently unconcerned about the impression he was making. With those who encouraged him or showed him friendship, he had a sharply different personality. The impression is unavoidable that he responded to others only in terms of his own desire for attention.

This personality trait seems to explain the occasional person who thought well of Pothier. For instance, he made the acquaintance in Tacoma of a Mrs. Herman Watson, whom the newspapers describe as a respectable matron, a member of the school board, and a social leader of the city. These two people of widely different backgrounds and social classes met through Pothier's singing; he was invited to perform for various civic groups in Tacoma. Mrs. Watson was on friendly terms with him for several years, apparently viewing him as a sort of protégé. He wrote to her for assistance after he was arrested, and she may have been the person who loaned or gave him money to help with his legal expenses. After his acquittal in 1924, he stayed at her home for several days while his transportation home was being arranged. That a man of Pothier's type could make a favorable impression on this sort of woman can be explained, I think, through the basis of their meeting. Pothier was proud of his voice and genuinely liked to sing. Anyone who admired his ability and respected him for it would give him just exactly the sort of attention he apparently craved and needed.

It would seem a plausible analysis that Cannon and Richards also provided what Pothier desired: an interested audience. Both men spent much time with him, were interested in everything he had to say, and patiently questioned him for hours at a time. Unlike Lee, they treated him with consideration and politeness, and suspicion cannot be avoided that their prisoner probably enjoyed the attention. Richards, in fact, remarked that he believed Pothier liked being in jail. He was much pleased when he was given five dollars by an official in New York to use for candy and magazines over Easter weekend and was clearly delighted by the fine meal bought for him in New York. Pothier himself referred to this in his press interview: ". . . they took me down to Childs—down there near the office of the Department of Justice for dinner. They fed me you bet your life they fed me. I made 'em cough up all right enough."[35]

Similarly, Pothier's reaction to the New York visit implies he had hoped for attention and had failed to get it. He was locked up at night in the police station under the name of Joseph Brown, and spent his days handcuffed to a chair in the offices of the Justice Department. He complained bitterly of the boredom of this routine and felt strongly aggrieved when the expected hearing did not take place. Furthermore, he discovered while in the city that he had been tricked. Agent Harris revealed himself as a Bureau of Investigation employee, not a friend of Rosenbluth, and someone—probably Deputy Marshal Jordan—told him that Rosenbluth had been arrested because of his confessions and no other charge lay against him.

If Pothier expected to testify as an important witness, this goes a long way toward explaining his insistence on going to New York and his failure to retract his confessions to Cannon in Providence. Obviously he anticipated the trip with pleasure. That he retracted his confessions involving Rosenbluth as soon as he learned the truth (and stuck to this retraction thereafter) suggests he had been deliberately misinformed by Agent Lee about Rosenbluth's position. Unfortunately, his failure to retract while being interrogated by Cannon and Richards in Providence, coupled with his lack of complaint about the way the confessions had been obtained, finally convinced these two officials he must be telling the truth, or at least part of it. Both men repeatedly insisted that Pothier convinced them by his steady assertion of guilt when being questioned under circumstances allowing him ample opportunity to retract his confession if he wished.

Pothier's inclination to brag, to talk about himself, and to weary his acquaintances by his "mouthiness," became a factor in the case. The temptation to remain in the spotlight was too great. Without denying that his initial stay in jail was unpleasant insofar as he was harrassed by Lee, by his priest, and by his family, the experience seems likely to have had its pleasant side. He had an audience at last.

In addition to the pleasure derived from being an important witness, another personality trait was also involved. Pothier was extremely aggressive—a trait often found in very short, stocky men—and most of his life he was in a position where he could not release aggression except in socially unacceptable ways—by sullen behavior, egotistical talk, or almost open dishonesty. His success in gaining a promotion to sergeant-bugler was undercut by the open dislike of his fellow sergeants. After the death of Major Cronkhite, he was reduced to the ranks again by Colonel Thomas's rather capricious order; after his discharge he returned to an obscure job and the routine life of a laboring man of the lower middle classes. Thus his arrest and the false information provided by Agent Lee gave him an outlet; it permitted him to get back at an officer—one of the lordly class which had, except for Major Cronkhite, rebuked him, ignored him, and despised him.

A further anecdote about the man reveals his basic attitude toward life and his capacity to derive great emotional pleasure from the very simple rejection of help from a man he felt had betrayed him. Pothier did not mind taking assistance from those he thought were well disposed toward him, but he reacted strongly to handouts from those he distrusted. When he was taken to the Pennsylvania Hotel to be interviewed by Mrs. Cronkhite and Captain Jones, he went as a prisoner. " 'I was wearing my handcuff on one wrist, but when we got in the hotel and upstairs in the corridor they snapped it on the other wrist too. I saw what they were going to do, and so I put my matches in one vest pocket and my cigarettes in the other so's I could get at them—like this.' He crossed his wrists and showed how it was done." Later in the conversation he was able to display his foresight. "For the first time during the interview Pothier smiled as a thought struck him. 'Billups Harris offered me a cigarette,' he said, chuckling, 'and I told him, 'Thanks, I'll use me own.' Again he went through the motions of reaching, handcuffed, for his cigarettes and matches, and repeated, 'Thanks, I'll use me own.' " The reporter who took down this story described Pothier as being very sullen and withdrawn during the entire interview, except for this one very pleasant memory.[36] Harris had tricked him by pretending to be an agent of Rosenbluth's, and he had Pothier in his power; but even under this handicap, his prisoner managed to assert himself.

Pothier may possibly not have been in an entirely normal mental state at the time of his initial arrest. A reporter, who did a series of articles on the case two years later, mentioned that Pothier had been struck by a freight train a few weeks before and had sustained a head injury that kept him in the hospital for two weeks.[37] If he were recovering from a concussion, his erratic behavior is partially explained. He was under great emotional stress as well. Lee's accounts of his interrogation referred over and over to Pothier's abnormal mentality. Lee, of course, wanted to show that Pothier was a weak-minded person who would readily yield to the suggestions of a stronger personality, and his remarks must be read with that in mind. But if Lee's report is reasonably accurate, it is clear that Pothier was behaving somewhat strangely. Certainly others who questioned him later did not observe any signs of mental retardation or confusion. The two reporters who took his story several years apart agreed that though uneducated he was shrewd and perfectly normal.

Lee, however, constantly referred to Pothier's peculiarities. "He has traits which are peculiar to a small boy . . . is calm and collected, only that he cries continually for his wife's sake . . . he is the type of man whose mind is absolutely blank at times."[38] Lee seemed convinced, like Richards, that Pothier did not mind being in jail and did not worry about his own predicament except as it affected his wife. No one else who knew Pothier at any point of the case remarked about his crying or mental blackouts.

Whatever factors operated to produce Pothier's series of confessions, Lee's methods of interrogation were without doubt seriously at fault. But the combination of Lee's "detective mind" and the structure of the Bureau of Investigation, which permitted him complete autonomy, began Rosenbluth's four-year struggle to clear his name. Those in Providence who knew or suspected how the confessions had been achieved or doubted Rosenbluth's involvement in spite of them, found interference difficult and did not protest.

CHAPTER FOUR
FEDERAL
MURDER CHARGE
MARCH 23, 1921-
JULY 19, 1921

CAPTAIN ROSENBLUTH was arrested and charged with murder on March 23, 1921, the day after Sergeant Pothier had signed the statement asserting that the captain had ordered him to kill Major Cronkhite during the hike. Special agents Hoeckley, Harris, and Navarro appeared at the Civic Club—Rosenbluth's residence in New York—served him with a warrant, and took him to the Tombs where he was interviewed by a Justice Department official, Thomas Reddy, and locked up. No real case against him existed at this time, as shown by the fact that the agents in Providence continued to grill Pothier in an attempt to produce a more convincing confession. The arrest follows the classic pattern in cases of this kind: without any real investigation of the accused nor evidence suitable for a jury, a man was arrested and charged, with the case for the prosecution still to be constructed. At the time of the arrest, the basic "evidence" against Rosenbluth personally was Pothier's second confession—one that Attorney Cannon asserted no sane man would believe—and the twisted suspicions of Major General Cronkhite. Other data—the opinion of Dr. Schultze and Captain Jones that the wound could not have been self-inflicted and the garbled suspicions of Agent Lee—did not point to Rosenbluth directly.

The Justice Department did not interview men and officers of the 213th Engineers, nor did they make any effort to investigate Rosenbluth's general reputation. Insofar as any witnesses were questioned, the interviews followed rather unorthodox lines. An article which appeared later in the year in *The Nation* (written, Rosenbluth tells me, by Norman Thomas, then associate editor of that magazine) described the ordeal of Harry Bradshaw, a former sergeant in Rosenbluth's company. Bradshaw was taken to a hotel room by Justice Department agents and asked to reconfirm testimony he had given to General Cronkhite earlier. Bradshaw emphatically denied having said anything to Rosenbluth's discredit and added that the general had been drinking at the time of their earlier conversation. The general himself then burst into the room and threatened Bradshaw with arrest if he refused to give the desired testimony. Pressure was lifted only after he proved he had been in the hospital on the fatal day.[1] This interview indicates that the investigation was being conducted along lines suggested by General Cronkhite; suspicions somehow raised in private letters had led to Bradshaw. In other words the agents were not trying to find out what had happened by questioning men in a position to know, but were engaged, at Cronkhite's insistence, in collecting gossip about Rosenbluth.

When testifying before the grand jury, Bradshaw admitted that he had been asked by Rosenbluth to sign an affidavit describing this interview and had refused to do so. He agreed that the affidavit reported the event accurately but said he was reluctant to appear to be making a complaint against the Justice Department.[2] One difficulty Rosenbluth faced consistently in his efforts to prove that unfair methods were used was the quite human reluctance of men like Bradshaw to get involved in a fight they felt was no concern of theirs.

As soon as Rosenbluth was safely under lock and key, daily press releases highly prejudicial to him were issued by the department. The following day, the *New York Times* headlined a front-page article as follows: "Captain Arrested in Cronkhite Death. Robert Rosenbluth, A.E.F. Officer of Engineers Locked up Here on Charge of Murder. Hint of Camp Lewis Plot. Mystery of Major's Slaying Deepened." In the text of the article, slanting can be easily observed. After a few details about the alleged plot, an effort was made to suggest that the accused man was a dubious character: 'Mr. Rosenbluth, who says he is an expert in forestry, was locked up in police headquarters last night." In conclusion Chief Baley of the Bureau of Investigation, was quoted as saying that the arrest was delayed many months because they had to track Rosenbluth through Europe and Asia.[3] This assertion implied he had been a fugitive from justice. On the following day the headline read: "Establish Motive in Cronkhite Case. No Bail for Rosenbluth." The text explained that the motive could not be revealed for fear of impeding the investigation, but the impression was created that a genuine case against Rosenbluth was actually in existence.[4]

The motive was implied a few days later in an interview with Rosenbluth's lawyer, Jonah Goldstein. Goldstein placed considerable emphasis upon his client's good service record, mentioning that his company, Company D, was the banner one of the regiment. This is borne out by the *Divisional History* which reports that this company escorted the colors in a parade as a reward for their marksmanship record.* The lawyer also said Rosenbluth had not been due for a promotion or a rating period until the January following the tragedy.[5] These remarks hinted at the case that the government and General Cronkhite were trying to construct: in an effort to provide a believable motive, an attempt was made to show that the captain had reason to fear for his rating and Major Cronkhite was disposed of to prevent a bad or failing service report. Whether Cronkhite in fact would have been the officer entitled to rate Rosenbluth's performance is uncertain; Rosenbluth appeared to be attached to the First Battalion under the command of Major Zajicek. But since General Cronkhite believed that Rosenbluth and Zajicek were in league, disposing of an antagonistic officer was still necessary. However, Rosenbluth's story of how he avoided a major's commission which would have kept him in the United States to go to France as a first lieutenant does not suggest a man to whom rank and promotion were overwhelmingly important. Certainly no evidence was ever produced; "there is not a single word of authentic caliber to substantiate any of [these] rumors."[6]

The publicity given to the arrest produced an immediate and strong response from Rosenbluth's friends and business associates; a number of prominent men and women wrote at once on his behalf. First to protest was Dr. Katherine Bement Davis, a distinguished sociologist, who had served in New York in various important posts, including that of commissioner of correction in New York City. She described her professional relationship with Rosenbluth and the great assistance he had rendered in several prison reform projects, and she expressed the gravest doubt that he could be concerned in such a crime. Other letters were immediately forthcoming. Among those who wrote to express their belief in Rosenbluth's innocence were Herbert Lehman, then a member of a banking firm and later governor of New York; Felix Warburg of Kuhn, Loeb, and Company, a distinguished philanthropist and financier; William E. Allen, director of the Institute of Public Service; Professor E. Stagg Whiton of Columbia University; Lewis Strauss, former aide to Herbert Hoover; and Walter Frank, a prominent lawyer. These men also protested the continued refusal to set bail and offered to contribute funds for this purpose.[7]

---

* This is an error, Rosenbluth tells me; Company D's honors were won by superior performance on the drill field.

Although bail for Pothier had already been set, Rosenbluth was held in the Tombs for a week. The Civic Club gave him a vote of confidence, and he was visited by a delegation of correction officers who called to express their sympathy and to ask his assistance in getting their salaries raised. On March 29 he was finally released on bail of $25,000, his bond guaranteed by Felix Warburg, Herbert Lehman, and Walter Frank.[8] He waived his right to a formal hearing and agreed to appear when summoned before a grand jury on the west coast. (Ironically enough, this willingness to dispense with formality—a noticeable tendency in Rosenbluth—was a serious mistake. Had he demanded the hearing, the case probably would have been dropped, since Pothier after being brought to New York to appear against Rosenbluth had told his captors that he would not stand by his confessions involving Rosenbluth. Rosenbluth had no way of knowing this and was more concerned to show his readiness to cooperate with the authorities.) He emerged from his week of confinement confident that the confusion could be cleared up. It seemed that a few weeks of research would readily clarify what really had happened and settle the matter to the satisfaction of all concerned. But it became rapidly apparent that this would be a very difficult task.

The disintegration of a relatively simple case into a morass of conflicting testimony and almost total confusion is an object lesson to anyone who has studied the details. Again and again, one is forced to see that had the Justice Department constructed its case *first* and then made its arrests, the whole affair would never have occurred. The fundamental flaw in the original decision to arrest was that the government did not have a case and in fact never was able, even after three years of effort, to bring convincing evidence before a jury.

But there were many other aspects tending to complicate the affair. One was a simple matter of geography; Rosenbluth was arrested in New York City; Pothier was held in Providence, Rhode Island. The case was directed from Washington, D.C., and since the alleged murder had occurred in Camp Lewis, the U.S. attorney in Seattle was involved. In addition, General Cronkhite resided in Baltimore, and the witnesses and experts concerned were scattered all over the United States and its possessions. As a result even a very simple inquiry had to be routed through a maze of offices and officials, with duplicate copies sent to still more offices.

Furthermore, an amazingly large number of persons were involved in the case due to changes in personnel from various causes through the years that the case was under investigation. To add to the confusion, the investigations of the Justice Department were actually carried out by various agents from the Bureau of Investigation, whose reports were forwarded to the department. When we consider further that the War Department and the General Staff were closely involved in the case, that President Harding and his personal secretary George Christian also took an interest, and that a large number of congressmen intervened in the affair, it is in no way surprising that confusions multiplied, that documents were lost or misplaced, and that frequently no one seemed to know what anyone else was doing.

Another factor in the confusion was the issue of anti-Semitism. Rosenbluth was of Jewish descent, and many but by no means all of his supporters were also. This aspect of the case took more than two years to develop fully but was introduced almost at once. In the Justice Department file on the case is a photostatic copy of an anonymous letter received by General Cronkhite shortly after Rosenbluth's arrest. The letter is written in pencil on rough paper in an effort to make it appear as an illiterate scrawl, but the handwriting is that of an educated person. The letter reads as follows: "Ex-Capt. Rosenbluth is an ex-convict from Dannemora, I am pretty sure." Thus Rosenbluth's work in forestry training for convicts became part of the "evidence" against him. Most interesting, however, is the envelope and the address, which reveal the motivations of the writer. Although the letter is in favor of the case against Rosenbluth and in sympathy with the General, it is addressed—obviously a slip of the pen—to Major General Cron*kike*.[9] In addition to such malicious communications, the *Jewish Tribune* entered the case and helped to stress the racial aspect of it. It repeatedly called the affair a "Dreyfus case" and published the totally false story that Major Cronkhite's tombstone contained the opprobrious initials S.I.W., "self-inflicted wound," it alleged were required by military rule.[10] This and similar articles paved the way for the future charges that American Jewish interests were protecting Rosenbluth and the countercharges that the case against him was motivated by anti-Jewish prejudice.

But the primary source of the continued confusion was the problem that arose almost at once concerning the jurisdiction of the case. It was assumed at the time of the arrests that a crime commited on a military reservation would necessarily come under federal jurisdiction. But doubts arose immediately. Camp Lewis had not been transferred by deed to the federal government until about a year after the death of Major Cronkhite, and the immediate opinion of the officials concerned was that the government did not have jurisdiction over what technically had been state property in 1918. Two days after Rosenbluth's arrest a telegram was sent to the attorney in Seattle by Attorney General Daugherty, asking him to look into the jurisdictional question. After receiving a reply, Daugherty wired on March 30:

> Agree with you no federal jurisdiction. You authorized confer with state prosecutor. Give him benefit information now in your possession. Suggest to him issuance of state warrant for both parties and start extradition proceedings. Entire file covering investigation will be forwarded bureau office at Seattle for delivery to state prosecutor. You authorized do likewise. Please keep this phase of case confidential—not permit same to get to press until state authorities think advisable.[11]

Subsequent letters to Seattle make it clear that Daugherty's authorization had been communicated to various officials in Washington. On April 6, for example, Chief Baley wrote to the Bureau of Investigation office in Seattle to say he was forwarding data on the case—maps of the area, one drawn by hand by Captain Rosenbluth; Rosenbluth's interrogation by Attorney Joyce; and statements made by Pothier. His letter concludes: "You will please deliver the Cronkhite file to the United States Attorney for delivery to the State Prosecuting authorities and continue to cooperate with the State authorities in connection with the investigation of this matter."[12] Regardless of later denials it seems clear that Saunders, the attorney in Seattle, was specifically authorized by the Attorney General to turn over the case to the county attorney in Tacoma. Baley's letter indicates his understanding that the government did not intend to prosecute and did intend to give the matter to the state of Washingon. Furthermore, despite Daugherty's warning against premature press releases, the government's doubt of its right to try the case was known. On March 28 the *New York Times* carried a statement from the state prosecuting attorney in Tacoma, James Selden, announcing he would file charges against the two men accused as soon as the government dropped charges.[13]

A slight complication arose immediately, however; Pothier and Rosenbluth had both been granted bail with the condition that they agree to appear when summoned before the U.S. district court on the west coast. The county attorney in Tacoma refused to issue extradition warrants before he received the complete files on the case, and apparently the only way to get the pair to the west coast was to bring them there under federal warrant. While this problem was being considered and Saunders in Seattle was indicating his serious doubts of the evidence available, Attorney General Daugherty, prodded into action by Republican Senator William Calder of New York, decided to investigate the matter for himself. Orders went out to New York, Providence, and Seattle that no further action was to be taken until the Attorney General had reached a decision.[14] As a result, Saunders stopped forwarding material to Selden and did not, in fact, give him any additional information after the middle of April. Rosenbluth and Attorney Goldstein were pressing hard for a hearing on the case, spurred on by the publication of portions of Pothier's confessions by Selden and his refusal to act on the basis of the evidence then in his possession. Rosenbluth did not want the case to be transferred to Tacoma because the state of Washington could not subpoena witnesses from other states, and such an investigation could not possibly be complete. This jurisdictional issue haunted the case for the next three years and produced a cloud of confusion that was never entirely dissipated.

The month of April also revealed a basic problem of the case—the fact that the evidence in the affair ultimately turned on the reputation and character of the two men accused. Fundamentally, the case depended on the question of who was telling the truth, Rosenbluth or Pothier. If Pothier was truthful in his assertion that he also was firing his revolver, then Rosenbluth's testimony before the board of inquiry was clearly false or mistaken. If on the other hand, Rosenbluth had accurately described the events leading to the fatal shot, then Pothier had lied and had not been using his weapon. Since there were no other witnesses to the scene, there was no way to determine this except in terms of the reliability of the two men. No one, at any stage of the investigation, who really knew Rosenbluth was able to believe he was in any way involved. But men who did not know him were less concerned with his character than with the various contradictions in the record.

Since character was of crucial importance, Rosenbluth and his lawyer became increasingly alarmed at what appeared to be deliberate attempts to denigrate his reputation, combined with an apparent reluctance to accept materials favorable to him. Rosenbluth was informed by various officials that this man and that had given strong evidence against him. He was told his present statements were greatly at variance with his original testimony before the board of inquiry.[15] Stories began to appear in the press hinting at international intrigue, labeling him a "dirty German Jew spy," and asserting he had enjoyed a sinister relationship with a Russian ballet dancer. At the same time officials in the Justice Department showed they were not impressed with the growing body of favorable testimony. Assistant Attorney General Stewart commented to Senator Calder: "Why are you defending this fellow? Don't you know that nobody that knew him before the war has a good word to say for him?"

As a result of these and other reports Rosenbluth and his lawyer became increasingly convinced he was being made the victim of a deliberate plot and the Justice Department could not be trusted to deal fairly with him.[16] His problem was increased by the fact that he was unable to inspect the various documents in question. The War Department, for example, refused to give him a copy of the board of inquiry testimony, leaving him in the dark about the exact degree of variation between his testimony in 1918 and his statements in 1921. He had no way to verify allegedly adverse testimony given by others, except by correspondence, since the witnesses were scattered over the United States.

In addition, I believe, the personal antagonism he discovered massed against him came as a severe psychological shock. Rosenbluth for thirteen years had enjoyed a distinguished professional career and was accustomed to take for granted the goodwill and respect of those around him. He found it very hard to suppose that anyone could disbelieve him and tended unconsciously to insist on personal interviews and hearings on his own behalf, confident that he could convince his opponents easily if he could only reason with them. This inclination to brush aside legal procedures to settle the matter informally was unquestionably irritating to some Justice Department officials who took a stricter, more legalistic view of procedure.

There is evidence of a sustained effort to blacken Rosenbluth's character and reputation, and he openly expressed this feeling in a press interview in April in which he called Pothier "the willing tool of the rotten decaying system of the Bureau of Investigation" and asserted "there are men in the Bureau of Investigation in the Department of Justice who are willing to hang a man to hang on to their jobs."[17] The basis for such statements can be documented.

One of the officers formerly attached to the 213th Engineers was a regular army officer, Captain Eugene Caffey, later the Adjutant General of the United States. Caffey had no direct knowledge of the events leading to the shooting since he had not gone on the hike, but he was approached by a special agent of the bureau, shortly after Rosenbluth's arrest, for information about the accused man's character. Caffey later described the interview in a formal affidavit:

> the agent stated among other things that Captain Rosenbluth was a man of no standing, that he had "travelled with a pretty shady gang," and had "nothing good in his record." Deponent states that such statements are lies. They were a very evident attempt to influence deponent to make statements against Captain Rosenbluth. . . . Major Zajicek was approached AFTER the arrest of Captain Rosenbluth, by agents of the Department

of Justice, who attempted to blacken the character of Captain Rosenbluth.[18]

Captain Caffey was outraged by this attempt and went with Rosenbluth and Senator Calder to visit Stewart at the Justice Department. While Caffey remained outside in the corridor, Rosenbluth and Calder protested the use of such tactics. Stewart flatly denied that any agent of his had visited Caffey. The angry officer then burst into the room, contradicted this denial, and called the charges "a damned lie." Another department official, William Herron, subsequently explained this confusion by claiming that the agent's report was not submitted until a day after this visit; thus Stewart did not know, at the time of the conversation, that Caffey had been interviewed.[19] This is a possible explanation; however, as Goldstein pointed out, it was hard to believe that an interview taken near Washington would take more than two weeks to reach the files.

Nevertheless, there were signs toward the end of April that the Justice Department was not anxious to press the case. Senator Calder received a promise from Daugherty that he would investigate fully, calling the case "a hangover from the past adminstration."[20] Chief Baley gave a press interview to the New York *World* in which he stressed the role Mrs. Cronkhite had played in collecting the evidence upon which the case had been built.[21] Both statements can be taken as signs the department was attempting to disclaim responsibility.

Secretary of Commerce Herbert Hoover wrote to Attorney General Daugherty in support of Rosenbluth.

Two communications received by the department during this month probably encouraged a reconsideration of the matter. On April 5 Herbert Hoover, then Secretary of Commerce, wrote to Daugherty to assure him that Rosenbluth had been employed since the war in various relief organizations in Europe with which Hoover was connected. He protested the charge that Rosenbluth had been a fugitive from justice, labeling it "absolutely untrue. I know the young man and it seems to me incredible that such a suggestion should be made."[22]

On April 20 Davis Arnold, Pothier's attorney, visited the department and told an assistant attorney general that Pothier had retracted his confessions implicating Rosenbluth and would not testify against him in any way.[23] To whom Arnold spoke is not specified, but probably Stewart, who had been in charge of the case at first before Herron was assigned to it in the middle of April. Later the same day Stewart wrote to the U.S. attorney in Providence, and mentioned Arnold's visit and relayed his request that Pothier's removal to Tacoma be postponed until July. Stewart neither referred in any way to a statement of retraction nor suggested that Arnold had given him information affecting the case. Since Herron later insisted he had no knowledge of any retraction, it is possible that Stewart deliberately concealed Arnold's statement for a time.

Arnold later conveyed this information to Rosenbluth in a letter written August 23, which implied that Arnold had expected the government to act on this information when he gave it to them, but since it had not, he was prepared to give it directly to Rosenbluth:

> As you know, I have refused before now, to state to you just what Pothier's attitude was in regard to this matter, as I felt that the information which I received from him should be handled directly by the department of justice. Mr. Pothier regrets the connection of your name with the killing of Major Cronkhite, and assures you that as far as he knows you had nothing to do with Major Cronkhite's death. The department of justice has been in possession of this information since April 20th last, when I visited Washington.[24]

On April 23 Rosenbluth was hopeful he would be exonerated within a few weeks. Daugherty had promised a hearing with Herron in charge, rather than the antagonistic Stewart. There was, Rosenbluth remarked, no case "excepting how things like this can happen in America in 1921."[25] On April 29, Major General Cronkhite was assigned to the command of the army in Panama, "a most important overseas post."[26] Altogether, things looked reasonably promising: a full investigation with a new staff had been promised, the damaging confession had been retracted, and the leading force behind the prosecution had been ordered abroad. Furthermore, men like Hoover were writing to protest the manner in which the investigation had been handled. It was true enough that Daugherty did not like his fellow cabinet member, but it was also probable that he did not wish to offend him or ignore his wishes.

II

THE EXPECTATIONS of the defense, however, proved premature. The month of May passed without any action being taken by the Justice Department. General Cronkhite bombarded the Attorney General with demands for immediate action and a personal interview. Goldstein asked that Rosenbluth's bail be discharged, arguing that several grand juries had come and gone without his being called and the government apparently did not intend to press charges. The department refused to admit the motion to discharge bail, taking the position that bail had been granted on the condition that Rosenbluth had guaranteed to go to Tacoma when summoned. The accused had not been summoned to Tacoma, Stewart asserted, because he had demanded a new investigation in Washington. Having been granted this new inquiry, and his removal to Tacoma having been delayed in consequence, he could not logically demand that bail be discharged.

Goldstein withdrew his motion a few days later because he had been promised that the investigation would be placed in the hands of Colonel Hayward, U.S. attorney in New York, and he wished to give Hayward an opportunity to review the case. The matter was not, however, turned over to the New York office. Instead a department attorney, Neale, submitted a lengthy memorandum to Assistant Attorney General Guy Goff, urging the Justice Department to continue its investigation from Washington, despite Neale's opinion that the government did not have jurisdiction in the case and could not bring it to trial.[27]

A new element entered the affair on May 23 when the New York *World* published a long interview with Roland Pothier. The reporter, Austin Parker, first obtained permission from Pothier's attorney, who was also present during the conversation. Parker agreed to avoid any questions involving Pothier's part in the alleged crime and confined his questions entirely to the methods used to persuade Pothier to implicate Rosenbluth. In the article Pothier described his ordeal, insisting his confession of having accidentally shot Major Cronkhite was ig-

nored and he was put under heavy pressure to "tell the truth."
He described his interviews with Special Agent Lee:

> Lee kept calling me a dumbbell all the time—that was his fa-
> vorite word for me. And he told me that if he had his way
> about it he'd tie me to a truck and drag me through the streets
> until I came clean. He said he'd like to knock my block off,
> and he was all the time telling me that he'd put me in the
> sweat box.

Asked if Lee ever actually struck him, Pothier replied:

> You're damn right he didn't. I'd have hauled off and knocked
> him cold and he knew it. But he was always shooting off his
> face about what he'd like to do to me, and he was always pes-
> tering me. . . . I got so sick and tired of having him ask
> questions that I was ready to say anything just to have a little
> peace.

The article also described Pothier's visit to New York,
and his being taken to the Pennsylvania Hotel for an interview
with Mrs. Cronkhite and Captain Jones. Deputy Marshal
Jordan, who had been sent from Providence to protect Pothier
from undue harassment, was left outside in the corridor and
the conversation began:

> Jones began to talk to me. He said that Cronkhite couldn't
> have shot himself, and that I couldn't have shot him. And he
> said, "For God's sake, if you're trying to shield anybody come
> out with it."
> And then Mrs. Cronkhite, she started. She told me how
> much she loved her son and all that sort of stuff and she asked
> me not to shield anybody. She was pretty excited, but she
> didn't cry. She just asked me to tell the truth about everything,
> and I stuck to my story that I had killed the Major acciden-
> tally. . . .
> After they were tired talking to me they asked if I would
> talk to General Cronkhite, and I told them, "Sure, I'll talk
> with anybody." Mrs. Cronkhite and Harris left me alone with
> Jones, and after a while Harris came back and said that the
> General wouldn't come up.

The defense side of the case was particularly outraged by the
fact that a federal prisoner had been left alone in a hotel room
with a private dectective, unguarded and exposed to any sort
of pressures Jones wished to use. It was later alleged that
Pothier had been told to throw himself out of the window
and had been encouraged to kill himself to eliminate the
embarrassing retraction of his confessions.

Pothier maintained he had first notified Justice Department officials in New York that he would not stand by his story

implicating Rosenbluth after he discovered that Rosenbluth had been arrested as a result of his confessions. The article concluded with criticism of the handling of the affair, emanating from "experienced operatives in the Department of Justice." These men told the reporter that Lee should not have interviewed Pothier without witnesses being present, that Rosenbluth should not have been arrested before the case was properly investigated, that Pothier should not have been brought to New York without a court order of removal, that Agent Harris should not have tried to trick Pothier by pretending to be a friend of Rosenbluth's, and that Pothier should not have been taken to a hotel and left unguarded. That these criticisms were solidly based in fact is borne out by statements made by Attorney Cannon and Marshal Richards in Providence.[28]

Immediately after Parker's article was published, the *World* interviewed Chief Baley who announced his firm intention of making a complete investigation into Pothier's charges.

> "The Government is entirely too big to use that kind of methods," said Baley. "The idea is to protect citizens when they are right just as much as to prosecute them when they violate the law. So far as I am able to control it, we will not have any third degree methods or 'rough stuff'. The Bureau of Investigation does not have to do things that way in order to get results, and it isn't the best way, anyhow. . . . If it is found that the men handling the case were doing things which were not proper and entirely consistent with the way things ought to be run, I shall make a recommendation to the Attorney General to get things straightened out. We want to get the truth and we don't care whom it helps or hurts."[29]

The article also announced that the case had been turned over to "an experienced high class man," Special Agent Edward Chastain. Agents Lee and Harris had been taken off the case.

Despite Baley's forceful promise of a detailed investigation, nothing further was done. Presumably neither the bureau nor the Department of Justice wished to investigate the conduct of their agents or to reprimand them nor did they wish to consider the possibility that Rosenbluth had been the victim of a serious error. Lee was quietly fired in October 1921 by William Burns; Lee's own explanation was that Burns wiped out an entire department because of his dislike of its senior officer.[30] Despite this, Lee was subpoenaed to appear before the grand jury and at the trial, as was Agent Dunn; other agents associated with the early stages of the case—Hoeckley, Navarro, Starr, and Callaghan—testified at the trial only. But Billups Harris simply vanishes from the record. Whether he continued in the employ of the bureau is not known. Rosenbluth requested in 1924 that Harris be called as a witness to the trial, but he was not summoned.

One possibility exists to explain this odd omission. Harris was attached to the bureau office in Atlanta, Georgia, at the time of Rosenbluth's arrest and was apparently assigned temporarily to New York for this case. The name "Harris" was prominent in Georgia politics. Nathaniel Harris was governor of that state from 1915 to 1917 and campaigned during Leo Frank's trial on a pledge to punish "Jew perverts, capitalists, and Northerners."[31] William J. Harris was a senator from Georgia from 1919 to 1925. It seems at least possible that political protection was extended to shield Agent Harris from criticism.

Several days after publication of the interview Goldstein charged that Pothier was being persecuted for his retraction, having been twice arrested in reprisal. Goldstein also claimed that department agents had suggested that Rosenbluth and his "rich friends" contribute to Pothier's support, a suggestion which the lawyer interpreted as an attempt to make Rosenbluth appear to be bribing Pothier or paying him for his retraction.[32] The agents appeared most anxious to trace some connection, financial if possible, between Pothier and Rosenbluth; Richards mentioned Pothier's having received a thousand dollars for his expenses, and although Richards did not know the source, he speculated it might be a payoff from Rosenbluth. Before Pothier's arrest Agent Lee had doggedly tracked down a registered letter received by Pothier and was disappointed to learn it contained only a small payment from the Rhode Island veterans' bonus fund.

On June 18, after Rosenbluth had been held for two and a half months without any noticeable progress, the hearing he had been requesting finally took place. The government was represented by Herron and Chastain and the defense by Rosenbluth, Goldstein, and Caffey. The hearing consisted almost entirely of a lengthy list of complaints read by Goldstein, charging the Justice Department and the Bureau of Investigation with improper and illegal conduct in their investigation of the case. This statement did not concern the charge of murder against Rosenbluth; it was directed toward forcing an inquiry into methods within these organizations.

It must be kept in mind here that neither Rosenbluth nor his lawyer believed for a moment there was a case of any kind in existence; they assumed he was in no particular danger of being indicted and tried. However, they were mistaken in this belief, even though the department never possessed evidence of any real significance to connect Rosenbluth with the death of Major Cronkhite. But neither were the accused and his counsel in a position to know the details of the contradictions and puzzling variations in testimony which could be used to suggest there was perhaps some mystery to be solved.

Goldstein's charges fill nearly twenty typewritten pages, but summarized briefly they are as follows:

1. That Agent Lee had refused to record Rosenbluth's request for a lawyer during his interrogation on March 18.
2. That Rosenbluth on a visit to Washington on March 19 was trailed by seven special agents.
3. That Rosenbluth was refused counsel the night he was arrested.
4. That he had been at first refused bail, in spite of the fact that Pothier's bail was already set.
5. That Agent Harris suggested to Rosenbluth that he could rescue himself from his predicament by signing an affidavit admitting Pothier had been shooting but had concealed this out of pity for the man.
6. That Harris also suggested to Rosenbluth that he could help his own cause by providing evidence Major Zajicek was the real organizer of the murder.
7. That Captain Caffey had been interviewed by an agent who tried to get him to blacken Rosenbluth's name and this interview was later denied by Stewart.
8. That Pothier had been illegally confined in police headquarters under a false name, Joseph Brown.
9. That when Rosenbluth's bail was set, Harris did not inform the court of retraction of the confessions.
10. That Pothier had been taken to a hotel, turned over to a private detective, and encouraged to "throw himself out of a window."
11. That Chief Baley refused to trace the origin of the "German spy" story which emanated from his office.
12. That Baley had neglected to inform Daugherty on April 5 of the retracted confessions.
13. That important witnesses like Dr. Tucker, Frank Turner, and Arthur Miller had not been interviewed.
14. That Rosenbluth had been pressed to undergo questioning in a newly invented "truth machine."
15. That Selden in Tacoma had not received any word of Pothier's retraction.
16. That Baley had released the false story of Mrs. Cronkhite's travels around the country seeking information to create prejudice against Rosenbluth.
17. That the department had made no attempt to correct its stories about Rosenbluth's allegedly "shady" past, despite elaborate evidence of his utter respectability.

18. That Daugherty on June 3 had promised to transfer the case to Colonel Hayward in New York, but this had not been done.

These charges vary considerably in quality. Some of them, however offensive to the accused, were hardly illegal—to ask a man to take a lie detector test may be insulting, but it is hardly an abuse of authority. Many of the charges concerned the actions of men attached to the Bureau of Investigation, and its relationship with the Department of Justice was at this time very ill-defined. Several of the charges rest upon the word of one man and could not be proved accurate. Points 9 and 10, for example, depend upon Pothier's statements concerning the date that he retracted his stories, and his treatment while left alone with Captain Jones in the hotel room. And Pothier was not a reliable witness, regardless of which side he was supporting.

Except with the active cooperation of an official anxious to improve investigative methods and in a position of sufficient authority to undertake such a task, these charges were not likely to be followed up. And Herron, as his response to the hearing and his later letters showed, was not inclined to cooperate. Whether his motive was personal dislike or prejudice or he was simply handicapped by his own position is uncertain. In fairness it should be added that Herron took no active part in the case after November 1921 and died a year later. Possibly his bad temper resulted from physical causes.

Goldstein concluded the hearing by pleading that the case either be turned over to the state authorities or pushed to a definite conclusion by the department. He and Rosenbluth wanted a prompt trial; the delay and uncertainty were unfair to the accused and prevented him from seeking employment or leading a normal life. Over and over he returned to a main theme: He charged that the failure of the department to exonerate Rosenbluth stemmed from its desire to punish a man who had attacked its agents' methods; the department knew very well it had made a serious mistake and should be fair enough to admit it.

Evidence indicates that many officials were gravely concerned about the weakness of the case and the department's position in it. The reporter who interviewed Pothier said in a September letter to Rosenbluth:

> I interviewed numerous officials of the Department of Justice, all of whom seemed quite aware of the fact that Pothier had repudiated his confession involving you. In certain quarters . . . I found the feeling that the investigators had overstepped

themselves, and brought discredit upon the department. . . .
I was told various things in confidence, all of which led me to
the firm conviction that the Department had no evidence against
you, except Pothier's statement, and that the officials were at a
loss to know what to do without bringing further discredit
upon the Department of Justice. I was told that they would
probably pass the case along to the local authorities in Washington on the ground that the federal government lacked jurisdiction.[33]

Some of the "evidence" in the case was a natural result of
elapsed time and faulty human memory. Since Rosenbluth and
his lawyer were denied permission to inspect the original records of the case, they were forced to depend upon what Rosenbluth and others could remember. As a result mistakes were
made. As Rosenbluth later remarked with understandable bitterness, General Cronkhite was permitted access to all documents, confessions, and records, while he was not, thus giving
the prosecution side of the case a distinct advantage over the
defense.

In addition, since the government could control the transcript of the records, alterations and omissions were easily
arranged. A week after the hearing Goldstein sent a long letter
to Herron, listing mistakes and omissions in the transcript and
asking that the record be corrected. He pointed out that many
of Herron's remarks were not printed in the record, particularly
his answer, "No questions to be asked," in response to Goldstein's invitation to question Rosenbluth as freely as he wished.
Also Herron's assertion that he had no knowledge of Pothier's
retraction or of the methods used to acquire his confession, was
omitted in the transcript. Goldstein also criticized the proposed
government plan to have Agent Chastain travel around the
country examining witnesses, when letters and telegrams would
be faster. Chastain or any other single agent would require
years to complete the job, and in the meantime, Rosenbluth
would be forced to wait for a settlement.

Herron delivered the papers on the case, the record of the
hearing, Goldstein's corrections to it, and a set of affidavits submitted on Rosenbluth's behalf to Attorney General Daugherty.
He denied the accuracy of the various charges brought against
the department by Rosenbluth and his lawyer, asserting they
were either incorrect in fact, in inference, or both. But the
letter ended with a formal recommendation on the case:

I have finally come to the conclusion that, under the peculiar
circumstances existing and under the embarrassing conditions
which confront this Department, that this Department would
not be justified, having in mind its proper duties under the
statutes, in pursuing the matter further.

Herron then recommended that the proceedings against the accused pending in Washington be dismissed, that removal proceedings against them in New York and Rhode Island be dismissed, and that all materials in the case be turned over to the state prosecuting attorney for Pierce County, Washington.[34] A letter from Colonel Hayward in New York supported this view, stating it was improper to continue to hold men on bail and to investigate a case, however convincing, that the government would never be able to bring to trial.

Herron notified Goldstein on July 18 that the government was dropping its charges against both men and would transfer all materials to the state prosecutor in Tacoma. The press was notified the following day that charges were to be dropped for jurisdictional reasons. Rosenbluth and many of his friends protested that the insistence upon jurisdictional reasons created a strong impression that a case actually existed, and they expressed regret that the government had not seen fit to admit it had, in fact, no really convincing case. The attorney in Tacoma announced he would not attempt to press charges unless he was given significant new evidence; he would wait until the government forwarded all of its materials.[35]

A stalemate had thus been reached. Selden felt unable to act without additional evidence, and the Justice Department did not carry out its promise to forward it. Throughout the remainder of 1921 Rosenbluth remained in a kind of limbo, still accused of a serious crime, but unable to achieve a trial or hearing where he could defend himself.

CHAPTER FIVE
IN LIMBO
JULY 1921-
JANUARY 1922

IN JULY AND AUGUST of 1921 General Cronkhite and Rosenbluth alike waited for the government to turn the files of the case over to the attorney in Tacoma. William Allen, director of the Institute of Public Service in New York City, exchanged a series of letters at this time with William Herron and George Christian, secretary to President Harding, trying vainly to persuade them that the Justice Department was guilty of a serious injustice. Allen wrote to Christian protesting that to drop the case for jurisdictional reasons created the impression that a case actually existed. He urged the President's concern for a man of high reputation and distinguished public service who had been branded a murderer for six months, only to have the matter dropped without explanation. Christian did not, as far as is known, take the matter up with the President but turned the letter over to Herron. The latter's reply was indicative of his attitude. After a brief paragraph acknowledging receipt of the letter, he concluded: "As your letter clearly indicates that you have no real knowledge upon the subject regarding which you write, except what may have been told you by interested parties, this Department does not believe that your letter requires any further answer."

Allen, dismayed by this curt and inaccurate response, wrote again to protest. He explained he had been interviewed by agents about Rosenbluth's reputation and, since he had expressed the highest opinion of the man, could not understand why the department released materials tending to blacken his reputation. He also expressed indignation over the various stories in the press concerning Rosenbluth's hiding out in Europe and Asia to avoid arrest. "Frankly, your letter suggests you wrote in a hurry and in a temper."

Herron's reply was considerably longer than his first letter, but equally rude in tone. He repeated his statement that Allen had no actual information about the case and complained that his various allegations were too vague to be investigated or represented only Allen's personal judgment—which, the tone of the letter implied, was nonexistent. Allen replied, thanking Herron for his promise to investigate if given specific data but reminding him that he, as an official with a large staff and access to records, was in a much better position than Allen to do such checking. Again he referred to the allegation that Rosenbluth had been a fugitive from justice:

> Captain Rosenbluth came out to Ohio between his discharge from the army and his going to Siberia for the relief service, to help me make a study of correctional institutions for the Joint Legislative Committee on Administrative Reorganization. His coming was announced in the Ohio papers and in New York. His report was published. Was that ever made known to superior officers in the department of justice before his arrest or during the weeks when the claim was made publicly that the department had found it necessary to trail him through Europe into Siberia, etc.?*

After assembling his materials, Allen wrote again on August 6 and attempted to give Herron the exact data he had demanded. He listed a series of dated press stories which gave misleading or false information, and quoted Selden's statement that he had not been notified of any retraction. Allen's point was simple: These stories either were known to be untrue and had never been corrected; or they contradicted what Herron had stated at the hearing.

Herron's reply to these specific materials was stubbornly resistant to any inquiry and totally disclaimed any department responsibility in the matter:

> the Department knows nothing whatsoever about the statements published in certain newspapers referred to by you, does not admit their correctness, does not admit that they were even given by any person authorized to speak for the Department of Justice, and does not see their relevancy to the matter raised by you. Of course, if Mr. Lee had ever made the statement referred to in your 4th paragraph, [Allen quoted Lee's calling Rosenbluth a "dirty German Jew spy"] it would have been a highly improper statement for him to make, but Mr. Lee denies having made any such statement, and this Department believes him.

---

* It is possible, I think, that Rosenbluth's work in Ohio had made enemies for him. Reforms of state institutions usually involve interference with accustomed ways of doing things and established personnel. Herron was a native of Ohio and probably a political appointee of Daugherty's. His strong antagonism to both Rosenbluth and Allen may reflect a grudge against two men who had worked under Democratic governor James Cox. Cox's autobiography makes clear that he was a personal and political enemy of Daugherty; those associated with him in reform work may have offended the Republican party machine.

He dismissed the question of the failure to interview certain witnesses by saying, "Captain Rosenbluth's statements in this regard do not seem to this Department to be worthy of notice." He flatly denied he had been told of any retraction of the confessions and that Rosenbluth had been arrested prior to Pothier's confession. Here, as we have seen, the assertion depends upon which of the confessions is meant. He concluded his letter:

> It is sufficient to say that the Department dismissed the proceedings pending against Captain Rosenbluth before the United States Commissioner, simply because it was finally advised by those who had investigated the matter that, for purely technical reasons, the United States courts had absolutely no jurisdiction whatsoever over the case, and the prosecution would have to be in the courts of the State of Washington. There was no other reason which influenced this Department in its action.

Allen tried in several letters to both Herron and Christian to alter what was clearly departmental policy, as well as Herron's personal antagonism. He pointed out, for example, that if numerous agents had worked for many months on the case it was odd they had not discovered that the jurisdiction was in question and Rosenbluth's prewar reputation was excellent. He quoted letters from Dr. Tucker and Davis Arnold, contradicting Herron's statements, and said to Christian "either Mr. Herron is being egregiously imposed upon or . . . he is willing to mislead an inquiring citizen." He concluded the correspondence with a request that Christian agree to see Senator Calder on the matter and the whole affair be turned over to William Burns, head of the Bureau of Investigation, for a fresh and impartial inquiry.[1]

This correspondence is of interest because it supports the contention of the defense that the Department of Justice showed no interest whatsoever in trying to straighten out the matter. Herron's angry and offensive replies revealed a total lack of concern for the personal position of Rosenbluth and a complete refusal to correct misstatements which clearly emanated from the department. Despite Herron's lordly denial of official responsibility, the various newspaper stories about spies were not simply invented by a host of different reporters representing different papers. His attitude was the more offensive in that the department actually was not in the process of turning over the files to the state authorities. Perhaps it was planning to do so in August, but the files remained in Washington while Selden waited to receive them in Tacoma.

The failure of the Justice Department to carry out its announced intention of forwarding all the materials to the state authorities was never satisfactorily explained. Donald Ewing, a reporter for the *Chicago Tribune,* later analyzed the peculiar vacillation that characterized the government's actions. Ewing quoted an explanation he received from a Justice Department official:

> the case was placed in the hands of W. C. Herron. . . . Herron held that because the deed to the reservation had not been given the government prior to the shooting, the government held no jurisdiction, and the case should go to the county officials. Daugherty wired Saunders at Seattle to turn it over to them, but when this became known around the department, other assistant attorney generals differed with Herron's opinion. . . . so we decided to hold up the evidence we had pending a thorough investigation of the law on the subject.[2]

This, however, does not fit the record. Daugherty's directive to Saunders was sent March 30; the case dragged on in Washington until July 18, when the government decided to drop charges. It is not possible that "other assistant attorney generals" discovered in July, nearly five months after the arrests, that the jurisdiction was in question. This is particularly evident since the correspondence and memoranda on the case show that everyone in the department worked on it. The explanation Ewing received is not sufficient to explain why the department, after five months of investigation, dropped the charges and then failed to transmit the papers to Tacoma.

The correspondence of the Justice Department in August, September, and October of 1921 is filled with inquiries from various sources. General Cronkhite, Goldstein, Senator Calder, the Veterans of Foreign Wars, and others wrote to ask: Have the papers been sent to Selden? General Cronkhite was also concerned about the assignment of a necessary witness, Major Zajicek, to duty in the Philippines; in August Herron wrote to the Secretary of War requesting that Zajicek be held in the United States, since the case was being assembled for transmittal to Selden. A few days later Daugherty, replying to an inquiry from Senator Calder, assured him the department would be happy to send any papers that Selden requested. After an inquiry from the Veterans of Foreign Wars in early September, Attorney Ridgeley explained that the case was being "closed up." A further letter asking the meaning of "closed up" produced the response that the attorney in charge of the case was out of town and would reply later. General Cronkhite, still under orders to report for duty in Panama, sent letter after letter demanding information on plans and received brief replies to the effect that the attorney in charge was on vacation or out of town. Obviously considerable confusion existed; either these letters contradict each other, as do Herron's and Daugherty's, or they display uncertainty and reluctance to make a positive statement.[3]

An exchange of letters between the Justice Department and H. J. Wright, editor of the *New York Globe,* further indicated that some change in policy was being arranged. Wright wrote in August to Postmaster General Will Hays asking for his assistance with the Attorney General in settling the case promptly. Hays passed the letter along to Daugherty with a penciled note: "This is an *important* editor. It would be fine if you would write him personally." In late September the letter was passed to Guy Goff, with a memo from Daugherty asking him to write "as nice a letter as you can." Daugherty said he did not want to ask Herron to reply, since the letter implied criticism of him, nor could he write himself, "as I am not myself familiar with all the details of the case."

Goff's letter, dated October 14, is a masterpiece of federal prose. After admitting that the department had decided to send the papers to the state authorities in Washington, he qualified that decision:

> In order to avoid, however, any semblance of injustice, which it was suggested following the implication arising from that course, the question has been taken under review, and the Attorney General has requested me to assure you that the Department has at heart a purpose not to wrong Capt. Rosenbluth.

Postmaster General Will Hays intervened in Rosenbluth's behalf to urge prompt settlement of the case.

Replying on October 20, Wright expressed his thanks for the information that the department "has under review its earlier decision to transmit to local authorities in the State of Washington the papers in the case of Capt. Rosenbluth."[4] The next day Goff enclosed the letter in a memo to Herron and suggested they talk later on the question of sending the papers to Tacoma. Despite this clear evidence that some officials were apprised of a change in plan, Crim, who was shortly to be named head of the criminal division and placed in charge of the case, wrote to General Cronkhite on October 25, assuring him the papers would be sent within the next two or three days to the state prosecuting attorney in Tacoma.

The failure of the Justice Department to carry out its promise can be explained in only one way: it did not have anything to send. Selden had expressed himself forcibly on several occasions concerning the case and had made it abundantly clear he would not extradite the accused unless he was shown convincing evidence.* The government was well aware that Selden could not be persuaded to act against his own judgment nor coerced into concealing the weaknesses of the case. If the handful of unconvincing reports and exhibits had been turned over to him in July, he would have undoubtedly reported at once there was no case to be investigated.

The longer the delay lasted, the greater were the chances that the matter could be compromised in some fashion without embarrassing publicity. In the decision to delay, the government seriously underestimated several things: the strength of General Cronkhite's obsession, Rosenbluth's determination to achieve an exoneration and to force an investigation into the methods of the department, the volume of criticism which would be created by the delay itself, and the honesty and sense of justice of State Prosecutor Selden at Tacoma.

II

WHILE THE JUSTICE DEPARTMENT sought a decision on procedure, the two men genuinely concerned with a rapid settlement struggled steadily. Although Rosenbluth believed that Cronkhite was the primary force behind the case and his prestige as a general was operating to keep it open, the record shows that the general was experiencing difficulties of his own. Without

---

* For example, the *New York Times* reported Selden's statements on the case on April 19, 1921. Selden is quoted as saying, "My own opinion in the matter is that Pothier has a screw loose." He went on to argue that Pothier had never claimed that Rosenbluth gave him a direct order to shoot Major Cronkhite and no sane man would have shot without such an order. In any case, he believed that the confessions alone were not sufficient evidence upon which to act.

doubt the War Department was unhappy about the whole affair and most reluctant to pursue it. There also appears to have been a clash between Secretary of War John Weeks and the General Staff headed by John Pershing. Weeks was not a military man; although he had graduated from the United States Naval Academy, he resigned his commission and divided his time between Congress and the brokerage firm of Hornblower and Weeks. Thus by training and experience he was somewhat oddly placed and not likely to be congenial to staff officers. Weeks was intimate with Daugherty and inclined to cooperate with him; Pershing and other senior officers tended to be contemptuous of nonmilitary affairs.

In addition there are signs that General Pershing did not care for Major General Cronkhite. The two men were contemporaries and had served together in the last of the Sioux Wars in 1891. A photograph of the Sixth Cavalry, printed in *World's Work,* shows Cronkhite standing next to Pershing.[5] But in the extended biography of Pershing which appeared in the magazine for many issues, Cronkhite is never mentioned, although reference is made to many other officers of Pershing's acquaintance. Similarly, in Pershing's two-volume history of the war, Cronkhite is referred to only in parentheses, identifying him as a division commander. In an interview published in the *Dearborn Independent* in 1923, General Pershing is quoted in a way that shows his lack of sympathy for the whole affair: 'His son was killed, maybe murdered, probably was, and he has the deepest sympathy of everyone. But this matter has dragged along for two whole years, and the Department cannot afford to consider the personal affairs of its officers.''[6] At least some of the opposition General Cronkhite met probably resulted from personal antipathies as well as from the fear of military scandal.

When Cronkhite received orders to report for duty in Panama, he protested vigorously to Weeks, arguing that his rank and record of service entitled him to more consideration. Weeks agreed that the order was too abrupt and talked with Pershing, who nonetheless wrote to inform Cronkhite that the order could not be changed. Later he was granted a delay until October, but a request in July for a cancellation of the order was disapproved, again by Pershing.

Already in trouble with the War Department, General Cronkhite was beginning to experience definite coldness and lack of attention from the Justice Department as well. He was outraged by the announcement in the press that the charges against the accused were being dropped by the federal government and wrote a long and angry letter to the Attorney General demanding to know why this had been done. Daugherty's reply was lengthy, but cool in tone. The general was informed that the government did not have jurisdiction in the case, that any statements or promises made to him by Herron were merely personal opinion and not binding, and that Cronkhite's mass of evidence—which, he was reminded, he had refused to turn over to the department—did not alter the jurisdictional situation.[7] After a series of letters requesting personal interviews, always refused, the general lost his temper and wrote to Weeks complaining that Daugherty had refused to see him, and more seriously, that the charges had been dropped because Daugherty had yielded to political pressure brought to bear on him by Secretary of Commerce Herbert Hoover and Senator Calder.

This letter brought a very sharp reproof from Major General Harbord. Cronkhite was told he had no right to make "loose allegations" against the Attorney General and only the sympathy the War Department felt for him in his bereavement prevented prompt disciplinary action.[8] The general felt that his honor was impugned by these remarks and demanded a court of inquiry to examine the whole affair. He was notified on October 10 that his request for this court was refused. (Curiously enough, the *West Point Biographical Register* lists under the general's name a court of inquiry held on October 12, 1921, to which Cronkhite was called as a witness by order of the Secretary of War.[9] What this court concerned will apparently never be known. The National Archives, the Judge Advocate General's office, and the office of the Adjutant General all report they have no record of such a court being held. While it is possible the *Register* is in error, it is more likely that the court records were not filed officially. General Cronkhite's mental balance was beginning to be affected; his decline can be traced progressively as the case continued. There was perhaps a natural reluctance to file, as a matter of record, evidence of the disintegration of a senior officer.)

Unable to persuade the War Department to assist him, the general appealed to President Harding, and on December 1 Harding asked the Secretary of War to give Cronkhite a three-month leave of absence. The letter commented:

> I quite agree with the department of justice that the case is not one for that department. I would not wish to see the matter completely dropped. If Gen. Cronkhite, with his particular interest in this case, can secure evidence to bring about an indictment for trial, I think the service would be well worthwhile.[10]

Harding had apparently been advised in December that the Department of Justice did not have jurisdiction, even though

the department had decided to review its decision in the matter in October and November, and in early January turned
the case over to the U.S. attorney in Seattle. His letter also
implies his understanding that the government in December
1921—nine months after Rosenbluth's arrest—was not in possession of sufficient evidence for a grand jury indictment.

General Cronkhite became increasingly convinced he was
being blocked in his researches by hidden forces and antag-
onisms. Obviously the War Department was trying to quiet
him and the Justice Department was ignoring many of his
requests for information. He was, nevertheless, given privi-
leges that were refused to Rosenbluth, who was, in particular,
greatly handicapped by being denied access to documents in
the case. The War Department supplied the general with
photostats of the board of inquiry testimony but replied to
Rosenbluth's request as follows:

> Any action with an incriminatory tendency which may have
> been taken in the case of Capt. Robert Rosenbluth was insti-
> tuted by the department of justice and is a matter over which
> the war department has no control and one in which it has no
> real interest. Consequently, it would be contrary to a rule of
> long standing to permit Capt. Rosenbluth to inspect personal
> files of another officer for the purpose of clearing his name.[11]

Similarly, other materials were supplied to the general to use
as he wished. In a letter to Assistant Attorney General Ottinger in October 1921, Rosenbluth complained of an announcement carried in the *Seattle Post-Intelligencer* of the
paper's plans to publish "evidence" from General Cronkhite,
apparently the Pothier confessions. "Will Mr. Crim find out
how the General got from the Department this 'evidence' and
is permitted to give it or such parts of it as he sees fit to the
newspapers?"[12]

III

DURING the last half of 1921 Rosenbluth and his friends struggled vainly to persuade the Justice Department to send the
materials of the case to Selden and to collect evidence on their
own. Their experience with Lee, Stewart, and Herron had
convinced them they could not expect honesty, fairness, or
justice from the Justice Department. Although the department
later displayed great irritation at "trying the case in the newspapers" and at repeated interference by various civic and professional groups, there is no doubt that the defense had to as-

semble what help they could from whatever sources were
available.

Rosenbluth assumed that the published notice of Pothier's
retraction removed any personal threat against him and believed it was his duty as a citizen to insist upon an investigation of departmental methods. This attitude toward the case
was expressed at the conclusion of an article which appeared
in *The Nation* in October:

> It is not a matter merely of private concern. Captain Rosen-
> bluth is no longer in jeopardy. What he has suffered he has
> suffered. He fights now for principle rather than for himself.
> . . . we must know plainly whether this mighty arm of the
> Federal Government is a Department of Justice or of Persecu-
> tion. . . . Captain Rosenbluth will not have suffered in vain
> if his experience opens the eyes of the American people to the
> necessity of protecting themselves from the various bureaucra-
> cies which they have set up in the name of their own safety.[13]

A similar article in the *Literary Digest* in January 1922 quoted
from an editorial in the *Brooklyn Eagle:*

> Captain Rosenbluth has been the victim of a gross miscarriage
> of justice, and but for the repudiation of the false charge against
> him, might have suffered much greater injury.
> He is still seeking vindication and justice, but he is basing
> his demand for an investigation on broader grounds in order
> that his case may serve to prevent such injustices in the future.
> . . . the Department cannot afford to rest under the suspicion
> that it is willing deliberately to ignore a wrong which had been
> perpetrated by its agents. And the investigation itself should
> be followed by the creation of some form of recognized pro-
> cedure that will prevent the repetition of such a wrong as has
> been done Captain Rosenbluth.[14]

The certainty of the defense that no shadow of a case
existed was produced in part by the refusal of access to certain
documents and by Rosenbluth's gradual discovery that men
alleged to have borne witness against him had not in fact done
so. There were, however, certain problems presented by the
evidence, even disregarding Cronkhite's wilder theories. The
expert opinion of the autopsy surgeon and Captain Jones (a
pistol expert licensed in most eastern states) that the wound
could not have been self-inflicted had to be considered valid.
Dr. Schultze was a member of the medical staff of New York
County and an experienced man. There is no reason to suppose his opinion was anything but honest. Secondly, Pothier
did not retract his first confession that he had accidentally
shot the major while trying to unload his own revolver. In
the interview published in the *World,* he made it clear he

withdrew all confessions implicating Rosenbluth but did not deny he fired the fatal shot. While it is possible to argue that Pothier was originally forced to confess by the "third-degree" methods of Agent Lee, it is more difficult to explain why he did not later retract *all* his confessions and return to the original assertion that the major had accidentally shot himself. Nor is it entirely clear why Pothier did not make his retraction in the form of an affidavit, rather than verbally through his attorney.

This possibly may have been a matter of legal tactics. His attorney, Davis Arnold, forbade Pothier to make further statements to anyone and asked that the government refrain from further interrogation. Probably Arnold hoped his verbal notification to the department combined with the permitted interview with the New York *World* would remove suspicion from Rosenbluth without further compromising his own client. But when Pothier's first confession was set beside Rosenbluth's board of inquiry testimony there was an obvious difficulty. If Rosenbluth was there, how could he not have known that Pothier was shooting? Or, if Pothier's story was a lie, why did he not retract it when he was out of Lee's clutches?

The matter is further clouded by occasional references to the fact that both Pothier and Cronkhite were shooting at the target. H. J. Wright's letter to Will Hays, for example, described the scene in this way. He was clearly sympathetic to Rosenbluth; where did he get this version of the story? In an editorial written after the trial in 1924, Louis Marshall also says both men were shooting.[15] Similarly, two witnesses asserted with great positiveness that Rosenbluth did not go forward until after the shots ceased. Both men, Elmer Kieffer and Frank Turner, sought out Rosenbluth voluntarily after his arrest and made affidavits in his behalf. Turner, who testified before the grand jury in 1922, was asked if he would change his story if he knew Rosenbluth claimed to have been present and said he would not. Turner appeared to have been a far more reliable witness than Kieffer, but the real difficulty with their affidavits was that they were apparently contradicted by Rosenbluth's statements before the board of inquiry, in which he said he was present when the fatal shot was fired.[16]

This raises the obvious question of the accuracy of the board of inquiry transcript. Some evidence exists to suggest that the testimony was edited before it was filed—not falsified, but rephrased to emphasize Rosenbluth's position as an eyewitness to the tragedy. If this was really done, then the War Department's refusal to supply copies of this document to Rosenbluth or to Prosecutor Selden is explicable. The department could hardly risk the possibility that those present at the tragedy might question the record. The board of inquiry seems to have been motivated entirely by a desire to avoid a blot on Major Cronkhite's record. But whatever the intent, the results were unfortunate. There is little doubt the War Department was attempting to impede the investigation to protect itself, and the growing suspicions of this in the Justice Department had some basis in fact.*

Rosenbluth was the man in the middle. Lacking the board of inquiry transcript, he could not raise any questions about its accuracy nor even realize the specific contradiction between that transcript and the affidavits of Kieffer and Turner. Nevertheless, there is reason to believe he discovered during the spring and summer of 1921 that the question of his exact position was a danger point. The last reference I have discovered which places him at the scene of the tragedy is contained in the *World* article of May 23, 1921, which mentioned that Rosenbluth caught Cronkhite as he fell. After this date, no reference is made to the question by anyone connected with the defense. Also, we have the two affidavits of Dr. Seaburg. In his first, dated March 26, 1921, he reported that Rosenbluth had told him about the accident, speaking as if he supposed Rosenbluth had been an eyewitness. In his second, dated June 2, 1921, he corrected this assertion and merely said, "the captain, as a matter of speculation, told me how it might have happened."[17] In his testimony before the grand jury, Seaburg admitted to having corresponded with Rosenbluth between the two affidavits, and making a definite effort to clarify his statement as a result.

No one would suppose that this conflicting testimony is in any sense a "case" against the accused man, but it does appear to raise questions that need answers. The Department of Justice could have raised these questions directly with Rosenbluth had it wished to do so; he could have been shown the board of inquiry testimony and asked to explain. But instead the department continued collecting damaging gossip about Rosenbluth, attempting to discover something sinister in his past, and giving him false information about testimony collected against him. Rosenbluth has told me that during this time he and his attorney were in touch with an agent in the Bureau of Investigation who reported back to them the frequent conferences on the case and the struggles to find something, anything, that could be used to bring pressure to bear on Rosenbluth to ensure his silence.

---

* The full text of the board of inquiry testimony is included in the Appendix, together with an analysis of its inaccuracies and omissions which point to alterations having been made at some time subsequent to the actual hearing.

The bureau also made use of another tactic during this period; it was for a time searching Rosenbluth's mail. This was apparently a common practice; the *Congressional Record* from 1922 on is filled with complaints that various congressmen had their offices and mail searched in an effort to find material to be used for blackmail. An amusing incident resulted from this search order. Rosenbluth decided to play a trick on the bureau and prepared a fake secret message by marking leaves of toilet tissue with meaningless symbols and gluing the stack together. This was mailed to a friend in Cincinnati—and arrived in a somewhat damaged condition three weeks later. Even after fifty years the perpetrator of this hoax was delighted at the vision of harried special agents struggling to decode a mass of fragile paper. He also admitted that his lawyers pleaded with him not to do such things.

This, however, was almost the only light note in the second half of 1921. Rosenbluth began the laborious task of corresponding with men and officers of the regiment in a desperate attempt to gain support for his cause and to unravel the various allegations supposed to have been made against him, even though grand jury testimony did not bear these out in some cases—Rustenbach's, for instance.[18] Rosenbluth was in the painful position of a man who had taken for granted the goodwill, respect, and affection of his acquaintances and was suddenly forced to believe that those he trusted had betrayed him. Many of his letters during the fall and winter of 1921 ring with relief at the discovery that one more supposed "witness" against him had never so testified; yet in some cases they reflect anger and distress at what seemed to him a cowardly neutrality.

Excerpts of his correspondence written between August and December show the strain under which he lived and the enormous task he had set himself: to unravel truth from lies and facts from fiction; to straighten out misunderstandings; and to find out who, if anyone, his enemy actually was. His letters are very long handwritten scrawls which go over and over the same points with different correspondents. In a letter written to ex-lieutenant Morrison his anger at the Justice Department is shown:

> Then I believe letters from you to the two U.S. Senators, your Congressman; and any editorial support you can get for a Congressional inquiry, and we'll clean out this bunch yet, who carry on so recklessly and then having done their dirt, carelessly shrug their shoulders and say, "We're tired of this—give it to the County Prosecutor at Tacoma," after holding me 4 months under arrest on a murder charge! I submit that this isn't American—it's the Czarism of old Russia; and we've simply got to wipe it out.[19]

This letter also reveals the sustained and almost impossible effort made to verify his own memory of events more than three years in the past:

> There is one pt. [point] more that I've not been clear on myself in relation to you. I know, and it's corroborated by Dr. Seaburg and many others, that he was attending the Major within 2 minutes of the shot; and of course he was in charge, and it was while he and the non-coms assisting him were giving him artificial respiration that they found the bullet wound. First they thought the Major had died of heart-failure.
>
> Now the point is when I sent you into headquarters, was it before or after the bullet wound was discovered, or can't you remember either. And of course it was long enough after the accident that you would have had time to hear the general talk, such as that the Major had been shooting at the tin can, and that there was absolutely no talk, or whisper or knowledge that anyone else there was even shooting at all. . . . Do you remember Root's saying "If only I hadn't lent him my gun," etc.

In another letter, written to ex-lieutenant Saunders thanking him for sending an affidavit, Rosenbluth accepted Saunders' refusal to comment about the relationship between Rosenbluth and Pothier because of his personal lack of knowledge of the latter: "As to Pothier, you have nothing on me—I couldn't identify him if I saw him on the street either, altho I dare say I'd remember the face, if it were pointed out to me."

Rosenbluth must have written literally hundreds of lengthy letters during the second half of 1921, in a desperate struggle to straighten out the tangles of the case single-handed, greatly handicapped by not knowing exactly what case was being constructed against him.

His letters also reveal the natural distress he experienced in his gradual discovery that at least some members of the regiment were prepared to spread malicious stories about him. In the letter to Morrison, he remarked:

> I too know Rusty talked, but thought it was just his irresponsibility, and certainly as far as I can remember, never treated him unfairly. I just can't make it out. Moreover, knowing him as we do, is there any human way of accounting for the fact that . . . he never told the Col. or others on me, if he knew anything? No, I think he's pure scatter-brained, or worse. [Rustenbach, whatever stories he may have told informally, did not testify against Rosenbluth before the grand jury.]

In a letter written about the same time to ex-sergeant Little, the same idea was expressed:

> I was certainly very glad to get your letter. Do you know that's the first one I got from any of the old "D" Co. boys.

But really I thought that with all the efforts I made and sincere liking for our old gang entitled me to at least an expression of sympathy and confidence from them. And unquestionably, some of the crowd was traitor to themselves as well as lying about me. It lies between Twisselman, Thompson, and you, and you're now out of it. Some one told a long tale about how I was no good, and that Major Cronkhite had to remove me from command several times, etc. . . . Just why anyone should tell such lies, I can't even imagine. Did either of the other two bear me a grudge? If so why? Or was there really such talk about me (no matter how false) and was my pride in the crowd a misplaced confidence? I thought particularly when we won the competitions, there was a feeling that we—all of us—were "pretty good."

The bitterest exchange, however, was a series of letters with ex-sergeant Kreutz, then a medical student at the University of Wisconsin. Rosenbluth had been informed by someone in the Justice Department of Kreutz's assertion that Pothier had informed him on the morning of the hike he had been sent by Captain Rosenbluth to borrow a revolver and ammunition for it. In several memoranda submitted to the department, Rosenbluth demanded that Kreutz be asked about this testimony, particularly to explain why he did not report this most unusual request. Kreutz was not a supply sergeant, nor even in Rosenbluth's company, and should have recognized Pothier's request (if it had been made) as completely unlikely. In addition to this alleged testimony, Rosenbluth had another reason to be suspicious of Kreutz. After several letters had been exchanged between them, Rosenbluth asserted:

> At this point, let me inform you that my investigations long ago secured some of the original signed letters which you sent last April to various former members of the regiment. To say the very least, these require a tremendous amount of explaining.*

After the department had dropped its charges in July, Rosenbluth wrote to Kreutz, asking him frankly to explain whatever reasons he had for his apparent suspicions.

> I'm sure though, that you will not want me to go thru life bitter at your part in bringing this trouble on me, or with unallayed suspicions on your part that either you unjustly have done me wrong, or that what you conceive to be a crime has gone unpunished.

---

* Exactly what Kreutz had said in these letters is not known. But it is highly probable that he and his friends, who knew that Pothier had borrowed the revolver, were puzzled by the lack of official mention of this. Speculation about it would be natural in letters exchanged between friends.

In his reply, Kreutz denied having given any statements on the case to government agents, although he had written several letters to General Cronkhite. He explained he had no information to give and said he felt he should be neutral in the case.

The word "neutral" caused a violent reaction in a man undergoing the strain Rosenbluth was experiencing. He attacked Kreutz's statements vigorously:

> "Had I information that a man, not guilty of murder, was being tried for murder, I would feel duty bound to do everything in my power to see him acquitted" and then go on to say "In this case, I felt that it was my duty to remain neutral." In effect you say that you suspect me, altho you have no evidence either way.

Rosenbluth then demanded to know why Kreutz had not reported his suspicions at the time:

> If you had doubts of my innocence at least after I left the regiment (which was a full month before the rest got off) why didn't you tell some one then. Or if you had no suspicions then, why in Heavens name do you find it necessary to be neutral now? . . . Can't you realize that I'd rather be convicted, even on perjured testimony which in time I could definitely refute than to go thru life with people remaining "neutral" and a cloud of suspicion resting on me forever.

He tried repeatedly to make Kreutz understand his need to know exactly what had been written to the general, since he had discovered that many perfectly innocent letters had been distorted:

> In the unhealthy atmosphere of the grief-stricken general, anything you may have written was given a rotten twist to mean something against me, you probably never meant. . . . I know, for example, that innocent letters Father Harron wrote were so twisted, albeit almost immediately after the junk was published in the papers, Father Harron rushed forward to my aid and right up to the minute had supplied affidavits nailing every lie that appeared and nailing it hard and in detail, and offered to go to Washington and see the Attorney General.
>
> The situation is such that, sad as it is that it must be said, that such specific affidavits in refutation, or at least duplicates of them, must be in my hands to be useful to me, as, altho unfairly, anything I can't disprove in black and white is passed as facts.

Kreutz finally wrote to the Justice Department asking them to supply him with a copy of any testimony given by him against Rosenbluth. Kreutz was apparently extremely reluctant to make an affidavit refuting testimony which he had not made, possibly enmeshing himself in a legal tangle of some sort. When the department refused him a copy, he asked that

Rosenbluth show him bonafide copies or newspaper use of his supposed evidence. This was impossible, of course, since Rosenbluth's information had been acquired verbally. Finally, Kreutz wrote to deny any testimony he was alleged to have given, and the unhappy series of letters came to an end.

A final pair of letters illustrating the general pattern of the affair was received by ex-lieutenant Fred Reeves, who had been the personnel adjutant of the regiment. Rosenbluth wrote to Reeves in the summer of 1921, but the letter apparently did not reach him and no reply came. In November a second letter was sent, and revealed the bitterness Rosenbluth was unable to avoid entirely:

> I take it that you wish me to, or are willing to let me, believe that you are one of those who bore false witness against me. You are the only one of the former officers not heard from. I hope you enjoy the distinction, and that you only may continue to be sufficiently hardened that you may never feel qualms of conscience, either over "false witness", or that you are unwilling to help a comrade, falsely and grievously hurt, by even so much as a word to help put the whole matter straight.

This letter produced an immediate response; Reeves wrote at once to explain he had not received the earlier letter and was willing to do anything he could to help.

Rosenbluth's reply was prompt and whole-heartedly apologetic. He began by explaining why he had supposed that Reeves had testified against him:

> it was alleged that the "personnel officer" had testified that my efficiency was something less than zero, that there was to have been the final half of the examination on which $\frac{1}{2}$ I had already been "flunked", and that Cronkhite was to have "finished" me that day; etc. Does the fact that not having heard, in answer to a letter that apparently never reached you, [explain] that I lost faith a bit, and felt hurt.

These allegations were part of General Cronkhite's attempt to demonstrate that Rosenbluth had a strong motive for doing away with his son. Who, if anyone, actually made them is not known, but obviously Rosenbluth had been informed they were a matter of record.

The letter then described the struggle:

> Honestly, it's a tough fight. Just a few days ago got affidavits from others who were threatened, importuned, and what not, to agree to implicate me—and directly by agents of the Dept. of Justice; General Cronkhite's agents; and the general himself! . . . And if you knew the unfairness of the procedure, the cold brutality of the refusal to help clear up the matter, at the same time lending the machinery and power of government agencies to General Cronkhite, who is even today con-

ducting a "propaganda campaign" in the Seattle papers against me.

The letter concluded with a request for an affidavit making any statements about the case within Reeves' knowledge. The affidavit was subsequently drawn up, and like most of the others, denied that Reeves had ever heard of any bad feeling between Cronkhite and Rosenbluth or any doubts expressed about the verdict of the board of inquiry, and it asserted Rosenbluth's reputation for moral worth and integrity was very high indeed.

Rosenbluth did not give up all attempts at communication with the Justice Department and was receptive to any official who seemed prepared to show even moderate consideration. In September and October he wrote to and met with Assistant Attorney General Ottinger and, for a time at least, was able to believe that Ottinger wished him well and was trying to help. A letter dated September 25 said:

> Not that, after all, personal feelings are at all relevant to the case, still you may care to know that your attitude has gone far to lift the bitterness which, fight it though I have to the utmost of my ability, I found weighing upon me. I think you will agree that to become embittered is to be lost, as while there may have been cause enough, yet the world takes only the results. You know "Hope long deferred maketh the heart grow sick."[20]

At the conclusion of the letter Rosenbluth enclosed copies of an article on the case and expressed the hope that this, together with the goodwill of Ottinger and Burns, "can make Mr. Crim 'see the light' of justice as the ordinary American citizen sees it." Ottinger and Burns, whatever their good intentions, were nonetheless unable to influence the policies of the Justice Department significantly.

The various letters and affidavits were turned over to Norman Thomas of *The Nation,* and on October 19 an article was published summarizing the case and attacking the department for its procedures and apparently deliberate falsification. The article contained lengthy quotes from a letter from Herron, which were shown to be either false or misleading. Herron's statement "Pothier's attorney never stated to this department that Pothier had retracted his confession," is in flat contradiction to a letter from that attorney to Rosenbluth. A later statement saying Selden "could not have had any retraction of said confession, since this department had none itself" is technically correct; the Justice Department repeatedly took refuge in the fact that the retraction was given verbally, not in written form. Herron ignored the published account of this re-

traction and Chief Baley's subsequent promise of an investigation. A third statement asserting that Dr. Tucker had refused to be interviewed, saying he had nothing to add to former
testimony was denied by Tucker. He said an attempt had been
made to reach him by phone just as he was leaving for the
summer, but no further attempt had been made, although the
agent had his summer address.

The *Nation* article was submitted to the Department
of Justice by editor Oswald Villard for corrections and emen-
dations, but despite repeated requests, no reply came. Subsequently, after the article had appeared, Daugherty commented
loftily: "In so far as your article contains statements of fact
they are in every fair sense and purport incorrect. In so far as
your article contains inferences of your own they are incorrect
because based upon incorrect facts."[21]

The Justice Department file for the month of November
1921 contains a solitary letter, in marked contrast to the heavy
barrage of letters, memoranda, and documents for other months.
In the letter that survives, Norman Thomas wrote to Daugherty making several suggestions about the Rosenbluth case and
concluded with an inquiry of his own. Thomas had been in-
informed that prisoners in Atlanta, Eugene Debs among them,
were not being permitted to receive *The Nation*.[22] Thomas
wanted to know what federal statute permitted such an order.
Hardly avoidable is the conclusion that the files for this month
are not complete or the suspicion that they once contained material which would explain why the department reversed its
decision.

The only trace of activity for November was recorded in
Ewing's articles in the *Chicago Tribune*. He reported that
Rosenbluth had enlisted the aid of Congressman Harold Knutson of Minnesota; in November Knutson's secretary, David
Berg, wrote to Rosenbluth to tell him that William Burns
had turned over all the papers in the case to John Crim, new
head of the criminal division of the Justice Department. Crim,
asked about the matter, replied that the papers had been sent
to the court which had jurisdiction. Since Burns had assured
Rosenbluth in September that the papers had been sent to
Selden, Crim was asked again where they were. He replied
that his phrase "the court which had jurisdiction" did not
refer to the county court but to the federal court at Seattle
where the papers had in fact been sent.[23] On October 25 Crim
had told General Cronkhite the papers would be sent within
a few days to the state prosecutor in Tacoma.

By December no pretense was made. Further frantic inquiries from General Cronkhite resulted in a curt reply from
Crim that Selden had never been sent anything except a few

materials from the Seattle office the previous spring.[24] Obviously the Justice Department had privately reversed itself and had reopened the case without any formal notification to anyone. That it was reluctant to go on record on the matter was suggested by an exchange of letters between Assistant Attorney General Goff and Bruce Bliven, managing editor of the *New York Globe*. Bliven wrote to ask some questions about the case, including an inquiry about the failure to send the papers to Selden. Goff finally replied in December 1921 that he would advise Bliven later about the matter. A lengthy letter prepared by Goff, but not sent (each page is marked from corner to corner with an "X") indicated the line of argument the government intended to use. Goff asserted that the attorney in Seattle had the agents' reports of Pothier's "recantations" at the same time as the confessions, and both had been turned over to Selden. ". . . the Legal Division of this Department, as distinguished from its Bureau of Investigation, has never authorized the turning over of any papers whatsoever to the said Prosecuting Attorney, nor had any communication with him as to the evidence in this case." He concluded by explaining that the department was still examining evidence to get it into a clear and definite form to submit to the "authorities" having jurisdiction.[25] Goff's review of the case is of interest also in that it was used later by Crim when he prepared an analysis for the grand jury; similarities of phrasing and of argument indicate the source. Crim, naturally enough, depended upon reports made previously by responsible officials; any errors of fact or misrepresentations of fact or interpretation were thus passed from one hand to the next, without much chance of being noticed and corrected.

In the meantime, Selden in Tacoma was becoming more and more outraged by the government's failure to submit the materials he understood he had been promised, and he was concerned for Rosenbluth's position. Selden did not know Rosenbluth, but had corresponded with him and had been visited in September by ex-lieutenant Morrison on his behalf. After waiting many months for additional evidence, Selden lost patience and wrote a lengthy analysis of the case. This document, entitled 'An Exoneration of Captain Rosenbluth in the Matter of the Death of Major Cronkhite," was published in three installments in the *Tacoma Ledger* and later was issued in pamphlet form by Rosenbluth's friends. Selden, gravely annoyed at the Justice Department and strongly persuaded that Rosenbluth was being persecuted, acted as he felt was right.

The exoneration began with a presentation of the legal argument on jurisdiction; the lawyer whose brief was reprinted was a friend of General Cronkhite and believed there was evidence of murder, but he was equally certain that the state of Washington had jurisdiction over the offense. This material was followed by a description of the materials which had not been received, particularly a copy of the board of inquiry testimony and a statement of Pothier's retraction. An analysis of Agent Lee's diary followed, and Pothier's various confessions were shown to be confused, mutually contradictory, and valueless. Selden then reprinted a long series of affidavits and letters, showing the character and reputation of Captain Rosenbluth and the unlikelihood that he had had anything at all to do with Cronkhite's death. The pamphlet concluded with Selden's formal opinion as prosecuting attorney for Pierce County:

1. There is no reason shown why the findings of the Military Board of Inquiry, made shortly after the death of Major Cronkhite, should not be accepted as final and conclusive. . . .
2. All of the statements made by Pothier must be repudiated. They do not ring true. . . .
3. Captain Rosenbluth . . . should be and is, so far as we are able to do it, entirely exonerated from any connection, whatever with the death of Major Cronkhite. . . . We adopt it as an established fact that Captain Rosenbluth rendered a valuable service to his country, both at home and abroad, during the late World War, was an efficient, capable and untiring officer, was an intimate and close friend of Major Cronkhite, and that from the record of his life and service he is not the kind or type of a man who would entertain in his mind for one moment any such crime as that attributed to him by Pothier; that nothing in the way of a motive has been shown; that a great injustice has been done him, which should be righted; that there is nothing which in any manner approaches the dignity of evidence to connect him with the killing of Major Cronkhite, and we are firmly convinced that he should be again restored to public confidence to the same degree that existed before the happening of this very unfortunate incident.[26]

The publication of this forceful statement produced a predictable reaction. Since the Justice Department had never officially or publicly removed the case from Pierce County jurisdiction nor admitted that it had resumed investigation, Selden's exoneration was accepted, reasonably enough, as a final answer from the court empowered to reach a decision. There seems to be no doubt that Selden did have the authority to make this decision. He was later alleged to have acted without authority and on the basis of a few documents to have tried the case himself without judge or jury. But in an exchange of letters with Herman Chapman, secretary of the Yale Forest College Alumni Association, Selden explained that in his

county the prosecuting attorney was legally entitled to decide
whether or not a case was strong enough to be presented to a
jury. Grand juries were not called, he said, to evaluate routine
criminal cases; such juries were considered an expensive and
unreliable method of evaluating evidence. Selden, therefore,
was not deciding whether or not to bring the case before a
grand jury; he himself was empowered to decide whether or
not to bring the case to trial.[27]

Selden's reasons for his decision were further explained in
an interview in the *Chicago Tribune:*

> I am not now, and never have been, prepared to state that Ma-
> jor Cronkhite was not murdered. I cannot say that he shot
> himself, intentionally or accidentally, or that he did not. I was
> told by the government that the case was turned over to me. I
> was furnished certain documents and I understood that I got
> everything the government had, for those were the instructions
> issued. In that evidence there was nothing to implicate Rosen-
> bluth except Pothier's confession, which evidently is the child
> of a disordered mind and which I was reliably informed had
> been retracted, although the government sent me no retraction.
> While I had not seen Pothier, his silly statements were ample to
> judge by. After the uproar over the case, I felt it my duty to say
> there was nothing in my hands on which I could prosecute and
> that there was nothing against Rosenbluth at all and I said it.
> . . . If any one can show me one bit of evidence on which to
> prosecute, I will forget that statement and do my best to put
> Rosenbluth or any guilty person on the gallows. But nothing
> has been given me except in exoneration of Rosenbluth.[28]

Selden was not refusing to try the case absolutely; he was
refusing to try it on the evidence he had. The exoneration was
the more convincing in that he did not know Rosenbluth, and
his statement was manifestly the result of his sense of justice
and his strong indignation at the federal government's vacillation and delay. As the *New York Times* commented, this courageous effort to right a wrong challenged Daugherty to restore
confidence in the Justice Department by officially accepting
Selden's opinion.

The Justice Department, however, declined the challenge,
although it wavered somewhat during the month of January.
An inquiry from Congressman Jeffers urging action "within a
few days" received a polite but noncommittal reply. A letter
from Congressman Burdick requesting a definite statement
about the present status of the case was filed with an attached
memo from Herron to Crim asking "Can any answer be made
at this time?" Crim delayed answering Burdick's letter for
nearly a month, then limited his remarks to an apology for the
letter's having been misplaced.[29]

On January 4, 1922, *The Nation* published a second article

on the case entitled "The Department of Injustice," which described the Selden exoneration, printed Daugherty's curt response to the October article, and concluded with a serious warning:

> Congress should institute a searching investigation at once. It ought also to pass legislation giving to innocent men redress which they now lack even after systematic persecution by public officials. There is too much reason to fear that Captain Rosenbluth's case is not unique. The Attorney General's last report acknowledges the existence of a Bureau of Investigation with elaborate files of alleged information about sundry citizens suspected of radical affiliations. After these revelations can we trust it with such power? . . . It is time to clean house in Mr. Daugherty's department even if that should, perchance, end in the impeachment of high officials.[30]

On January 10 a letter from Senator Calder was sent enclosing a resolution passed by the Annual Encampment of the Veterans of Foreign Wars urging a full exoneration for Rosenbluth. Calder advised Daugherty that if he believed Rosenbluth innocent he should say so promptly. "Your Department arrested him, inconvenienced him, referred his case to the authorities in the State of Washington, and have never attempted to set the matter right."[31] On January 11, however, Daugherty wrote to the U.S. Attorney in Seattle, Thomas Revelle, directing him to reexamine the jurisdictional status of the case and enclosing certain evidence for his use: the board of inquiry testimony, records of Rosenbluth's military service, and the tobacco can and shells presumably picked up at the scene.[32] The forwarding of these exhibits strongly implied that the government fully intended to reopen the case in federal court.

The following day Senator Calder wrote to Daugherty again, enclosing a copy of one installment of Selden's exoneration from the Tacoma paper, and delivering a serious warning. The letter is friendly in tone, but warned of the political dangers of delay. The articles in the Tacoma paper are "most damaging to the Department of Justice. . . . Rosenbluth's friends and also the Legion will keep this thing stirred up, and several months from now when the situation will be greatly magnified, it will be embarrassing to acknowledge his innocence. . . . I know scores of people who believe Rosenbluth was very badly treated." He concluded by remarking that numerous senators were interested in an investigation of the Justice Department and all this awkward controversy could be avoided by prompt settlement. "Frankly, I believe the matter is of considerably more importance than you realize."[33] For Calder, it was. As a result of the growing criticism of the administration he lost the 1922 senatorial election to his Democratic opponent.

But Senator Calder's advice was not followed, and the Justice Department continued its course. The decision to bring the matter to trial was undoubtedly stimulated by the determination of the principals to achieve a definite settlement. Neither Cronkhite nor Rosenbluth was prepared to take the Selden exoneration as final settlement of the matter. Cronkhite still believed wholeheartedly in Rosenbluth's guilt and was determined that a "murderer" not escape justice. Rosenbluth, who all along had insisted there was no case, now considered his position clarified and began in 1922 to proceed against the Department of Justice. He wanted, reasonably enough, a public statement that it accepted Selden's analysis. Undoubtedly his efforts to obtain such a statement precipitated the next stage of the affair. If he had not continued to exert pressure, the department very likely would have allowed the case to lapse.

CHAPTER SIX
RENEWED
FEDERAL ACTION
JANUARY 1922-
SEPTEMBER 1922

AFTER THE SPATE of newspaper editorials attacking the Justice Department and the articles published in *The Nation* and the *Literary Digest,* discussion of the Cronkhite case vanished from the press until fall. Friends had tried to persuade Rosenbluth that he was engaged in a hopeless struggle. He was physically and financially exhausted by the time the Selden exoneration appeared, having spent almost a year unable to obtain permanent work and constantly engaged in the effort to clear his name. After the exoneration he relaxed briefly by signing on as a common sailor on a tanker to Mexico, but he was unwilling to give up entirely. As he told his friends, "I am single, I have no responsibilities to others, and if the Department of Justice could do that to me, think of its action against others who are really helpless!"

Efforts to silence him were immediately put into effect. Jonah Goldstein recalled a conversation with the U.S. Attorney for Manhattan, in which that official said, "Look, Johnny, your client Rosenbluth is making a lot of trouble for us and we will have to shut him up, some way or other. Why don't you persuade him to lay off and we will see that he is cared for by our exoneration?" To this Goldstein replied, "I certainly agree with you that he should quit and get back to normal life. . . . But I looked up his genealogy and in a previous incarnation, he was a mule, and I have no hope of persuading him to stop—he is a tough one when he has a fighting cause."[1] It is interesting to note that this conversation implies the attorney's belief of the department's willingness to drop the case if Rosenbluth could be silenced. Correspondence within the department at Washington, however, shows that definite plans to prosecute were going forward.

A stronger attempt was made to secure a compromise early in 1922. Rosenbluth was invited to lunch at the National Republican Club in New York City by an assistant attorney general, a stranger to him. This man began by warning him that if he ever dared to repeat their conversation, he would deny it ever took place; and he, not an accused murderer, would be believed. He then made his offer: The Justice Department was prepared to issue a full exoneration to Rosenbluth if he would first give them a statement exonerating it from any and all charges of improper conduct. If Rosenbluth would not accept this compromise, he continued, the department would reverse itself on the jurisdiction question, indict him before a federal grand jury, and jail him in Tacoma. This time, he was told, he would not be admitted to bail, and they would delay the trial indefinitely, leaving him to "rot in jail" until he was so badly smeared that he could never recover.[2] But Rosenbluth refused the offer, by this time completely determined to clean up the Justice Department and the Bureau of Investigation and not ready to believe that the department could carry out its threat to press the case.

Rosenbluth, of course, had no way of knowing that in January 1922 the authorities in Washington were planning to reopen the case in federal court. He no doubt supposed that the formal press announcement the previous July ordering the case turned over to the state authorities would make reentry of the federal government into the case an impossibility. He interpreted this offer as an attempt to bribe him into silence, not as a threat of continued prosecution. But it would seem the offer was even more dubious than it appeared. Had he agreed and given the department a statement that he had no complaint to make against it, the department still could have, and probably would have, gone ahead with its plan to indict Rosenbluth and Pothier before a federal grand jury. A retraction by Rosenbluth of his repeated charges against the department would have been a considerable advantage to those intent upon prosecuting the case.

Even granting the offer was what Rosenbluth supposed, obviously at this point the question of his guilt or innocence had become irrelevant. The department was clearly concerned with protecting itself and obtaining "evidence" that would defend it against a growing tide of criticism. Perhaps the offer was a fair one, but the possibility exists that it was the answer to the problem raised by Senator Calder. Once the department had Rosenbluth's affidavit attesting to its honesty and fairness, no Senate investigation of the affair could hope to succeed. And department pursual of the case would be a useful demonstration of the falseness of the current charges that it was reluctant to prosecute.

At this point, the Cronkhite case became entangled with the political situation and Daugherty's personal struggles with Congress. As early as July 1921 Senator McKenzie protested the failure of the Justice Department to press the various war fraud cases before it. Similar protests continued to grow in volume and climaxed on April 11, 1922, when representatives Woodruff and Johnson introduced a resolution calling for an investigation of the Justice Department for its failure to prose-cute war fraud and alien property act cases. These congressmen received much of their evidence from two employees of the department, Captain Scaife and Major Watts, both of whom had worked preparing briefs against dozens of business firms, only to find that there was no serious intention of bringing these cases to trial.

Captain Scaife resigned from the department in disgust and gave the two congressmen what help he could. In a letter printed in the *Congressional Record,* he charged:

> Half of the time spent during this investigation has been in efforts to overcome obstructions and fighting to get a chance to fight. . . . The Government is being overthrown, not by bolshevists, but by crooked politicians and trusted officials who know what is going on and have not the courage to fight or expose the conditions. So far as the Department of Justice is concerned, it no longer functions except in the capacity of first aid to crooks.[3]

Scaife continued by exonerating certain officials, Goff, Crim, and Burns, from his charges: "Your hands are tied the same as mine." Major Watts, who also gave information to the congress-men, was summarily fired by the department—the letter of dis-missal charging him with "disloyalty" to the department's interests.

The *Congressional Record* for May 1922 is filled with references to alleged interference by business and political in-terests into Justice Department cases. Scaife and Watts were particularly concerned at the antics of two department employ-ees, Lenihan and Myers, who seemed to control the files on fraud cases and openly joked about the failure to prosecute, calling their department "the department of no cases." Watts claimed that Lenihan was visited by a lumber contractor named Phillips who was also the Republican state chairman of Geor-gia, and as a result the Phillips-Stevens fraud case was dropped.[4] Frequent mention was made also to Daugherty's generosity with pardons for federal prisoners.

Most of these cases were never fully investigated, and it would be impossible now to determine the exact degree of negligence or corruption involved. But there seems to be little doubt that political and business interests were intervening in the Justice Department and it was not overly zealous in prosecution of such cases.

These attacks were accompanied by a growing protest in the press; even papers sympathetic to the Attorney General felt that the Woodruff-Johnson resolution should have been openly investigated. The growing cynicism and lack of respect for the Justice Department were clearly shown. The *Baltimore Sun* reported that a newspaper in Daugherty's hometown had offered a prize of $2,500 for every convicted contractor placed in the penitentiary through Daugherty's efforts—with a costly automobile thrown in if the contractor was a Republican.[5] The upshot of these attacks was to suggest that Daugherty was not prepared to prosecute anyone and was in fact pardoning every malefactor in sight.

Daugherty's failure to agree to Senator Calder's suggestion for department acceptance of the Selden analysis and the attempt to have Rosenbluth drop his charges against the department must be evaluated against the political scene. In 1922 Daugherty was under heavy fire both from outraged citizens and from political rivals. Not only were the Democrats in full cry but Henry Ford was gaining substantial support as a rival of Harding for the next presidential nomination. Ford's rivalry gained additional force early in 1922 when a book was published claiming the Harding family was of Negro ancestry. The last thing Daugherty, the Department of Justice, and the Republican party needed at this moment was an enforced demonstration that the department had persecuted an innocent man.

When the prosecution side of the case met in April to consider future plans, the Woodruff-Johnson resolution charging Daugherty with deliberate delay in war fraud cases was before the House. The political advantages of dropping the case must have seemed less important than the advantages of pushing it. Perhaps the staggering list of cases Daugherty had not pursued encouraged him in his decision to bring the Cronkhite case to trial. He seemingly had no apparent interest in the rights and wrongs of the matter. But to abandon it would be a weakness, and since some of those supporting Rosenbluth were men of great wealth, dropping the case could lead to further charges that wealthy criminals or their protégés could "buy their way" in the Department of Justice.

These charges were being made with regularity. On May 5, 1922, Senator Caraway had printed in the *Record* a long list of complaints written by Captain Scaife, challenging Daugherty to deny or explain them. The third one read: "Is it not a fact that you have personally granted hearings to alleged male-factors of great wealth to determine whether or not their cases are to be handled by the courts, and are similar hearings granted to all classes of citizens?"[6] Rosenbluth was not person-ally a rich man. But since several of those who publicly sup-ported him—Felix Warburg and Herbert Hoover in particular—were men of great wealth, interpretation of the government's action in this way was easy enough. It will be recalled that in 1921 Rosenbluth was granted a special hearing by the Justice Department, after which the government dropped its charges against him. To make this action appear the result of financial pressure would be a simple matter.

Pressure may also have been applied indirectly from the Bureau of Investigation. The impact of the Red raids early in 1920 produced "growing opposition, from important sources, to the general intelligence activities of the Bureau of Investiga-tion [during] the years 1921 to 1924."[7] The bureau had been organized rather casually in the first place and had been devel-oped more or less by chance, rising to public notice during the Bolshevik scare and the attempts to enforce the Prohibition amendment. Early Attorney Generals like Bonaparte and Wick-ersham assured Congress that abuses of power in this organiza-tion could be prevented by an alert official who could oversee his agents personally. But by 1920 Attorney General Palmer asserted the rapid expansion of work and personnel in the bu-reau made personal supervision by the Attorney General im-possible. Although bureau head William Burns and Daugherty claimed that the organization had grown in efficiency during their administration, its many abuses were manifest. Particu-larly objectionable to many was Gaston Means, a special agent who doubled as confidence man. The growing outcry against him was too open to be ignored, and in 1923 Crim was assigned to investigate his operations. Means was eventually tried, and despite his defense by Daugherty's dubious legal friend, Thomas Felder, he was convicted. The story of his years with the bu-reau, *The Strange Death of President Harding,* is one of the curiosities of the period, particularly in its scarcely veiled as-sertion that Harding was murdered by his wife to save him from disgrace.

Crim, testifying before the Wheeler Committee in 1924, asserted that after eighteen years with the Department of Jus-tice, he thought it advisable to "do away with nine-tenths" of the Bureau of Investigation as presently organized.[8] When J. Edgar Hoover was appointed head of the bureau after Daugh-erty had been replaced by Harlan Fiske Stone, he at once reorganized his staff, removing many employees who had been given jobs for purely political reasons, establishing clear requirements for employees, and tightening the chain of command to prevent the autonomy of agents like James Lee.

The bureau, as it existed under Burns' administration, was extremely vulnerable to criticism. And since it was an established agency wishing to survive, it no doubt resisted strenuously any plan to admit, however tacitly, that its agents or its policies were at fault. However, Burns did intervene briefly in Rosenbluth's behalf; his son and Rosenbluth had trained together at the army camp in Plattsburg, New York. But his efforts produced no tangible results; he finally told Rosenbluth he had been directed not to interfere in the case in any way.

A more puzzling cause of the continuation of the case (or at least its vigorous prosecution) was John W. H. Crim, the new head of the criminal division of the Justice Department, who by all accounts was an honest and dedicated official. He has the negative distinction of being almost the only assistant attorney general during these years who was *not* attacked by a congressman for corruption or neglect of duty. Crim appeared to believe in Rosenbluth's guilt and in addition seemed to be personally quite antagonistic to him, which no doubt reinforced his belief.

Crim's conviction that there was a case to be investigated was the result of various department memoranda prepared by different officials. Admittedly, a document like Neale's analysis of the case prepared for Goff in May 1921 would convince most people with little or no background on it that something needed investigation. Crim did not have anything to do with the Rosenbluth case until November 1921 and probably did not know in detail how it had been handled earlier. He apparently depended upon reports of assistants for his initial information and did not investigate the agents' reports covering the early stages of the case until much later. J. Edgar Hoover, for example, reported in 1924 that the files on the case containing reports from agents Chastain and Lee had been checked out to Crim in 1923. In other words, in early 1922 Crim had just taken over as head of the criminal division and was no doubt engaged in handling a variety of cases and problems. He could not investigate each of them in detail from their beginnings. Convinced by his assistants' reviews of the case and worried, as he later implied, that the War Department was trying to stifle an investigation, he was determined to get to the bottom of the affair.

His personal antagonism may have resulted from his conviction that Rosenbluth was trying in every way possible to influence departmental decisions in an unethical and reprehensible way. At this time the Department of Justice was repeatedly being accused of failing to prosecute cases, of being vulnerable to pressures from political and business sources, and of profiting from graft and corruption. Because Crim was an honest man and undoubtedly knew that these charges had ample basis in fact, he was doubly determined to stay in the Rosenbluth case. He eventually resigned from the Justice Department in 1924 when the investigation of the Old Hickory Powder Company, a subsidiary of the DuPont Company, was blocked. Crim believed, although he did not allege this publicly, that forces in the War and Justice departments had interfered with the case. In a letter to the U.S. attorney in Nashville he said of the case: "It now appears from what transpired that there cannot be any question that it was the intention of someone to frustrate any investigation. . . . I have prevented such tricks being worked a great many times."[9] It seems likely that the Rosenbluth case was one to which he referred. Rosenbluth's array of senators, representatives, and business organizations; the growing number of articles in the press charging anti-Semitism; and the constantly threatened Senate investigation appeared to Crim as just the sort of improper interference with the duties of the department that he so utterly despised.

From Rosenbluth's point of view he had received completely convincing evidence that the department had no case worth mentioning, and he was entirely certain that only through continued use of pressure could he possibly clear his name and bring about needed reforms in the department. In addition, he was temperamentally inclined to disregard formal procedures and to attempt to straighten out the tangles of the case through personal conversation. Thus circumstances and pressures combined to convince two honest and stubborn men that the other was corrupt.

The sort of confusion that irritated Crim and clearly antagonized him was shown in an exchange of letters with Goldstein in December 1921. Goldstein, having been told that Crim would like to talk to him, wrote a friendly letter, expressing his pleasure at the suggestion and saying that this was the first indication that he and Rosenbluth had had that any official of the department wished to communicate with them. Rosenbluth had been informed, he said, that Goldstein was not acceptable to the department, and was advised to obtain a different lawyer. When Crim asked in a very serious way to be told exactly who had advised Rosenbluth that Goldstein was not acceptable, Goldstein's reply was a bit evasive. Crim was left with the impression that Goldstein had made an unfair allegation and then backed rapidly down when challenged about it.[10]

Crim's antagonism and its partial cause is again revealed in a letter to Emil Fuchs, an attorney:

> Captain Rosenbluth called me on the telephone this morning and asked me if he could see me with regard to this matter. . . . I declined to see him, just as I would decline to see any other man who has a matter pending here and who has an attorney handling his matter.

After explaining that he would be glad to see Fuchs if necessary, he continued:

> I regard it as absolutely inimical to proper procedure in this Department to have men under investigation coming in here unaccompanied by counsel, when they have a counsel in charge of such matter. Now, Captain Rosenbluth is just the type that cannot comprehend the reason for my attitude, and I have no doubt that he will turn up at some newspaper or magazine office complaining. That, however, does not disturb me.[11]

Crim also received a long letter from Senator Calder, who asserted among other complaints that he and Fuchs had been told by Crim in a private interview that Rosenbluth should take his case to the state authorities in King County, Washington, and ask for a grand jury hearing to decide the matter. Calder stated Rosenbluth had done so and had been notified by an astonished state prosecutor that King County had no jurisdiction and no intention of investigating the case. The state attorney in Pierce County was also approached, and he had replied that grand juries were not called in his county except in extraordinary cases and none was contemplated in the Rosenbluth case. Calder also protested the department's "quibbling," its refusal to admit knowledge of Pothier's retractions, and its excuses for failure to reexamine Pothier (based on a request from his lawyer, made over a year before, that he not be questioned further by the Department of Justice). Crim's reply was brief and unhelpful. He did not refer to any point raised by the letter except the grand jury suggestion, and then either deliberately or by accident he misinterpreted it. He implied that Rosenbluth had dictated the entire misleading letter and denied he had said the case was being sent to the state prosecutor in King County. Calder's letter had not so stated; he claimed that Crim told them to have Rosenbluth approach the state authorities personally.[12]

A further exchange of letters in June again demonstrates Crim's growing resentment of interference in the case. A letter from the Detroit Bureau of Governmental Research inquiring into the delay received a very brief reply stating the case had been referred to the federal authorities in Seattle. A second letter from the Bureau of Municipal Research of Akron, Ohio, asking that Rosenbluth be exonerated and expressing doubts of the fairness of the department, drew a much firmer reply. After acknowledging receipt of the letter, Crim said:

> if you have any evidence in the so-called Rosenbluth matter that will exonerate Captain Rosenbluth, or in any way tend to exonerate him, this Department would like very much to have it as promptly as possible. If you have any evidence that will show, or tend to show that Major Cronkhite was not murdered, this Department would like to have such evidence as promptly as possible. If you have any evidence as to how Major Cronkhite came to his death, by accident, or design, this Department would like to have such evidence as promptly as possible.[13]

There seems to have been a growing conviction in Crim's mind that the War Department was trying to stifle the case, presumably to protect itself and its officers from criticism. The War Department had steadily refused to become involved and in various ways had refused its cooperation both to Rosenbluth and to General Cronkhite. Very likely the department was indeed concerned to prevent any real investigation into the pro-

Secretary of War John Weeks and the War Department refused to cooperate with either Rosenbluth or General Cronkhite in pursuing the investigation.

cedures of the original board of inquiry. This resistance served
to confirm Crim's belief that there was a case to be investigated.

Shortly after plans had been made for a conference on the
case in April in the Justice Department, Acting Secretary of
War Wainwright notified the department that General Cronkhite could not be given additional leave of absence:

> General Cronkhite has been under orders to proceed to
> Panama since April 28, 1921, where his presence is much
> needed. At the urgent request of General Cronkhite frequent
> delays have been granted. . . . The last of these was a delay
> of ninety days, at the instance of the President, to enable him
> to gather evidence in this case. This ninety days will termi-
> nate the 5th of March. . . . The Government has had no
> value received from General Cronkhite since last April, [and
> has] given very explicit orders that if General Cronkhite de-
> sires to remain on the active list of the Army he must go to
> Panama . . . [by] the 14th of March.[14]

This letter was followed on March 2 by a memorandum for
Daugherty written by Crim. This communication is of interest
in that it makes clear his own personal determination to press
the case and suggests some reasons why this was advisable:

> The action of the Acting Secretary of War throws a mon-
> keywrench, as it were, into our machinery that I did not contem-
> plate. The investigation of the Cronkhite matter has been go-
> ing on in an orderly way, and we expect the United States
> Attorney here about the fifth of April. . . . I feel that the
> Cronkhite matter must be submitted to a Grand Jury. If it
> fails to indict, the matter will be settled. On the other hand, if
> the evidence developed is so strong that, in the opinion of the
> United States Attorney, there should be a trial, then by that
> process the matter will be decided.
>
> A number of Congressmen are just as insistent that this in-
> vestigation continue to some legal determination as the friends
> of Rosenbluth were that the matter be abandoned. We were
> advised a few days ago by Col. Fair, Secretary to Mr. Wain-
> wright, that General Cronkhite would be kept here for the
> purposes of this investigation. . . . Our information is meagre,
> but it indicates that after the Secretary of War had made an
> order directing General Cronkhite to remain here to assist this
> Department, the General Staff took the matter up and put a
> stop to it, by demanding that he be sent to Panama. . . . The
> Army organization is so strong in matters of this sort that I feel
> this situation should be handled by you and not by one of
> your assistants.[15]

Daugherty's letter to the Secretary of War a few days later also
suggests reasons for the change in department policy in the
fall of 1921:

It was not until late in the fall of last year that the Criminal
Bureau in this Department was fully organized. Almost immediately after the appointment of my Assistant, Mr. Crim, he
took up the investigation of the death of General Cronkhite's
son. The facts developed by General Cronkhite and from other
sources are of such a character that the evidence was forwarded
to the United States Attorney at Seattle, Washington, for appropriate investigations.

Concerning the General's absence from duty, Daugherty wrote:

This Department desires to be held responsible for that seeming
neglect of duty on his part. He has been indefatigable in his
efforts to ferret out the cause of the death of his son. Through
such efforts on his part, facts have come to the attention of this
Department that it cannot afford to neglect. It is the intention
of this Department to pursue this investigation unremittingly
until more is known about the death of Major Cronkhite.[16]

The letter concluded by saying that if the War Department
insisted upon sending the general off to Panama, he would be
subpoenaed back to the mainland by return ship.

Weeks apparently agreed to cooperate, but the General
Staff was not so inclined. Later in the month Daugherty sent
a memorandum to Herron, inquiring about the status of the
case and whether Cronkhite would be needed. Then a letter
from General Cronkhite arrived: "I have been directed by
Gen. John J. Pershing, commanding the Armies of the United
States, to inform him when I will be ready to proceed to Panama under orders existing in my case on March 28, 1922." In
his reply, Crim apologized for the embarrassment to the general, but said that nothing could be decided until the case was
thoroughly discussed at the forthcoming April conference.[17]

Perhaps a basic criticism of the department's handling of
the case can be made at this point. It did not, apparently, notify
Rosenbluth or his attorney that the department had officially
resumed jurisdiction of the case and planned to bring it before
a grand jury. It made no public announcement on the Selden
exoneration; and since it had stated the previous July that the
case was to be turned over to the state authorities, Rosenbluth
and his supporters could hardly be blamed for supposing that
the Selden exoneration settled the matter as far as legal problems were concerned. The various "under the table" attempts
to persuade him to drop his attempts to force an exoneration
from the department completed the misunderstanding. Rosenbluth had no way of knowing until the summer of 1922 that
the department had resumed jurisdiction. He believed the department was activated by malice and embarrassment; the de-

partment believed he was endeavoring in every possible way to protect himself by bringing pressure to have the charges dropped.

II

PLANS WITHIN the Justice Department to prosecute the case were well organized as early as February 1922. Daugherty wrote to the Secretary of War, asking him to hold Major Zajicek in the United States, since he would be wanted to appear in Tacoma before the grand jury. Representative Lamar Jeffers wrote again to Crim urging a speedy conclusion to the affair and was told "the matter is developing in a satisfactory way." In March a conference was arranged for the following month in Washington, D.C., and letters went out to Revelle, the attorney in Seattle; General Cronkhite, Lieutenant Colonel Howard; Captain William Jones; and Major John Richards, formerly the marshal at Providence, asking them to attend. At this meeting the formal decision was reached to bring the case before a federal grand jury.[18] Statements were taken from Jones, Howard, and Richards; and analyses of the alleged facts in the case were prepared by Cronkhite and Crim, for the use of Revelle in preparing the case for the grand jury scheduled to meet in late September.

These materials did not present any new information, but do make more explicable the feeling that the matter could not simply be dropped. Lieutenant Colonel Howard repeatedly denied any belief in Rosenbluth's involvement or knowledge of reasons that might possibly explain its existence. He made many admissions about the original board of inquiry and expressed his continuing doubts about the findings. His concluding testimony explained his actions at the time:

> I do not think that it was my conclusion after thinking it over seriously that the wound was self-inflicted, and I so stated before the officers at Camp Lewis that it was a great mystery to me how Major Cronkhite could have shot himself with the weapon as exhibited before the Board. It was my opinion that he was shot by some party unknown to me. It may seem strange to you that in view of the conclusions since reached and stated to officers at that time, that I should have signed that report as I did, but we were governed entirely by the testimony offered before the Board and I did not feel like disagreeing with the other officers especially as the officers were positive in their opinions that the facts were as stated by the witnesses.

Howard's reluctance to interfere with the decision of the other officers probably was interpreted as another hint of army conspiracy. Howard, a civil engineer whose rank resulted from participation in the state militia rather than army service, was considered a more reliable witness than the regular army officers of the regiment.

Another damaging statement included in the files of this hearing concerned an informal interview with Pothier's attorney at the time of the April conference. Internal evidence suggests that the speaker was probably Major Richards; the page is apparently part of a longer report and is inserted into the record following Richards' testimony. The implications of the statement, in any case, are unfortunate.

> On April 12, 1922, I met Davis G. Arnold, attorney for Pothier in the Shoreham Hotel [in Washington, D.C.] dining room, and subsequently I had a talk with him in the corridor. He sent for me. He told me that he recognized Mrs. Cronkhite, who was with me at the time, and said he wished they would get that succor [sic–the word meant is apparently "sucker"]. I said, "Who?" He said, "Pothier because," he said, "he killed Major Cronkhite." He said, "There is no question about it." He said, "I do not know what connection Rosenbluth has with the matter, but that fellow killed the Major." He said he wished them success—that he did not represent Pothier any more, and he said, "You have his written statement to the effect that he did shoot him." I made no reply. He said that in itself is enough to try him on.

If the speaker is indeed Major Richards, the statement shows he was acquainted with the Cronkhites and was sympathetic to their views of the case. The statements made by Arnold are somewhat puzzling. He had been assigned to represent Pothier by the Veterans Bureau in Providence and, in spite of evident dislike of his client, continued to represent him after this date, appearing for him in district court, the circuit court of appeals, and in the Supreme Court in 1923 and 1924. He was perhaps trying to abandon his client at this time, but his statements, made to a representative of the prosecution, are certainly open to criticism.

Arnold's irritable comments may have reflected a conflict of interest. Pothier was his client, whether he liked him or not. Arnold was also acquainted with Rosenbluth; the *New York Times* reported in 1921 that the two men had met in Constantinople in 1919 while doing relief work. In the summer of 1921 he conferred with Rosenbluth, two attorneys, and New York *World* reporter Austin Parker and reiterated his earlier assertion that Pothier had retracted his confessions and the Justice Department had been notified of this in April. In a letter to Rosenbluth written in August 1921 he assured him, "Pothier will take any steps necessary to vindicate you in this subject."

Why Arnold did not have Pothier make a formal affidavit retracting the confessions is not clear, but possibly he was also concerned to protect the department from as much embarrassment as possible. Arnold had connections with government circles. He had worked for the Senate Reed Committee investigating oil scandals, and in 1924 he was assigned to assist John Crim in preparing the case against Charles Forbes, former head of the Veterans Bureau. Crim, who had resigned from the Department of Justice, was reappointed as Assistant Attorney General for this very important case. The selection of Arnold (then assistant director of the Veteran's Bureau in Washington) strongly implies that he was known to the department and approved.

It is not really determinable what Arnold actually thought about the Rosenbluth case. In an interview published in the *Dearborn Independent* in 1923, he was quoted as saying, "Pothier thinks that a bullet either from the major's gun or from his own caused the officer's death. 1 don't believe he knows which."[19] That Arnold knew or thought he knew something decisive about the case is implied by his request to appear for the defense during Pothier's trial in 1924. He was not called however, and what he wished to say was never revealed.

In addition to these documents, two analyses of the case were presented to Revelle in Seattle. General Cronkhite's relatively brief study reflects his conversations with Howard, as well as the information he had collected from members of the regiment by letter and through interviews conducted by Agent Chastain. The general continued his refusal to turn over his collection of documents to the attorneys and persisted in making his own analysis. Except for Howard's testimony about the informality of the board of inquiry, Cronkhite's report is mistaken or misleading. He attempted to show that the hike was planned by Zajicek and Rosenbluth to dispose of Major Cronkhite, that Cronkhite and Rosenbluth had quarreled seriously during the hike and earlier, that the decision to turn right after the halt was insisted upon by Rosenbluth, and that the column was halted by Rosenbluth secretly to permit him to arrange the murder while the men were back on the road unable to see. He included "facts" showing that a fight occurred between Cronkhite and Rosenbluth to explain the scratches Mrs. Cronkhite believed she saw on her son's face, and he attempted to show that almost thirty minutes elapsed between the shots and the arrival of reliable witnesses. This document is marked in the margins in pencil with question marks and exclamation points, probably by Attorney Revelle, in recognition of the doubtfulness of many of the General's allegations.

A particularly large exclamatory mark appears at the side of one statement, which shows the general's tendency to jump from a factual statement to a very doubtful inference. Having observed, correctly, that the original autopsy report recorded the diameter of the bullet hole as three-fourths inch and Dr. Schultze's later measurements found the hole to be five-sixteenths inch to seven-sixteenths inch, the General asserted: "It is evident that this misleading statement in regard to the size of the wound is made with the willful intent to deceive and give weight to the close range shot construction and to provide the basis for the false finding of the Board of Inquiry." Apparently the general believed that not only the members of the board but the base hospital personnel were involved in a concerted plot. One can only wonder why they did not, if his allegations were true, do a better job of providing false evidence!

The long report written by Crim concluded the materials sent to aid in the grand jury proceedings. This report (not identified officially as being by Crim, but so marked in pencil on one of the copies) is a document of twenty-two pages and analyzes the various conflicts of the testimony exhaustively. It depended to a large extent upon the interrogations of Rosenbluth by Agent Lee and by Assistant Attorney Joyce in 1921. These records are not in the files, but Crim's detailed references to them help to show what they contained.

After a brief statement regarding federal jurisdiction in the case, based in all probability upon a brief prepared by Revelle, Crim examined the proceedings of the board of inquiry and was able to show without difficulty that they were extremely casual and ignored obvious conflicts in testimony made at the time. In particular, the prosecution case stressed the fact that neither Rosenbluth nor Pothier seemed entirely certain of the other's whereabouts; and yet if Rosenbluth's description of the scene was accurate, he must have known where Pothier was, just as Pothier must have seen him. The failure to examine the major's coat for powder burns was discussed, and Major Tucker's testimony in that regard was undercut by the observation that he "seems to be a strong partisan of Rosenbluth." The opinion of various pistol experts was given to show the uniformity of opinion that the wound could not have been self-inflicted; Pothier's story of accidental shooting was also claimed impossible. Pothier's later confessions involving Rosenbluth were summarized, with testimony from experts who believed that the shells on file came from two different guns.

Up to this point the prosecution case had, on paper at least, some merit. Anyone working with the documents of the case, if unacquainted with the principals, could hardly fail to recognize the various confusions in the record. But as the report proceeds to explain the federal government's vacillation in the matter, the argument becomes dubious. The report asserts that Pothier's retractions made no difference, since "a man confessing to a crime can have only one motive, viz., to tell the truth, while he may have many other motives for retracting his confession and denying his guilt." Granting that this is a possible generalization, it is not an absolute one. "Truth" is not always the motive behind a confession, and since the officials had access to Lee's reports on the case, they could not be unaware that the confessions had been obtained in a very questionable way. For example, James Osborne, attorney for the prosecution at Pothier's trial, described these confessions as having been "obtained under circumstances which I believe were unparallelled," and expressed his amazement that the judge permitted them as evidence. But in Crim's summary of the case, no mention is made of any improper techniques; the only reasons for the retractions are said to be Pothier's annoyance at being tricked by Harris, and his discovery that Rosenbluth had been released on bond while he remained in jail.

The report continues by asserting that the state attorney in Tacoma had never been officially involved in the case, but had been given occasional reports by the Bureau of Investigation office in Seattle through the U.S. attorney there. "He did so without any formal instructions from the Department." What level of formality was required is uncertain; the telegram of March 30, 1921, from Attorney General Daugherty, authorizing transmittal of documents to the state attorney and his notification that the case was to be transferred to his jurisdiction would seem to be sufficiently formal for most purposes. The report does not discuss the official announcement in the press in July 1921 that the case was being turned over to the state authorities. The report also asserts that it was "believed" that Selden, the state attorney, must have received notice of Pothier's retractions at about the same time he received the confessions themselves. This is on record as false in affidavits from Selden as well as in his exoneration statement. It also contradicts various letters from Herron, which asserted that the Justice Department had no knowledge of any retractions and had sent nothing of the sort to Selden. Crim seems to be depending here upon reports prepared earlier by Neale and Goff, where quite similar explanations occur.

Also included in the report is a very detailed analysis of conflicts in testimony between the original board of inquiry and Rosenbluth's later statements taken in 1921. Much emphasis is given the fact that information produced in the later statements was not mentioned before the board of inquiry—for instance, Rosenbluth did not give Cronkhite's illness as a possible cause of the accident. It is difficult to see, however, why these omissions were considered sinister. The members of the board had discussed the tragedy with Rosenbluth and Seaburg at length before the formal hearing. To go into details familiar to all those present was hardly necessary.

Crim was able to show quite easily that many details in Lee's and Joyce's interrogations of Rosenbluth did not entirely match with each other or with his testimony in 1918. As a sample of his argument, a few paragraphs will illustrate:

> In his testimony before Joyce, Rosenbluth testified that he heard a shot, ran forward, and in a few yards saw Cronkhite with a pistol in his hand, but he did not see Pothier. Rosenbluth reached Cronkhite and stood behind him before another shot was fired, "at his left rear in such a position that I could see along the pistol." Cronkhite fired twice and missed both times (although Rosenbluth had testified before the Board and before Lee that Cronkhite had missed only once after he got to him). On the third shot (fourth altogether) Cronkhite hit the can, and then swung around, his back to the post, facing Rosenbluth. He held the gun "with the upper arm close to the side and the forearm at a very acute angle almost vertical with the pistol upward, pointing in the air." The swinging around and weakness from the influenza must have let the gun drop back, "the muzzle of the gun backwards and downwards," and these same motions pulled the trigger; but Rosenbluth does not now believe that he saw the shot fired and merely assumes that Cronkhite shot himself in this way. . . . Rosenbluth testified before Lee and before Joyce that he did not go back in the ambulance, and that he never made any report or statements of the death of Cronkhite, except informally to the colonel; whereas he testified before the Board of Inquiry that he went back in the ambulance and made a written statement to the officer of the day at the base hospital; and Lieutenant Colonel Howard states that he was summary court officer for the regiment and that, as such, he sent for and questioned Rosenbluth the evening of the killing or the next day, Rosenbluth bringing to him the shells and the empty tobacco box. It is noteworthy that Colonel Howard, who was also president of the Board of Inquiry, further stated that he never heard of any written statement made by Rosenbluth; and yet the latter testified before the Board that he made one, and it is incredible that this testimony should have passed unchallenged if, in fact no such written statement had been made.

It seems fair to say that the author of these paragraphs is trying very hard indeed to construct some kind of case. The circumstances of the interviews, the friendly relations of the officers involved originally, and elapsed time tend to explain the various contradictions. At the original board of inquiry a group of intimately acquainted senior officers made a rather casual examination into the death and had no reason to doubt Rosenbluth's explanation nor to discuss peripheral details. Almost two and a half years later Rosenbluth voluntarily agreed to an interview with Agent Lee. This interview was recorded *before* Lee told him that Pothier had confessed to shooting the major. Thus Rosenbluth had no reason, during this questioning, to be overcautious or guarded in his statements. He was a voluble man, in any case, and could not have guessed that his memory of events years in the past might hang him if he were slightly inaccurate. The third interview, before Joyce, was held after Rosenbluth was under arrest for murder and had his attorney present. In a more formal session he would quite naturally make every effort to clarify his memory on details, to think back, and to try to be as accurate as possible. Crim complained in his report that Rosenbluth was vague and indefinite with Joyce and seemed reluctant to make positive statements. That he was well-advised to be reluctant is shown by the use made of these three interviews.

Furthermore, some of Crim's material appears to be unrelated to Rosenbluth. For example, he states that it was "noteworthy" that Colonel Howard did not recall any written statements being made, nor Rosenbluth's testimony to that effect. What Crim is getting at here is somewhat obscure, but he seems to be saying that despite Howard's present lack of memory of these statements they must once have existed, since no one challenged Rosenbluth's reference to them before the board of inquiry. Thus, Rosenbluth must have lied in his statement to Joyce and Lee that he had not written out a report at the time of the accident when he actually had done so. This inference seems highly prejudicial; if Howard could forget these statements three years later, why was Rosenbluth's failure of memory so significant?

A probable underlying motive for Crim's determination here was his suspicion of an army plot of some kind. The document was written to summarize the Justice Department's case against Rosenbluth personally, but an essential difficulty—establishing a *connection* between the casual board of inquiry procedure and Rosenbluth—is never tackled. Since Lieutenant Colonel Howard presided at the board of inquiry, he was assumed to be a reliable witness for the prosecution. But simultaneously Crim discussed military law regarding such investigations and showed that the board's organization and procedure were faulty. Major Zajicek was cited as a reliable witness to the events of the morning of the hike as a demonstration that Rosenbluth's testimony was false. Later, however, it was asserted that General Cronkhite believed Zajicek had falsified

Rosenbluth's rating sheet to raise it to passing levels and was suspected of "some concealed connection with Rosenbluth." Colonel Thomas was also disposed of as a dependable witness with the comment that he had filed erroneous information, claiming that Major Tucker had performed the autopsy and Major Cronkhite's coat was bloodstained. Thomas was mistaken on both these points, but no sinister purpose is apparent. In other words, the report wants to have it both ways: one officer's faulty memory is accepted, while another's appears suspicious.

The board of inquiry situation, however, was evidence against Rosenbluth only if the government could show an army plot, and one can hardly help suspecting that Crim was motivated by a strong desire to make sure that the War Department was not covering up a scandal involving several officers. That this was part of his motive was implied in a comment made in a letter to Revelle: "If murder, then it was most foul. If not murder, then it is of high importance that the Army be under no such black suspicions."[20]

In addition, from the tone of the document Crim clearly was genuinely convinced that Rosenbluth's statements were very suspicious, and he was prepared to discard material favorable to him quite abruptly. For example, he remarked, quite correctly, that none of the witnesses except for the accused claimed to have seen the major shooting at a target except Kieffer, "and his testimony is manifestly false." This statement is marked with a large question mark in the margin. The complete accuracy of Kieffer's statement does seem doubtful but it was never proved false in any definite way. Why Crim was prepared to dismiss it so casually is uncertain. His analysis does not explain his reason for this comment.

It would appear that the department was disinclined to investigate seriously statements made in behalf of Rosenbluth. For example, in the files is a letter, received shortly after Rosenbluth's arrest, from a former member of the regiment then living in Boone, Iowa. The writer stated positively that the major and Pothier had not left with the rest of the battalion and Pothier had told him he was alone with the major when the accident occurred.

Major Cronkhite took out his automatic and started to aim at the target. In so doing drawing his gun from his holster at his right side, bringing it high in the direction of the target, which was the practiced way he let the gun slip to far back in his hand, making the barrell point toward himself, seeing what was taking place he made an attempt to clutch the gun and discharged it, killing himself all most instantly.[21]

The writer of this letter was never interviewed as far as the files show, and he was not called as a witness to the grand jury or the trial. Even if his story depended only upon a statement of Pothier's made at the time, it would have had some relevance to the case. But apparently no inquiries were made.

By August of 1922 plans for the grand jury were under way. During the summer Rosenbluth and his friends discovered that the grand jury was being summoned, and Senator Calder wrote an extended letter of protest to Daugherty, suggesting strongly that the sudden assertion of federal jurisdiction must stem from the personal prejudice or malice of some official in the department. He reminded Daugherty of the previous decision to pass the case to the state authorities in Tacoma and protested his failure to secure an interview with the Attorney General. The letter was answered over Daugherty's signature but was drafted by Crim, as an attached memo makes clear. The reply called Calder's letter "astonishing," and asserted, "this office does not intend to be influenced one iota by the disingenuous implications set forth in your letter or the propaganda of Captain Rosenbluth."[22]

Calder's failure to produce results led to another exchange of letters, this time between Daugherty and Representative Ansorge of New York. Ansorge wrote to protest the reversal of jurisdiction, calling it persecution rather than prosecution and listing one by one the many official records where the government had acknowledged it did not have jurisdiction. This letter produced another sharp reply, signed by Daugherty but in all probability written by Crim:

> Why should Captain Rosenbluth be permitted the unheard of privilege of selecting the forum which is to investigate him? Why should not this matter take the ordinary course? Now that he is getting precisely what he prayed for at one time—a thorough investigation—he desires to take charge of it and run it.
>
> Within a fortnight he was procuring a Senator to place before this Department precisely what you have placed before it and receiving a reply that was unsatisfactory to him he appeals to you, and as soon as he has the reply I am writing you he will then appeal to some one else. . . .
>
> There are very serious issues of fact involved in this matter and I cannot permit them to be decided by any unofficial referee at New York or elsewhere. The matter must take its ordinary course. If he has done no wrong, he will undoubtedly be exonerated; if he has done wrong, he ought to be prosecuted.[23]

It having been made quite clear that the Justice Department was determined to proceed with the grand jury, Rosenbluth accepted the inevitable and wired the department as follows:

Will gladly answer subpoena appear before federal grand jury Tacoma September fifteenth Cronkhite case waiving immunity but explicitly leaving open question federal jurisdiction and reserving rights to full legal redress for this illegal move your department if you desire full inquiry will cooperate gladly I repeat here your records deliberately perverted even changing or omitting essential parts of my statements.[24]

This was followed by a letter to Revelle in Seattle from Crim, promising him full support in his prosecution of a difficult case. "There has been an enormous amount of propaganda and a great deal of political pressure brought to bear on this Department to prevent an investigation of the death of Major Cronkhite. . . ." The letter suggested that some of this pressure had resulted from the use of the case for "selfish purposes," a hint that political maneuvers were involved.[25]

After Rosenbluth and his lawyer approached Revelle in Seattle about appearing before the grand jury, Crim exploded: "I will make no such recommendation. Whether or not a man under investigation by grand jury will be permitted to appear before it is a question for the court to consider and most of the federal courts will not permit it."[26] In a later letter Crim's personal dislike of Rosenbluth again appeared: "I feel it ought to be handled in the ordinary way. Rosenbluth's ego is so big that he cannot reconcile himself to the ordinary processes of law."[27] However, the legal processes of this case could hardly be called "ordinary" by any stretch of the imagination if viewed in perspective.

In the meantime, arrangements proceeded for the grand jury and witnesses. Edward Chastain was assigned to the case as a special assistant, an appointment that appeared to the defense as highly unfair. Certain needed witnesses were unavailable; Dr. Tucker was in Europe and could not be summoned, and Elmer Kieffer proved to be elusive. His mother and his fiancée insisted they did not know his exact address. The search for him was finally abandoned, the department believing he did not wish to make the trip to Tacoma and had deliberately dodged the subpoena. A certain amount of comic relief was provided by expert witnesses Captain Jones and Dr. Schultze, who horrified the department by asking for $100 and $250 a day, respectively, for their services, payable from New York to Tacoma and back. Since their testimony was essential to the department, it could not refuse to call them and was finally forced to agree to pay, although the total sum was slightly reduced.

Even more amusing was a request from James Lee, who wrote to General Cronkhite asking that he use his influence to have Lee appointed a special assistant for the period of the grand jury; Lee desired this temporary post because it would entitle him to carry a concealed weapon. As the general explained the matter to Crim, Lee seriously believed he was in danger of attack because of his work on the case. Crim replied politely that the appointment was not possible, but he would assign a deputy to Lee as a special guard during his stay in Tacoma. Lee balked at this, obviously annoyed at the suggestion; he said firmly that he was accustomed to taking care of himself. To make absolutely certain no embarrassing nursemaid-deputy appeared, Lee also wrote the marshal at Tacoma that a guard would not be necessary.[28] That Lee relayed this request through General Cronkhite is further evidence that he and the general were still in communication, despite the fact that Lee had been fired from the Bureau of Investigation a year before.

The correspondence during September reveals the growing deterioration of Major General Cronkhite, through his refusal to turn over to the authorities the "mass of evidence" he had collected for use before the grand jury. From 1921 on the general had steadily asserted his willingness to release this information but had just as steadily refused to submit it when requested. Revelle directed a series of anxious telegrams to Crim inquiring about these documents, but Crim was unsuccessful in persuading the general to part with them. They finally accepted his assurances that he would bring the materials personally to Tacoma and present them to the jury. But he did not do so; as far as is known, these letters and papers were never examined in full by anyone except the general and his wife and perhaps some personal friends. The only materials he released to the Justice Department were his personal analyses of the case. His steady refusal to submit the original data hints at his almost conscious realization that objective examination would show their essential weakness as evidence of anything but his personal obsession.

The degree to which both prosecution and defense were convinced that the other was trying to influence a verdict unfairly is shown during the month of September. Just before the grand jury was about to begin hearing the case, a telegram was sent to Tacoma from Washington:

> Represented to Department that Colonel R. S. Thomas and Major John F. Zajicek now in your District may probably attempt to control certain witnesses as to prevent indictment in Cronkhite case. Suggest you have Department agents your District cover their movements.[29]

Again a military cover-up is hinted; the Justice Department persisted in its attempts to find evidence that Thomas and Zajicek were concealing something. At the same time, the defense side of the case was sharply criticizing the department for its unfair refusal to subpoena Rosenbluth. His lawyer remarked angrily that to hold the grand jury hearing without him was like giving *Hamlet* without Hamlet. Prosecuting Attorney Selden expressed his opinion in the newspapers after Daugherty's refusal to call Rosenbluth was published:

> Attorney General Daugherty is sore that an ordinary citizen should demand clearance from the Department of Justice. We know that if no demand had been made, the matter would not have come up again. . . . if Rosenbluth had called things even, everything would have been dropped. We know that the Attorney-General personally ordered this inquiry.[30]

The Veterans of Foreign Wars complained that a "closed hearing" of the affair did not meet their repeated requests for a full and open investigation. In addition to these critical statements, on September 23 the *New York Times* published in full the correspondence between Rosenbluth, Representative Ansorge, and Daugherty. On October 4, 1922, *The Nation* published another article in a series attacking the Attorney General and spoke of "the new chapter Mr. Daugherty is adding to the scandal of the Rosenbluth case."

> Mr. Daugherty has steadily refused a Congressional inquiry into the case; he has let Federal grand jury after grand jury come and go without presenting his evidence. Yet suddenly, at a cost of thousands of dollars in witness fees, he orders an investigation! Even now his subordinate refuses to subpoena Captain Rosenbluth who is told that he may appear at his own expense. There are only two reasons for this action: Either Mr. Daugherty is determined to save his own miserable face at any cost, or behind him are men intent on making a Dreyfus case here in America with a Jewish officer as the victim.[31]

To make matters worse, Daugherty was again threatened by a congressional investigation, this time initiated by Oscar Keller of Minnesota, who moved on September 11, 1922, to impeach the Attorney General for "high crimes and misdemeanors." Keller, according to Daugherty, was a front man for labor agitators and Bolsheviks and wished to discredit the notorious Wilkerson injunction issued to stop a nationwide railroad strike. Keller's motion of impeachment died eventually in committee, but it undoubtedly affected the department's nervousness over the bad publicity it was receiving.

The grand jury met in an atmosphere of mutual suspicion—the defense certain the government was planning to force an indictment and the prosecution certain the defense was formally organized to block a genuine investigation of the facts.

CHAPTER SEVEN
GRAND JURY
OCTOBER 1922

THE FEDERAL GRAND JURY, which on October 12, 1922, returned a secret indictment against Rosenbluth and Pothier for
the murder of Major Cronkhite, met for two weeks and heard
the testimony of 73 witnesses. These witnesses consisted of 45
men and officers of the 213th Engineers; 13 members of the
medical staff at Camp Lewis; 6 officers from other regiments,
including General Cronkhite; 5 officials of the federal government; and 4 experts who testified about the weapon and the
injury. Pothier was not called to testify before the grand jury,
and Rosenbluth, acting on his lawyer's advice, declined to come
to Tacoma, since he was not officially called as a witness by
subpoena. Almost all the witnesses were questioned by U.S.
Attorney Thomas Revelle and his assistant, Falknor. Edward
Chastain, the special assistant, played a very small part in the
proceedings, only occasionally handling a witness.

Although Attorney Revelle's claim that he conducted a
thorough and impartial investigation is amply proved by the
record, he was necessarily limited by the witnesses actually
called to testify. Far from trying to secure an indictment deliberately, as the defense perhaps understandably believed, by
the end of the hearings Revelle and Falknor were completely
convinced of Rosenbluth's total lack of involvement and made
every effort to display the flaws in the government's case. They
were assisted in their efforts by a jury whose questions showed
them to have been intelligent and alert men. A sincere attempt
was made to produce evidence which would support Pothier's
confessions and demonstrate the accuracy of General Cronkhite's allegations; the government was aware that neither
Pothier nor Cronkhite was a reliable witness and was anxious
to obtain independent testimony substantiating the prosecution
case.

Revelle did not succeed in this task—an impossible one,
since the evidence quite genuinely did not exist. But he also
failed to convince the jury that it would be improper to indict.
Here the explanation seems to be, as Rosenbluth stressed in a

conversation in July 1969, that certain key witnesses were not called. In addition to these omissions, the attention of the jury was at no time directed to methods used to obtain Pothier's confessions, even though these methods were a matter of public record, nor was his retraction given any real attention. Revelle's efforts to prevent an indictment, genuine though they were, were undercut by lack of material which could counteract the effects of the actual testimony.

Both jury and witnesses were handicapped also by the fact that four years had elapsed since the accident, and memories were both clouded and contradictory. In particular it proved very difficult for many witnesses to disentangle what they had thought and known in 1918 from what they had heard and read about the case since that time. But the testimony, taken as a unit, tends fairly definitely in one direction. Almost nothing was revealed during these two weeks that was not already known to the government.

The government did not succeed in its attempt to demonstrate motive. Testimony concerning the general reputations of Cronkhite, Rosenbluth, and Pothier and their mutual relationships confirmed what was already known. Major Cronkhite was highly regarded by men and officers; Pothier was universally disliked; Rosenbluth was liked and respected, but not considered an ideal military man. Colonel Thomas testified that he "was giving Rosenbluth hell all the time." It was generally agreed that Cronkhite and Pothier were friendly in a casual way, and no one could be found who remembered any association of any kind between Rosenbluth and Pothier.

A strenuous attempt to show that Cronkhite and Rosenbluth were on bad terms was unsuccessful. A good many of the men recalled some incident on the way to Camp Lewis involving an officer being reprimanded and relieved of his command by a superior for sloppy handling of his men, but there was considerable uncertainty as to the identities. The inquiry into this portion of General Cronkhite's allegations is an excellent illustration of the way his "evidence" vanished under sustained examination. Of the 35 men and officers who were questioned on this point, 20 flatly denied any recollection of such an incident; 8 men recalled Colonel Thomas scolding Rosenbluth for some mistake, but none stated he was removed from command; and 6 seemed to believe that Cronkhite had removed Rosenbluth from command of a platoon during the trip, but of these only 1 claimed any direct knowledge of the episode—the others "had heard" about it and were very vague in their memories. One man had been told Cronkhite was the one disciplined by Colonel Thomas.

Concerning the alleged quarreling between the two officers

Robert Rosenbluth as he
appeared in 1922 at the
time of the grand jury
hearing.

the day of the hike, only one witness, Samuel Moore, was found willing to assert that Rosenbluth had replied to Cronkhite's criticisms in a seriously insubordinate way.[1] His testimony must be put down to anti-Semitism, personal antagonism, or some other motive, since none of the many other witnesses could remember any talk or argument to support his statements.

This section of testimony was a considerable stumbling block to the government's case. It was impossible to demonstrate that Rosenbluth and Cronkhite had been enemies or Rosenbluth and Pothier had been friends. The total lack of motive was a serious flaw. Even those dubious about the wound being self-inflicted found it impossible to get around the improbability that two strangers would conspire to murder a man with whom they were both on friendly terms.

The testimony relating to the hike itself, the Major's death, and the immediate aftermath produced no new or significant information. The witnesses could not agree on the number of shots they heard, on Rosenbluth's position when the firing began, or on the approximate lapse of time between the shots and the call for help. The witnesses did establish that many of the men supposed the shots and the call for a doctor were part of a guard problem and did not pay special attention at first—a detail which further made exact memory unlikely. Furthermore, the column was strung out along the road in single file, and most of the men were not in a position to see anything. Testimony that seemed damaging to the defense was invariably canceled by substantial contradiction. No one could be persuaded to back up the solitary witness who claimed that Cronkhite had habitually criticized Rosenbluth, and that Rosenbluth bitterly resented this. The same witness testified that a friend of his had gone to the scene of the accident and paced off the distance between the body and the bushes, reaching certain sinister conclusions about the probable position of the gun that fired the shot.[2] The friend, however, when questioned about this, denied having gone to the scene at all and agreed that if anyone told this story he was a liar.[3]

In some cases, witnesses were called who had no knowledge at all. One Edward Tobacco was summoned to give information about the horse that Major Zajicek had used on the morning of the hike. Tobacco, however, denied that he had anything to do with the stables or knew anything at all about the major's horse. He also assured the attorney, in response to a question, that as far as he knew, he was the only man named Edward Tobacco in the regiment![4]

The testimony of the men who had gone on the hike is quite contradictory in many small details. Upon study of the complete written transcript, one can easily see that when all the testimony is taken into account, no real conclusions are possible. All one can do is assess the probabilities, using the principle that what a majority of the men recalled was more likely to be accurate than the testimony of a few. However, the grand jury listened to the witnesses one at a time only. Thus forceful testimony from a convincing, level-headed witness could have an effect out of proportion to its value. An illustration of this can be made by examining the testimony of two witnesses, George Root and Charles Wuthenow.

Both of these men were sergeants in the 213th Engineers, both were attached to the Intelligence Section under Lieutenant Arthur Miller, and both sang tenor in the regimental quartet. The picture of the quartet in the *Regimental History* shows they were nice-looking men, intelligent and clean-cut in appearance. Root strongly disliked Pothier and had been assigned the task of investigating him as a possible thief. These two witnesses were interviewed early in the proceedings because of their special importance. Root had loaned his gun to Major Cronkhite, and because of this and his connection with Intelligence, he was particularly observant of details. Furthermore he and Wuthenow had gone forward to give artificial respiration and thus, with the medical orderlies, were the first "independent" witnesses on the scene.

Wuthenow and Root gave essentially the same testimony on certain points, although their recollections are contradicted by the testimony of many others. They recalled, for example, that Captain Rosenbluth was out of their sight when the shooting began, and both were certain the major was not wearing his uniform blouse. However, so many others recalled that Rosenbluth had run forward after the shooting began and were sure the major was fully dressed, that this discrepancy was not crucial. Of interest to the jury was their testimony concerning the gun and shells and the medical treatment.

Root claimed to have made a deliberate attempt to investigate at the scene, as he was interested in his gun and in finding out exactly what had happened. His testimony came to three points: Cronkhite's gun had been fired. It did not, as far as he could recall, contain any exploded shells but held three unexploded cartridges. He picked up four exploded shells from the ground, two near the body and two near where Pothier was then standing. This testimony was damaging for several reasons, and also puzzling. The gun in use was a revolver which had to be unloaded manually. Root agreed that the major would wait until he was through firing before he unloaded his gun, and he could not have unloaded it after he was hit. This raised the obvious questions: How did the exploded shells get out of the gun? Who removed them and why?

The possibility that Root was maliciously lying to implicate Pothier is vitiated by the fact that he insisted the major's gun had been fired, thus confirming the target-shooting story. It is difficult to tell from a written transcript without the advantage of hearing the tone of voice, but certain details suggest that Root was not entirely reluctant to implicate Pothier, although he consistently denied this. His statement, for example, that he picked up two shells where Pothier was standing sounds damning until one reflects that Pothier was not rooted to a particular spot. Root did not see the accident and could not have known where Pothier was at the time it occurred. That he happened to be near where the shells were later found means nothing.

In any case, impossible as it is to work out any coherent explanation for Root's statements, they clearly worried the jury. He was asked again and again to repeat his statements about the weapon, and a juror finally voiced the obvious question: How did the shells get out of the gun onto the ground as the major fell mortally wounded? Root replied: "You fellows will have to figure that one out." There is no confirmation of Root's statements about the gun and shells. Various persons remembered shells being found or seeing them in someone's hand, but apparently no one else examined the gun at the scene or observed Root searching in the grass for shells. Possibly Root was simply mistaken; the three unexploded shells he recalled in the gun could have been exploded cartridges,

which were subsequently removed and given to Colonel Howard. And it is also possible that the shells he picked up from
the ground had nothing to do with the accident and had been
fired the previous day by some other casual pistol shot.[5]

In addition there is reason to believe that Root's memory
was not entirely reliable. Again we have a direct contradiction
in testimony widely separated in time, so that the grand jury
may not have noticed its oddness. Root testified with complete
certainty that Rosenbluth had been sharply rebuked by Major
Cronkhite for confusing the men in an exercise drill on the
trip west, and that the major had removed Rosenbluth from
command and placed Sergeant Root in charge of the platoon.
Root said that he remained in command of the platoon for the
trip, while Rosenbluth marched back with the file closers.
He did not assert that Rosenbluth appeared to resent this, but
stressed the unusual nature of the reprimand and the replace-
ment of a captain by a sergeant.[6] However, a later witness, ex-
sergeant Samuel Moore, reported the matter very differently.
He said he was placed in command of a platoon for the trip.
On one occasion Rosenbluth assumed command of the group,
and Moore fell back. Cronkhite, noticing this, inquired why
Moore was not in command and told him to resume his normal
place. Thus instead of a captain forcibly removed for mis-
management, we have a sergeant directed to resume command
for no other reason, as Moore told the story, except that he was
supposed to be in charge.[7]

Moore's version of the incident is particularly interesting
because of his clear antagonism to Rosenbluth. He also seems
to have been the author of another curious story—that Rosenbluth gave a talk about suicide to his company two weeks after
the hike and seemed to Moore to be implying that the major
had deliberately shot himself.[8] No one but Moore so testified,
but he certainly was not concerned about shielding Rosenbluth.
Thus his version of the platoon story is somewhat more believable than Root's. Most of the other men who remembered any
such episode occurring on the trip believed it was Colonel
Thomas, not Major Cronkhite, who corrected Rosenbluth.

The testimony of ex-sergeant Wuthenow was damaging in
some degree because it tended to suggest that the medical treatment given the major was at best criminally careless and at
worst, murderous. Wuthenow insisted, for example, that Captain Rosenbluth ordered them to continue artificial respiration
after he and Orderly Croy were sure the major was dead.
Wuthenow was voluble on the subject:

> I said to Croy, "This man is dead." Captain Rosenbluth said,
> "That makes no difference, you give him artificial respiration."

You know that is a hell of a sensation to be grabbing a dead man up and giving him artificial respiration. When you are moving that body you have got to be more or less calloused to pull a job like that off. I asked Dr. Seaburg, "What is the matter with the Major?" He said, "He has got heart failure." I said, "Jesus, that is funny."[9]

Wuthenow described his refusal to continue the respiration and claimed that suspecting the heart failure story was inaccurate, he opened the shirt and found the bullet wound. It is of some importance here to compare the later testimony of Medical Orderly Croy, who was questioned on the identical event:

Q. Was his blouse on when you got there?
A. Yes, sir. . . .
Q. How long did you give artificial respiration before you discovered the man was shot?
A. We did not discover that he was actually shot until after he was dead.
Q. How long did you give artificial respiration before he died?
A. Only a short time; until he quit breathing.

Croy also asserted that it was he who discovered the bullet wound in the major's chest—perhaps a more natural discovery for a medical orderly than for Wuthenow.[10] Croy's evidence contradicted Wuthenow's statements one by one, but his testimony was taken perhaps a week later. The impression made by Wuthenow probably stuck with the jury.

Wuthenow appears to have been a rather callous individual, or at least one insensitive to the probable effect of his phrasing. Without meaning to suggest any deliberate malicious intention on his part, his way of expressing himself contributed to the idea that the major had been neglected or carelessly treated. After the major had been pronounced dead, he claimed:

they got busy and went into this canteen and the doctor got busy and fixed up a hypodermic needle and they injected strychnine but he stayed dead just the same. They let him lay there for a while, and then when I figured he was fully dead—his eyes were open, and I pressed his eyelids down and I got some bandages and tied his arms together. Too bad I didn't have any money to put in his hand. Anyway that is the way we left him there. We started to get something to eat and started to shoot craps. Then the ambulance came and busted up the crap game.[11]

Again, it must be emphasized that Orderly Croy remembered the scene differently. He said the hypodermic injection was given as the major was dying, not after he was dead.[12] Wuthenow's statement created a mental picture of the body, man-handled after death, lying neglected on the ground with only Wuthenow in attendance. It further suggested that Seaburg and Rosenbluth were somehow in league. This impression arises more from his manner of speaking than from what he says, and seems to stem from a rather slapdash attitude, coupled, as some of his testimony implies, with a noticeable grudge against officers generally. He stressed the fact that none of the lieutenants volunteered to give artificial respiration and implied an officers' plot in his comment: "After that we hiked home. Everything was nicely forgotten."[13]

Just as the testimony about the hike failed to produce any single convincing picture of the events of the morning and revealed the very great confusion of memory the four inter-vening years had produced, testimony relating to the handling of the body at the base hospital did also. The hospital was working under emergency conditions because of the influenza epidemic and the need to prepare a greatly increased load of bodies. One mortician reported that they were working twelve hours a day to keep up and would leave at night with as many bodies waiting for attention as they had found when they re-ported in the morning. This condition probably explains one detail that worried the Cronkhites—the fact that the major's heart had been removed and was found to be missing at the second autopsy. Dr. Sommer testified he had removed the heart without explaining why, since the bullet had not passed through it. Morticians ordinarily replace organs removed in an autopsy; that they did not would appear the result of the haste and con-fusion. It seems reasonable to suppose that morgue conditions at the time were unsatisfactory, and any carelessness or inatten-tion to the body of Major Cronkhite could be attributed to this.[14]

Witnesses who testified about the proceedings of the board of inquiry and the following disappearance of some of the exhibits did not produce any significant clarification or new information. Lieutenant Colonel Howard repeated his earlier statements indicating his doubts at the time that the wound was self-inflicted but continued to insist he had not the slightest reason to suppose Rosenbluth had anything to do with the matter.[15] As he later insisted at the trial, Colonel Thomas was shown two tobacco cans and was asked to identify the one he had taken charge of; later witnesses were shown only one.[16] The origin of this second can is somewhat mysterious; possibly the sample cans prepared to demonstrate the angle of the bullet holes had been mixed up with the "real" can by this time.

The testimony of Major General Cronkhite proved a seri-ous disappointment to the prosecution. Despite the fact that he had been issued a subpoena on August 28 requiring that he produce his documentary evidence for the grand jury, he did not do so. Sharply questioned by Revelle, the general explained rather vaguely he had been told by Crim and Chastain that his evidence would not be needed, and in any case, he had not had time to collect it. His documents were stored in a box in Fort Monroe, Virginia, and his wife's illness prevented his leaving her for several days to travel there.

The remainder of the general's testimony was almost entirely subjective. He spoke fondly of his son: "He always devoted a great deal of time to things athletic; just a great big boy; still a boy when killed. That was his nature—just to be a boy." He repeated his belief that the senior officers disliked his son as well as his conviction that quarreling between young officers and older men they commanded was common. He strongly criticized the board of inquiry and Colonel Thomas's failure to return all of his son's possessions. But he did not say one word that could be used as objective proof of his suspicions.[17]

The testimony of the expert witnesses, despite the cost of procuring their services, was by no means totally antagonistic to the defense side of the case. Dr. Schultze and Captain Jones stated with great certainty that no human hand could have fired the revolver held in such a position to explain the path of the bullet through the body. This judgment was somewhat undercut, however, during Jones's interrogation. He demonstrated the way the gun would have to have been held, using Assistant Attorney Falknor as a "dummy." The following exchange then occurred:

> FALKNOR: Now, here, Captain, you say that the wound could not have been inflicted in that way. I can pull the trigger that way without any difficulty.
> REVELLE: I want you to observe that [gun] has not got a hair trigger anyway.
> JONES: It is pretty hard for a person to flex their hand around that way and do it.
> FALKNOR: You won't say, will you, that a man could not deliberately shoot himself in the way you have indicated here?
> JONES: The only way that I could see that a man could do it exactly right would be this way.
> FALKNOR: Why can't it be done that way?
> JONES: There is not one time in a thousand you could do it there.

It seems clear here, hard as it is to visualize what was being done with the gun, that Falknor could pull the trigger, and was not able to understand why Jones persisted in his rejection of this possibility.

Similarly, Jones's testimony about powder burns was not contradictory to the defense. He stated that a weapon held even as close as two or three inches from the body would not leave marks on the skin if protected by a coat, shirt, and undershirt. This opinion, if correct, explained the cleanness of the wound itself. He also presented samples of fabric at which he had fired from various distances and reluctantly agreed that an inexperienced person might not notice powder burns at the three-inch distance, since even that close they were relatively faint. He also could not honestly rule out entirely the possibility that a .45 bullet fired at close range might not pass through the body, although he considered this would be quite unusual. He contradicted Dr. Schultze's opinion that the wound suggested passage of a .38-caliber bullet; Jones thought a .45 was more likely.[18]

Two other experts, both military men, testified about the ballistics of the wound. Major Wright agreed with Jones that a .45-caliber bullet had about the same velocity from contact range to 25-yard range; only at greater distances did its velocity slacken measurably. As a result, it was not possible to determine from the failure of the bullet to leave the body that it had been fired from a short distance.[19] Another expert, Lieutenant Johnson, said that the bullet's not leaving the body was possible, although he agreed that a heavy caliber bullet usually did so when fired at close range. Asked to examine the shells introduced as evidence, he concluded they had been fired from a revolver rather than an automatic but was unable to be definite about whether they had been fired from one gun or two, since their corroded condition made examination difficult.[20] In his analysis of the case written in 1922, General Cronkhite asserted that the shells he had been shown at the War Department were clean and shiny. Again substitution is suggested, although for what purpose is unclear. Since the gun in use was never positively identified, the shells meant very little.

The interrogation of the officials from the Providence attorney's office was probably as damaging as anything else to the defense. As in earlier interviews, Cannon and Richards continued to assert they had been convinced by Pothier's adherence to his story in their lengthy sessions with him that he was telling at least part of the truth. Since both men made a good impression and were able to show they had not subjected Pothier to any harrassment, their testimony helped greatly to convince the jury there was *something* to be investigated.[21] Even Agent Lee's dark hints of Bolshevik plots may have assisted in producing the indictment.[22] Citizens in 1922 were trained to react with alarm to the slightest hint of radicalism, and the violent strikes and I.W.W. agitation in the Tacoma-Seattle area made the dangers of such activity more immediate.

II

THE GRAND JURY'S DECISION to indict both Rosenbluth and Pothier despite the apparently vigorous efforts of the attorneys to discourage this verdict can be explained in terms of the particular nature of such a jury, that is, a group of citizens without legal training who have the task of deciding if a crime has been committed. The grand jury system has been criticized for many reasons, the usual objection being that the prosecution can secure an indictment any time it wishes since it controls what is brought to the jury's attention. One cause of the indictment was the omission of certain witnesses known to be doubtful of the government's case. The jury heard Richards and Cannon assert they were convinced by Pothier's reiteration of his own and Rosenbluth's guilt; they did not hear the opinion of Agent Callaghan, who later at the trial said he had never believed in Rosenbluth's involvement, but believed that the major was shot accidentally by Pothier. They heard Richards's opinion that Pothier retracted his confession only to avoid a murder charge; they did not hear Austin Parker's description of his interview with Pothier. They listened to Agent Lee's lurid account of his visit to the Civic Club; they did not have the opportunity to question Agent Harris about his handling of the affair after Rosenbluth's arrest. Nor did they have the benefit of Selden's detailed study of the case. The defense, with some justice, claimed after the trial that "judging from the facts recently disclosed in court a study of the procedure resorted to [in the grand jury] would prove unusually interesting."[23]

The layman and the lawyer have a very different attitude toward evidence. Some of the witnesses who testified, both men and officers, acknowledged they had doubted the self-inflicted wound explanation at the time, or had come to doubt it after reading about the case later. Of 45 men and officers from Camp Lewis who expressed an opinion on the matter, 20 asserted their belief that the major's death was accidental, agreeing with the original verdict; 14 were not questioned in a way that elicited an opinion. Of the remaining 11, 4 believed that a bullet from an unknown gun had killed the major, 4 believed that Pothier had fired the shot by accident, and 1 man strongly implied his belief that the shot had been fired by Rosenbluth. Two men expressed their opinion that the death was suicide. A relatively small percentage, in other words, was prepared to go on record as disagreeing with the official findings. But most of those who did so were witnesses who were questioned at length, whose testimony was likely to be memorable. Those who favored the "unknown gun" theory were Lieutenant Colonel Howard, Lieutenant Saunders, Lieutenant Hastedt and Sergeant Wuthenow. Those who believed that Pothier had fired the shot accidentally were Lieutenant Miller, Lieutenant Morrison, Sergeant Root and an enlisted man, David White.

The layman, hearing a series of witnesses assert they believe a man did not die by his own hand, is likely to be affected by this testimony. The lawyer, in contrast, must ask the question: Can this opinion be substantiated by factual evidence before a trial jury? Regardless of the witnesses' beliefs, can they be shown to be objectively true? The layman, with the natural human wish for the resolving of contradictions, for the absolute clarification that is the appeal of the conventional detective story, will feel that conflicting opinions deserve further investigation. The lawyer is far more aware of the time, expense, and inconvenience of the trial procedure and is much more alert to the vast difference between the informal testimony the grand jury hears and the strictly controlled evidence submitted at a trial. Thus a conscientious prosecuting attorney will not seek an indictment unless he believes a successful prosecution is likely. To put it another way, the purpose of a trial is dramatic, not expository. Its purpose is not to find out the "truth" of an event, but to prove the guilt or establish the innocence of the accused. If the grand jury investigation does not produce the necessary evidence nor indicate where it can be found, the trial process cannot be expected to do so.

Selden had stated that his county almost never called grand juries, considering them a cumbersome and expensive method of procedure. Routine criminal cases were handled by the prosecutor, who was considered capable of deciding whether or not a case could be successfully prosecuted. This flaw in grand jury procedure, particularly in this sort of case, was a major reason for the indictment.

The testimony of Cannon and Richards was also influential in bringing the indictment. Pothier did not retract his final confession until after he reached New York because he feared being turned back to Agent Lee for further interrogation, and he was anxious to appear at Rosenbluth's hearing in New York as an important witness. When he found he had been tricked, he retracted the confessions involving Rosenbluth. His interviews with Cannon and Richards were held before the visit to New York, however. After that time Pothier's lawyer asked that he not be questioned further, and this request was strictly adhered to. Thus these men saw Pothier when circumstances had combined to hold him to his statements, and their honest description of his steadiness had a predictable effect.

Witnesses from the 213th Engineers, many of them sympathetic to Rosenbluth, made a somewhat doubtful impression on the jury because of the attempt to discover if they had been unfairly influenced. A second telegram arrived from the Justice Department in Washington during the hearings:

> What is the situation in the Cronkhite investigation? It is reported that the investigation is perfunctory, that it is a whitewash of Rosenbluth, that Rosenbluth and his friends are spreading propaganda among the witnesses furnishing liquor to witnesses and doing other things to interfere with a thorough investigation. Subpoena every witness that can throw any light on the situation.[24]

Again, the dual lines of pressure to stop the investigation, as the department saw them, are implied. Crim was absolutely determined to get evidence to confirm his suspicions that Rosenbluth's efforts to escape trial were being reinforced by the reluctance of the military to have him stand trial, presumably not for his sake, but for their own.

As a result, each witness from the regiment was asked if he had corresponded with Rosenbluth recently or if he had been approached in Tacoma by anyone purporting to represent Rosenbluth. No one had been approached during the grand jury investigation, but several of the officers had remained in Tacoma after they were free to go and Sergeants Rooney and Jepson were making a list of names and addresses of all the witnesses. Rosenbluth's friend Maelstrom, a newspaper editor in the city, had talked with Captain Caffey about the case, and some of the men were distributing copies of the *Nation* article. No evidence of any tampering with witnesses emerged, but the persistent questions asked one man after another may have had a damaging effect.

In addition, the atmosphere produced by bringing almost fifty members of the regiment to testify was rather like a homecoming or a class reunion. The officers and men quite naturally held get-togethers in various hotel rooms, talking about the past and singing songs. At times drinks were served, and some found themselves in trouble with the Prohibition authorities. This was perfectly natural and even inevitable, but the effect on the jury was unfortunate. The inquiry produced a picture of drinking parties in smoke-filled rooms, and since some of the jurymen indicated a sensitivity on the liquor question,* it

---

* After a series of witnesses had described the alleged sloppy drilling of the men and the rebuke it produced, a juryman inquired anxiously if "it was liquor that put them fellows off in their marching." The witness, obviously startled by the question, denied it.

is not unlikely there was some feeling that a man who drank
was not to be trusted.

Major Zajicek, Captain Caffey, and lieutenants Miller
and Sanborn were recalled for further questioning about their
drinking and talks with other witnesses. Miller had admitted
in his first session that drinking was going on and the case had
been discussed, although he firmly denied any prearrangement
or agreement about testimony, as did the others. Recalled before the jury, he showed considerable nervousness about his
earlier statements:

Q. Who furnished the liquor, Zajicek?
A. I did.
Q. I mean on all occasions.
A. Well, everybody did.
Q. Who furnished it in Zajicek's room?
A. I never had a drink in his room.
Q. In anybody else's room?
A. Yes, sir, I did, and somebody else.
Q. Who?
A. Oh, cheese this matter!
Q. You mean everybody—is that the idea, or what?
A. Oh, darn, it was in Colonel Thomas' room I had a drink.
. . . I slipped yesterday when I told you that and I have
worried about it since.

Later, asked if he intended to leave Tacoma, he said, "I am
afraid not. Say listen. About this prohibition case, am I in
trouble with that?"[25]

Sanborn, recalled immediately after Miller, was forced by
Falknor to confirm details about their meeting with Major
Zajicek at the hotel:

Q. While we were standing there talking, Major Zajicek came
up and spoke to us?
A. Yes, sir.
Q. He was pretty well under the influence of liquor at that
time?
A. Yes.
Q. Don't you remember right there while you were standing
there he made some statement that the officers should up-
hold the honor of the regiment?
A. No, I don't remember that. . . .
Q. Do you drink a little bit?
A. I have. I had one drink last night.[26]

Somewhat later in the hearings, Zajicek and Caffey were
reexamined; Zajicek was subjected to severe questioning, for
both the lawyers and the jury felt that his answers had been
deliberately uncommunicative. When Lieutenant Miller remarked, in answer to a question about Zajicek's evasiveness,
that his friend was "a wise old bird who doesn't tell all he

thinks," a juror replied irritably, "We discovered that yester-day!"[27] Zajicek, during his second appearance, denied that he had bought any liquor personally. It had been, he insisted, brought by others:

> At two o'clock Saturday night—I went to bed this Saturday night—I went to bed and planned to get up early Sunday morning and [go] to Ranier. About two o'clock in the morning there was a knock at my door, and there came the old regimental quartet and wanted to serenade their major.

Later in the session the attorney pressed him to admit that he had threatened to strike the marshal who served him with a subpoena to reappear and had been restrained by Captain Caffey. Zajicek denied this, insisting it was a ridiculous story. It would appear, however, that it was probably true; neither the marshal nor the attorney would have had any reason to invent it. Questioned about his drinking, this exchange ensued:

> Q. That is the only occasion you have been drinking?
> A. Col. Thomas had a little liquor; when he asked me to take a drink of course I am a man that wants to be sociable.
> Q. How much does it take for you to be sociable?
> A. Well, gentlemen, I am no. . . .
> Q. When you were talking to Mr. Falknor the other night you were pretty well under the influence of liquor?
> A. I don't know as to that. I was trying to be sociable with him.[28]

It is easy enough to imagine the probable effect of such testimony on a jury during Prohibition. Their failure to produce a good impression on the grand jury to a degree vitiated their defense of Rosenbluth and their certainty that he had had nothing to do with the death of Major Cronkhite.

After the grand jury's decision had been reached, Attorney Revelle wrote two letters to the Justice Department. On October 13 he wrote to the Attorney General testifying to the thoroughness of the investigation and its somewhat disappointing results:

> We were somewhat disappointed at the lack of any knowledge concerning the matter on the part of a number of the witnesses. Our greatest disappointment however, was in the attitude and lack of cooperation on the part of General Cronkhite. I regret to say that the money expended in bringing him to the Court was worse than wasted. The General, although having been subpoenaed, and having been served with a subpoena as early as the 28th day of August, 1922, and although he was granted an extension of time to prepare for, and to make this trip, yet he appeared before the grand jury and admitted that he had utterly disregarded and disobeyed the subpoena, which required him to bring all documents and other evidence. . . .

Revelle continued with a warning:

> In fairness to the Department, it should be stated that very little, if any evidence was obtained or resulted from this grand jury investigation that had not already heretofore been obtained by the Department of Justice or General Cronkhite, and that the Department should fully understand that in the presentation of this indictment, and in the trial of those indicted, no reliance whatsoever should be placed upon any supposition that any new or additional evidence was uncovered before the grand jury.[29]

Crim's reply a few days later thanked Revelle for his services and commented on General Cronkhite's failure to present his documents:

> I note what you say with regard to General Cronkhite. I do not place any reliance in General Cronkhite. I feel that the untimely death of his son, under the circumstances which he believes, has so impaired him mentally that he is not entirely responsible for his conduct. I am afraid that it is progressive. This is the only hypothesis on which I can explain his conduct.[30]

On October 16 Revelle wrote a personal letter to Assistant Attorney General Herron, advising him in detail about the unsatisfactory results of the grand jury. However, Herron died at this time, before receiving the letter. Revelle, writing to Attorney General Stone after the trial in 1924, enclosed a carbon of his first letter, remarking that the original sent to Herron had been mislaid or lost from the files. In the letter to Herron, Revelle urged him "that the true status of the case should be laid before Mr. Crim, and the matter should receive the very earnest thought of both him and yourself." He referred to his earlier letter, in which he had advised that Pothier be reexamined and had stated that no new evidence had been uncovered, nor was likely to be. Then he made a series of very definite conclusions:

> I am sure that you will recall that in one of our conversations in which General Cronkhite was present, I stated that the evidence developed up to that time was insufficient to secure any conviction. At that time, I was advised by yourself, if I recall correctly, that the General had a great deal of material evidence which he refused to deliver to your Department, but which he had promised to deliver to the grand jury. I recall at that conversation that I said if it was the matter of a private client, and if the client refused to reveal his entire hand to me or to you, we would refuse to go any further with the question. That was my position then, has been ever since, and is now. . . . Messrs. Chastain and Falknor, my assistants, and myself, felt that it should not be a perfunctory investigation. We therefore used every measure possible to bring to the grand jury's

attention every available bit of evidence that had the slightest
bearing upon the death of the major, but despite our best
efforts, as above said, we were not able to discover any additional facts whatsoever. We all three decided that the evidence,
even uncontradicted and unexplained, was not sufficient to sus-
tain the indictment or to secure any conviction. We very frankly, and fully informed the grand jury to that effect. In fact, I
think we possibly went a little further than the law justifies,
in trying to point out to the grand jury, that based upon the
evidence before them, there could be no conviction. The grand
jury fully agreed that there was not sufficient evidence to convict, but they felt that some wrong had been committed by
someone, that the major did not shoot himself, and that it was
up to us to further develop the facts. . . . Despite our protests
that we could not get anywhere in the trial of this case upon the
evidence before them, they returned the indictment, thereby
putting ourselves and the Department in a very embarrassing
position. I am sure that Mr. Chastain thoroughly agreed with
us in the position we took before the grand jury, even though
Chastain believes that both Rosenbluth and Pothier are guilty
of some wrong.

Our position before the Court will be an endeavor to convict men of a most heinous crime without any motive whatsoever, so far established, and without any testimony, documentary or otherwise, that can in the slightest possible way connect
Rosenbluth with the death of the major, if the evidence is admitted at all. Even the confession of Pothier cannot be used
against Rosenbluth.

So we have indicted a man on the charge of first degree
murder without a single fact to substantiate the charge. If he
insists upon a trial, in all good conscience and in honor and
because of necessity, the indictment will have to be dismissed.
This matter has greatly worried me. I have been thinking of
the Department, who I am sure would do no man wrong. I
have been thinking of the thoughtless criticism that will in all
probability be made against the Department, well knowing that
the Department had but little to do with the indictment. . . .

I am sure that if we attempt to try this case, which trial
will result in a fiasco of a most shameful nature, unless we can
gather some evidence that is worthwhile, the Department will
be criticized as well as this office. . . .

My firm convictions are that unless something new de-
velops very quickly, the indictment should be dismissed. As I
said above, unless some new evidence is revealed, we will be
obliged to dismiss the indictment or make fools of ourselves in
attempting to try the same. If, too, we are ever to dismiss
these indictments, the sooner the better. In other words, the
country should know that such action was taken upon our
part out of our own good conscience and fairness rather than
as a result of outside pressure.[31]

Revelle's letter is of considerable interest as a report of
a man who had studied all the evidence in the case exhaustively
and had in addition the advantage of talking face to face with
almost all the witnesses. He was in a good position to judge

their effect upon a jury, and he was not handicapped by prejudice in favor of the defendants, since he had met neither. His
conclusions are both stated and implied: He did not, nor did
Falknor, believe that the men were guilty; all three attorneys
were convinced the case could not be successfully prosecuted;
he was clearly disturbed at the bad publicity produced and
worried at the possibility that the Department of Justice was
persecuting the defendants. He was aware that the progress of
the case had resulted from pressure outside the department;
he hoped the department would act for itself at once, not
influenced by pressure from either side.

Since the case was substantially complete at this time, it
can be examined for strength in four categories:

1. The expert opinion that the wound could not be self-
   inflicted. This, while not meaningless, was undercut by two
   relevant facts: (a) Cronkhite was provably a limber man,
   with very flexible joints. (b) Some witnesses were able to
   fire the gun while holding it in the "correct" position—
   Falknor before the grand jury, and Captain Caffey later at
   the trial. Thus the expert opinion could not be correct in
   every case. Also, since Falknor had demonstrated his
   ability to pull the trigger before the grand jury, the government knew in advance that its experts could be shown
   in error.

2. Pothier's confessions. These are limited in value by two
   things: (a) The way they were obtained, particularly the
   ones involving Rosenbluth. This was a matter of public
   record, thanks to Selden's exoneration. (b) The published
   notice of retraction in the New York *World*. Of course, the
   retraction could be later denied, but the government had
   no reason to believe that Pothier would testify against
   Rosenbluth. He had steadily maintained that he would
   not do so. Nor, if the two men were tried together, could
   he do so.

3. The various mix-ups and evidence of lost exhibits at the
   board of inquiry. These could be clearly demonstrated, but
   it was impossible to show that Rosenbluth had anything at
   all to do with them. Since the government did not consider
   the possibility of trying to show a concerted plot existed
   involving several officers, the behavior of the board of inquiry, however careless or negligent, in no way reflected on
   Rosenbluth. Nor was any suggestion ever made that he was
   responsible in any way for the various missing items. Loss
   of this material, however instrumental it was in arousing
   suspicion in the first place, was simply irrelevant to the case
   as finally constructed.

4. The various confusions of testimony concerning the hike
and the tragedy, both among the members of the regiment
and in Rosenbluth's various interrogations. It is doubtful
if the prearrest interrogation by Agent Lee could be used
against him in court, since he was clearly at this time under
suspicion and was not warned or permitted counsel. But
the primary difficulty was the problem of proving these
variations were anything more than faulty memory of events
long in the past. Eye-witness memory of events in an emergency is extremely unreliable, as many trials have shown.
Studies have demonstrated that most serious miscarriages of
justice result from mistakes made by eye-witnesses—honest
mistakes in recall. People vary greatly in their capacity to
remember clearly and in their tendency to unconsciously
embroider and elaborate memory. When ex-sergeant Kieffer
told a reporter that the major fell, "blood spurting from
his neck," I do not believe he was lying. I think he actually
"remembered" a dramatic event in the most dramatic possible way or yielded to the temptation, strong in some people, to exaggerate the gory details, to tell a good story. In
any case, as the grand jury hearing showed, it was impossible
to put together a coherent story without including details
that were promptly contradicted by other witnesses.

When we add to these four points the fact that no motive
had been shown, and when we consider the enormous quantity
of evidence testifying to Rosenbluth's character and reputation,
it is obvious that the case was not a strong one.

Revelle's letter to Herron produced an immediate effect.
While Crim was considering removal proceedings against
Rosenbluth, having been warned that he would resist such
action, Daugherty wired Revelle as follows:

> If you are satisfied after mature deliberation that evidence is
> insufficient to sustain a verdict of guilty then you authorized
> to dismiss instantly and withdraw removal proceedings. . . .

Once again, it appeared the Cronkhite affair was about to
close, with the government prepared to admit, by implication
at least, that it was unable to construct a case sufficient for a
trial. And once again, the halt was nullified. Later the same
day (October 24) a second telegram arrived at Seattle:

> Disregard telegram sent you this morning Cronkhite case. I
> am requesting Colonel Hayward of New York to come to Seat-
> tle and confer with you and make a thorough investigation of
> situation.[32]

Felix Warburg, partner in
the banking firm of
Kuhn, Loeb, and Company,
twice posted bail for his
friend Rosenbluth.

A few days later, the orders were changed again, and Revelle
and Chastain were told to come to Washington, bringing with
them the grand jury transcript. Revelle's urgent request that
Falknor also be permitted to come was denied.

Again, the case was back where it had been. Revelle's
opinion that no real case existed—later proved correct at the
trial—paralleled the opinions expressed throughout the preceding year and a half of struggle by almost everyone who had
studied it objectively or was personally acquainted with Rosenbluth. But despite Revelle's convincing and formal warning
and Daugherty's order to dismiss, something or someone
blocked this. Just as in 1921 when Herron formally recommended to Daugherty that the government drop the case and
transfer it to the state authorities, Daugherty's acceptance of
this judgment was later reversed.

Rosenbluth and Pothier were rearrested in New York and
Providence. On October 21 Rosenbluth was released on bail,
set at $40,000 by Judge Learned Hand and provided by Felix
Warburg, who used his Fifth Avenue town house as security.
Rosenbluth, as Crim had been informed, was prepared to fight
removal to Tacoma on the grounds that the federal government
did not have jurisdiction over the alleged offense. In a press
interview Revelle had stated that the question of jurisdiction

might take years to settle, and Rosenbluth was understandably reluctant to spend years in a Tacoma jail waiting for this decision. Thus the case moved into its final stage: while lawyers of national prominence battled out the jurisdiction question in one court after another, the racial prejudice issue became a crucial factor. It had been waiting in the wings for more than a year; now the charges that Jewish organizations were protecting a murderer and the countercharges that the whole case was inspired by racist feelings came to full flower. It is only fair to say here that Rosenbluth was not personally responsible for these charges nor did he approve of the attempt to make the case an anti-Semitic one. But he could not prevent the issue from arising and being debated by others. He disliked the Dreyfus Case label; some years after the affair he refused an offer from a national magazine to write up the story, when he discovered that the reporter intended to use the title: "The American Dreyfus Case."

The Justice Department files contain, immediately following correspondence on the removal proceedings, two letters that show the way sides were forming in the case. The editor of the *Jewish Tribune* wrote to Daugherty and asked a series of hard-to-answer questions concerning the reversal of jurisdiction and the failure to investigate the behavior of department officials; he concluded with an inquiry about the paying of expert witnesses at the rate of $250 a day. The second letter came from an ex-naval commander, and deserves to be quoted in full as an illustration of the way some Americans thought and felt:

> Genuine Americans are sincerely hoping that in the case of "Our Martyr Rosenbluth" *or* "The American Dreyfus" (the French [?] Dreyfus was a scoundrel) which you have had the courage to begin, you will be proof against fear proceedings from the powerful jew system of gold and the pander press. The command having been given, the pander press side of said system is in full operation.
>
> Anti-Christian Bolsheviks don't want any Law unless it strikes the White Race and fails to strike the anti-Christian Bolsheviks. New York and vicinity is crawling with them. Barren of Victory buttons, they pick their noses while they read their anti-American, anti-Christian, anti-White Race newspapers and remain seated while Christian women stand.[33]

CHAPTER EIGHT
POLITICS
AND PREJUDICE
NOVEMBER 1922-
APRIL 1924

THE GRAND JURY INDICTMENT for murder and the refusal of the Justice Department to dismiss the charges led inexorably to the final pretrial stage of the case. It must be recalled that Rosenbluth had been told by the attorney who offered him a conditional exoneration that if he refused to cooperate, he would be indicted and held without bail and the trial would be indefinitely delayed. Whether or not this would have been done is uncertain, but Rosenbluth and his attorneys were convinced of it. Rosenbluth explained his refusal to accept extradition to Tacoma:

> Personally I would be glad to stand trial, but just after the indictment, Mr. Revelle, in a newspaper interview, said either side could raise the point of jurisdiction and that it might take four years for it to go through the various courts of appeal and be definitely settled. In the meantime I would be in jail under a murder charge and would not be permitted to give bail. So my attorneys insisted that the point of jurisdiction be settled before a trial was started.[1]

This opinion of the matter was confirmed after the trial in an editorial written by the distinguished jurist, Louis Marshall: "Had he been removed, he would unquestionably have been imprisoned and his admission to bail at Tacoma would have been extremely doubtful."[2] Granting the possibility, Rosenbluth naturally preferred to remain at liberty while the jurisdictional question was being argued.

His refusal to accept extradition, however, was misinterpreted by those antagonistic to him. This was a demonstration to many that he was trying in every possible way to avoid a trial and was using the debated jurisdiction as a legal trick to delay a real examination of the facts. Crim, for example, suggested a reply to a letter of inquiry from Senator Pepper: "Senator Pepper might be advised that Rosenbluth had appealed to every Senator and Congressman possible in his attempt to avoid a trial of this matter on its merits."[3] From a humbler source, the same suggestion is made. In August 1923 the outraged citizens of Hickory Valley, Tennessee, wrote to the Attorney General demanding to know the causes of the delay of the trial and urging that Daugherty remain the champion of "Right" and "Justice."

The jurisdictional aspect of the case continued to be discussed. The only published argument on the question was printed in Selden's exoneration of Rosenbluth. Author Hiram M. Smith, formerly U.S. attorney in Richmond, Virginia, was a personal friend of General Cronkhite and agreed with him that his son had been murdered. But Smith also believed the federal government was without power to act in the matter. Briefly stated his argument was this: The government has jurisdiction of such an offense if committed on land under the exclusive jurisdiction of the United States. The key phrase is "exclusive jurisdiction." The many lawyers, some famous and some obscure, who wrote briefs on the matter attempted to determine whether the government had "exclusive" or only "limited" jurisdiction over Camp Lewis at the time of the major's death. In Smith's opinion, it did not have exclusive jurisdiction. A sovereign state could lose territory to the federal government only by a deed.

Since the deed in this case did not pass to the government until about a year after the major's death, Smith concluded that the federal government had no right to "try or punish" the persons allegedly responsible for the crime.[4] This view of the matter was upheld by Louis Marshall; by Pothier's attorney, Davis Arnold; by U.S. Commissioner Samuel Hitchcock; by the U.S. circuit court of appeals; by James Osborne, the attorney eventually assigned to prosecute the case; and by *all* the Justice Department attorneys who commented privately on the matter.

Metaphorically speaking, however, half the lawyers in the United States spit on their hands and reached for the appropriate law books; the question is a fascinating and complex one for the legal mind and can be argued indefinitely. The government lawyers insisted that the passing of a deed was a mere formality. The land had been in use by the government for several years, the state legislature had approved of the sale, various condemnation proceedings had been begun, and no practical question existed about the federal government's ownership of the land in question. This side of the case was argued by Revelle, the attorney in Seattle; by attorneys Selig and Solomon in New York; by Solicitor General James Beck; and by a lawyer named Adkins, who represented General Cronkhite. While the briefs on both sides of the case were piling higher and higher—the average length is about sixty legal-size pages—the personal problems, stresses, and confusions of the case continued.

On the personal level Rosenbluth's position aroused much strong indignation. Writing in January 1923 to Albert Lasker, Chairman of the United States Shipping Board, Louis Marshall sketches the problem:

> Under the circumstances I cannot believe that it is in the interest of justice to continue the prosecution of Captain Rosenbluth. I have come in close contact with him during the past few months, and I am absolutely satisfied of his entire innocence. With the greatest sympathy for the unfortunate parents of Major Cronkhite, I cannot but feel that they are obsessed with a fantastic idea which is so abnormal in all of its phases as to be unworthy of serious consideration in any tribunal of justice.
>
> Rosenbluth, who is now approaching the prime of life, is practically precluded by the sword of Damocles that is hanging over him from engaging in any regular employment, and his entire career, which in the past has been in every way admirable, is threatened with ruin. I marvel at the self-restraint he has exercised. . . . after an experience at the bar of forty-five years, I have never known of a prosecution which is so devoid of merit as that which has been set on foot against this innocent man.[5]

Similarly, in April 1923 the Yale Forest College alumni published a review of the case and protested the extreme unfairness to Rosenbluth, held for years under an indictment without legal recourse, unable to continue his professional life, a worthy career interrupted and almost destroyed.[6]

In addition to the inconvenience of delay, Rosenbluth was entangled against his wishes in the racial aspects of the case. However, he could not prevent others from interpreting the government's actions as inspired by anti-Semitic prejudice nor protect himself from the charge that Jewish organizations were doing all they could to protect a murderer from justice. The racial issue became a powerful factor in the latter part of 1922 for several reasons.

While removal proceedings were under consideration in the fall of 1922, Goldstein charged in an interview with U.S. Attorney Hayward that ten weeks before the hearings "persons closely associated with the Department of Justice came to New York and made the direct proposal that it would be cheaper for Rosenbluth's rich Jewish friends to contribute to a fund to prevent the indictment than it would be to go to trial. I told them where they could go to." Later he asserted, "This indictment is an attempt to forestall the impeachment proceedings instituted against the Attorney General and to block the Congressional inquiry demanded by the Veterans of Foreign Wars."[7] These charges and others were brought before a federal grand jury in New York City, but were dropped almost at once.

Much of the substance of Rosenbluth's complaints was impossible to prove. The actions of agents in private interviews, the various offers of compromise, and the loss or alteration of government records were all matters that could not possibly be substantiated. Rosenbluth's story of the offer made to him by an assistant attorney general over the luncheon table rests on his word alone. Even today when the files of the case are public records, much remains mysterious; at the time, none of the records would have been available to those outside the Justice Department. This was a problem that plagued any group wishing to investigate the department. As various congressional committees found, the department could not be examined without access to its records; and these records could be refused, altered, or in some cases, simply lost altogether. The audits prepared by Captain Scaife, for example, disappeared from the files after his resignation.

In addition to Rosenbluth's attempt to initiate an inquiry into department behavior, other circumstances combined to raise hints of prejudice. The hearing on Rosenbluth's refusal to accept extradition to Tacoma was scheduled to be held before Commissioner Samuel Hitchcock of the U.S. court of appeals in October. A series of delays occurred, however. A postponement to November was granted to permit the government to assemble the records of ownership; a further postponement was made necessary by the absence of Attorney Joyce, and still another to wait for the arrival of Revelle from Seattle. These delays, the defense insisted, were deliberately arranged to prevent the case from being considered by the congressional committee then inquiring into Representative Keller's motion to impeach Daugherty.

Evidence of some unnecessary or deliberate delay is implied by the behavior of Commissioner Hitchcock. He was reluctant to rule on the matter, believing that such an important issue should be decided by a judge. Therefore, on January 4, 1923, he ruled:

> I repeat that I have not the slightest doubt that the Federal courts have no jurisdiction over the offense, assuming that one was committed, and the only testimony adduced before me as to the tragedy itself tended to show the innocence rather than the guilt of the defendant. Nevertheless, I feel that sitting as a commissioner, who is merely an appointive officer, I should not

undertake to pass on this most important question of jurisdiction. . . . For that reason only, I now direct the matter be placed before a District Court Judge. . . .[8]

For reasons that cannot be ascertained but apparently existed, the matter was not transferred to a district court. After more than a month of delay, Hitchcock agreed to rule on the issue, explaining that the decision had been delayed long enough and although he wanted to place the matter before a judge, there were "difficulties in the way of doing so."[9] As the quotation above implies, Hitchcock was sympathetic to Rosenbluth and annoyed at what appeared to be deliberate slowness.

Aware of the charge that Rosenbluth was being persecuted for racial reasons, before this hearing the Justice Department took the case away from Revelle, who had prepared a brief arguing for federal jurisdiction, and arranged that the government be represented by attorneys Selig and Solomon. A memo from a department attorney to Crim informed him that U.S. Attorney Hayward had sent the names "of those of Jewish faith he has appointed in the Rosenbluth case, of which I spoke to you today at lunch."[10]

This substitution did more harm than good, since neither side approved of it. The *Seattle Union Record* printed an article on the matter, laughing at the naiveté of the Attorney General, who appeared to believe that the use of Jewish lawyers would wipe out all suspicion of prejudice.[11] Those antagonistic to Rosenbluth believed that the government had lost the battle because Selig and Solomon were handed the case at the last moment at the insistence of Jewish pressure groups. These complaints gained additional force because Rosenbluth was represented at this hearing by Louis Marshall, a lawyer of very great reputation. Marshall's basic argument is perhaps the clearest statement of the issue:

> It [federal jurisdiction] would only be when the United States acquired the title to the lands referred to in the act. That title could only be acquired by the execution of a conveyance to the United States from Pierce County, after the latter had acquired the title to the lands in question.
>
> The nature of the conveyance was expressly specified. It was to be evidenced by the deed or deeds of Pierce County, signed by the Chairman of its Board of County Commissioners and attested by the Clerk of said Board under the seal of such Board. . . . In the meantime sovereignty over this large tract of land, lying within the State of Washington was not to rest *in nubibus*. It was not to be "no Man's Land," for jurisdictional purposes. Jurisdiction would follow the title. That was certainly not in the United States until conveyed in the manner prescribed by statute.

The execution of this conveyance was clearly a prerequisite to the acquisition of title to these lands by the United States, and to the cession of jurisdiction over these lands by the State of Washington to the United States. That controlling act not having taken place until more than a year after the alleged murder, the State alone had jurisdiction over any offense committed upon those lands when the title either still remained in the original owners, or was vested in Pierce County and had not been conveyed to the United States.[12]

Commissioner Hitchcock, who had earlier announced his entire agreement with the defense position, ruled on February 14 that the government did not have the right to try the case and ordered Rosenbluth discharged. Concerning his previous decision to pass the question to a district court, he explained that his ruling could not be appealed but *de novo* proceedings could be instituted. In other words, if it wished to do so, the government could rearrest Rosenbluth and bring him before a district court for a second decision.[13]

The government, however, showed no desire to review the question, and Rosenbluth was technically a free man in the early months of 1923. The anger aroused in many quarters by his release was sharply increased by the fact that Pothier remained in jail. His removal hearing was held before the U.S. district court in Rhode Island, and Judge Brown ruled in January 1923 that the government had jurisdiction. This decision was appealed, but bail was refused. Thus the impression was created that one man, supported by powerful racial groups, had received very different treatment than the other. General Cronkhite expressed the opinion of many when he stated, "Without trial they are liberated. . . . Today one is free again by reason of a technicality of the law."[14]

II

THE PREJUDICES of those who believed that Jewish groups were behind Rosenbluth's release were also stimulated by the entrance of Louis Marshall into the case. Marshall was at this time a jurist of great distinction, with forty-five years of service. He had been connected with many important cases, particularly with the trial of Leo Frank. Marshall volunteered his services when this case was appealed to the Supreme Court; although he did not win the appeal, his connection with the case served to convince some that Jewish organizations intervened to "protect" a murderer. The wide publicity given to the Frank case and Marshall's participation in it permitted parallels to be drawn between it and the Rosenbluth case. In both it was alleged that Jewish organizations and a Jewish lawyer protected criminals from justice.

Henry Ford's relentless pursuit of the "international Jew" helped prolong the case.

The intrusion of Henry Ford's periodical, the *Dearborn Independent,* into the Rosenbluth case provides the most detailed study of the anti-Semitic forces in the affair. The confusions in the case and the long delay in settling it made it a natural addition to Ford's growing structure of allegations against American Jews. Between 1920 and 1922 many articles appeared alleging that the Jews were responsible for almost every symptom of decay in American life: short skirts, jazz, the baseball scandals, the threatened decline of wrestling as a sport, the immorality of the younger generation, and the breakdown of American home life. Far worse, this group was alleged to be threatening the American legal and judicial system and secretly attempting to gain political control of the country. These articles were reprinted in four small volumes entitled *The International Jew,* and gained wide circulation in this country and in Europe, particularly Germany.

Ford stopped this series abruptly in 1922 and only occasionally reopened the attack. But the comment in a recent study of Ford, "After 1922, little was published to lacerate their [the Jews'] feelings," is not quite accurate.[15] The Rosenbluth case was useful evidence to a man with Ford's prejudices concerning the political takeover that he feared Jewish organizations threatened; the series of articles that resulted differed from the first only in that they restricted their attack to political and judicial matters.

The event that triggered Ford's articles was Rosenbluth's release on bail provided by Felix Warburg after his second arrest in October 1922. Warburg was a partner of the important banking house of Kuhn, Loeb, and Company and was further connected with Jewish banking circles through his wife, the daughter of financier Jacob Schiff. Shortly after his marriage Warburg planned and built a "fairy-tale house of Gothic spires" at 1109 Fifth Avenue, a building which is today the American Jewish Museum. It was thought by his father-in-law to be ostentatious, and undoubtedly became for those inclined to dislike Jews a symbol for the un-American display of wealth.[16] This house was used as security for Rosenbluth's bail of $40,000, and the *New York Times* carefully reported that Warburg was able to show it was free from mortgages and other claims. The *Independent* had this to say about the bail:

> When Mr. Warburg . . . ostentatiously offered his private residence as security, wittingly or unwittingly, he cast a reflection upon the people among whom he has elected to live. Mr. Warburg is of foreign birth and, therefore, it may be that he fails to understand national sensibilities. . . . *As a director of the Bond & Mortgage Guarantee Company, he could have provided bail for his protégé in a more tactful way.*[17]

Outraged by the combination of an alleged Jewish murderer allied with powerful Jewish banking interests and the appearance of Louis Marshall, who had previously been the object of direct attacks by Ford, the *Dearborn Independent* began in December 1922 to publish a series of eleven articles which concluded in May 1924. The author, Charles Albert Collman, made use of several sources of information; much of his material is drawn from General Cronkhite's collection of letters and documents, some appears to stem from Agent Lee's attempts to find a Bolshevik plot, and the remainder is drawn from the Selden exoneration pamphlet, despite the fact that Collman tries to discredit it. The articles attempt to prove three things. First, although it is repeatedly claimed that most Americans want a fair trial for the accused, the probability of Rosenbluth's guilt is assumed. Second, Collman tries to show that the long delay in the case has been caused by American Jewish organizations who make it their business to protect Jews accused of crimes by making martyrs of them. Third, he argues that this protection is extended as part of a deliberate plot aimed at undermining faith in American justice and government law officers, and more specifically destroying the Department of Justice as a functioning body.

An examination of these articles shows them to be a strange mixture of fact, fiction, half-truths, distortions, and contradictions. The writer was aided in his purpose by the fact

The Ford International Weekly

THE DEARBORN INDEPENDENT

By the Year $1.50   Dearborn, Michigan, December 30, 1922   Single Copy Ten Cents

RECEIVED JAN 4 1923 UNIVERSITY OF MINNESOTA

WHAT THEY CALL A DREYFUS CASE!

Here, for the First Time in Newspaper or Periodical, Are Presented the Facts in the Amazing Death Mystery Known as

The Rosenbluth Case

With Which Is Revealed the Audacious Attempt Now Being Made to Prevent the Administration of American Justice

We know of one great newspaper which printed the FIRST CHAPTER of what was announced to be a serial story of this soldier tragedy. The first chapter is ALL that it ever has printed. You will understand why after reading this and succeeding chapters in THE DEARBORN INDEPENDENT.

CHRONICLER OF THE NEGLECTED TRUTH

OTHER SPLENDID FEATURES IN THIS ISSUE:

That Billion of Gold—Who Owns It?

Bringing the World to Our Easy Chairs

Back Thro' the Centuries to Days of Sumer

The cover page of the December 30 **Dearborn Independent** announced the series of articles purporting to tell the "facts" of the Rosenbluth case.

that they did not appear consecutively or regularly. Thus even a fair-minded reader had ample time between issues to forget what had been asserted in previous articles. The issue that began the series (December 30, 1922) had printed on its cover the headlines of the piece: "The Mysterious Killing of Major Cronkhite and Amazing Actions of Captain Rosenbluth." It begins by bewailing the fact that "thousands of aliens, ignorant of our country's language and its ways, are being taught in their vernacular press that the United States is persecuting deliberately a member of their race." The writer then describes the fatal hike as General Cronkhite imagined it, placing great stress on the fact that friction between young academy-trained officers and older half-trained national army officers was very common. To support this analysis, Rosenbluth's age is given as forty, Cronkhite's as twenty-four. Rosenbluth, although he did look older than he was as indicated by press photographs, was in fact only thirty-one at the time of Cronkhite's death. The article concludes with the general's fundamental assertion: Pothier had confessed he was also shooting, and Rosenbluth had testified he was present when Cronkhite was shot. Why had he not reported that Pothier was using his weapon? The writer does not, however, point out that Pothier's reliability was highly questionable.

The second in the series (January 6, 1923), "Truth Crushed to Earth," depends heavily upon slanting and rhetorical questions for its effect. "Is it possible," the writer darkly inquires, "that any organization in this country has the power to obtain for racial reasons, the impeachment of a United States Attorney-General because he is active in the performance of his duty?" The article then attempts to show that Rosenbluth's two visits to Russia after the war have sinister implications. ". . . after he had been mustered out in January, 1919, Rosenbluth immediately made haste in getting out of the country." His travels are presented as private business backed by Jewish bankers, made more dubious by the fact that trade with Russia was at that time forbidden. Much is made of a secret code, allegedly found in Rosenbluth's possession at the time of his arrest, and dire hints are dropped concerning deals with the Bolsheviks.* "These facts incline one to the belief that this affair is more involved than may appear on the surface, that there may be 'men higher up'—men of wealth and importance—concerned in

---

* Portions of this allegedly "secret" code are reprinted in the *Independent* and in the *Chicago Tribune* articles of April, 1923. The code would appear to be similar in type to codes still used by business firms; standard phrases are reduced to numerical or alphabetical abbreviations so that information can be cabled as inexpensively as possible. Such codes are secret only in that they cannot be read without a code book; they are not intended primarily to deceive but to reduce cost.

enterprises which they are determined must not see the light of day."

The third article (January 13, 1923), "Trying a Case in the Newspapers," attempts to show that any questions raised about the validity of the government's case came from "organized racial groups" determined to make a martyr of the accused, or from those who knew little or nothing about the case. The retraction of Pothier's confession involving Rosenbluth is called into question: The New York *World,* the paper that reported the retraction, drew most of its circulation from the heavily Jewish Lower East Side. In addition, Pothier's attorney is quoted as saying that he had never officially filed this retraction with the Justice Department. The Selden exoneration "purports," the writer asserts, to be an official document, but it is "quite evidently the output of a printing establishment on the East Side of New York, the work of men ill acquainted with the proper usage of the English language." Reference is made to the yellow cover of the pamphlet, an apparent attempt to use the link between Jews and a color they had sometimes been forced to wear as a sign of their religion. (Perhaps some of the copies were bound in this color; the only one I have seen was bound in grayish white.) The writer remarks he does "not know who has approached Mr. Selden in this matter, nor whether his authority was obtained in giving a statement out in this form." It would have been, of course, an exceedingly simple matter to find out from Selden whether or not he had authorized the document and its distribution, but the writer is careful not to inquire. Nor does he mention that the first item in the pamphlet is a certificate from the Hon. William D. Askren, presiding judge of the Superior Court of the State of Washington, in which the judge attests to the validity of the document and to Selden's right to present the analysis of the case that follows. Neither does the writer mention at any time that the case was turned over to Selden for handling.

The fourth essay (January 20, 1923), "The Jewish Smoke-Screen of Falsehood in What Press Dubs the 'Dreyfus Case'," continues the attack on the exoneration, here labeled "fake." It is strongly hinted but not precisely stated that Selden did not write the pamphlet; that it was published by him in the *Tacoma Ledger* is not mentioned. The Institute for Public Service in New York City, an organization for which Rosenbluth worked before the war, is criticized for supporting him. The institute, which had earlier published a pamphlet titled "Teachable Facts about Bolshevism and Sovietism," was circulating materials on the Rosenbluth case meant for use in public schools. This, Collman asserts, is a clear attempt to "influence the minds of school principals, teachers, and school children

THE DEARBORN INDEPENDENT   9

The Jewish Smoke-screen of Falsehood
in What Press Dubs the "Dreyfus Case"

Another Chapter of the Revelations Being Made in the Cronkhite
Tragedy Brings Mr. Marshall of the Kehillah to the Fore

By CHARLES ALBERT COLLMAN

MORE than 70 witnesses were summoned, last autumn, before a Federal Grand Jury in Tacoma, Washington. They were assembled from widely separated parts of the country. On the strength of their testimony, the jury returned indictments charging Robert Rosenbluth and Rolland R. Pothier with the premeditated murder of Major Alexander P. Cronkhite. In certain quarters great fear is entertained of this testimony, and an organized effort is made to prevent the indicted men from being tried. But justice demands that these witnesses be heard.

Immediately on the news of the indictment, officers and directing heads of the American Jewish Committee and the New York Kehillah threw the mantle of their protection about Robert Rosenbluth in New York City. They provided him with lawyers to fight his extradition to the West, and with means for spreading an extensive publicity campaign, in an endeavor to prove his innocence without permitting resort to be had to the law courts of the country.

An avalanche of defamation was directed against the organization of the United States Army. A concerted system of attack was launched against the indicted heads and personnel of the prosecuting arm of the government. An "atmosphere of persecution" was created through, and in their vernacular press, a studied campaign to inflame the race hatred of thousands was begun, giving them shelter and "framing up" a murder charge against one of their people.

How Press Is Used

SHOULD the plans of these great racial organizations prove successful, a deathblow will have been struck at the administration of justice in the United States. For a better understanding of these plans, it is necessary to recapitulate the outstanding features of the case. Major Alexander P. Cronkhite was a West Point

The group that was shielding Rosenbluth now decided that it was urgently necessary for them to try to cast discredit upon the confession made by Pothier. They enlisted the services of a newspaper owned by members of their race, the New York World. The editor of the World first sent a reporter to consult Robert Rosenbluth and his attorney, Jonah J. Goldstein, in New York City. The reporter then saw Pothier in Central Falls, Rhode Island, but the latter would not speak until he had seen his attorney, Davis G. Arnold, of Providence. Mr. Arnold refused to have his client interviewed until he had visited New York. Subsequently the World man talked to Pothier in Mr. Arnold's office in Providence. The World then published an alleged retraction of Pothier's confession implicating Rosenbluth, but not retracting the statement that it was the bullet from his weapon that had killed Major Cronkhite. Publicity organizations, acting on behalf of Rosenbluth, gave this "retraction" a wide circulation.

Now Goldstein & Goldstein, attorneys for Rosenbluth, drew up a series of affidavits, consisting of some made by themselves, others by Pothier's lawyer, by the World man, and by other persons who knew nothing about the case. These they sent to J. W. Selden, a prosecuting attorney of Pierce County, Washington. Next a booklet of 62 pages was printed by an East Side press, entitled the "Exoneration of Robert Rosenbluth." This was a "faked" exoneration, since Mr. Selden had not been in possession of the evidence in the hands of the Department of Justice, had not examined the witness nor tried the case. This booklet was circulated by thousands of newspapers of the country at a great expense. In other words, a man charged with murder, was "acquitted" by his friends, without recourse to law court, judge or jury, and without his accusers being heard.

There are two very good reasons why this persecution against me on this four-year-old incident is renewed by Attorney-General Daugherty:

1. Because if the matter is in the courts while the impeachment proceedings against him are pending, Congress will not be able to take up this case with its evidence of incompetence and misfeasance in office by Attorney-General Daugherty personally and his department.

2. Because I have refused to respond to the many suggestions that my "rich Jewish friends raise a fund to dispose of the matter."

In spite of rebuffs of suggestions that settlement could be effected if my "rich Jewish friends would raise a fund," 10 weeks before this present grand jury met in Tacoma, Washington, from sources whose authority cannot be questioned, came the direct proposition that "everybody could be happy."

It was warranted "that this would be cheaper than a trial." I still believe that it is a good American motto. "Millions for defense, but not one cent for tribute."

Agents of the Department of Justice taunted. "What are you going to do about it?" As soon as they discovered that they had made a mistake and had taken some one with a lifetime record in public service and that my bail was furnished by persons as well known and highly respected in the country as Felix M. Warburg and Colonel Herbert Lehmann, they started on a new track. Cash!

What Happened Before Jury

OF COURSE, nobody takes seriously the allegation that Rosenbluth is being "persecuted because of his race." The fact that the United States Army is a stern

The fourth essay in the **Dearborn Independent** fanned the flames of prejudice.

against officials of the government." The article concludes with a description of the hearing before Commissioner Hitchcock, and much stress is placed on the number of Jewish lawyers present. In addition are newsmen, "strange, exotic types, reporters for the vernacular press of the East Side. The scene, with its figures and faces, is worthy of one of Hogarth's ancient prints." Louis Marshall is insultingly described as sneering and imperious.

The fifth in the series (January 27, 1923), "The American Jewish Committee Would Substitute Itself for Country's Laws," attempts to show that this organization was engaged in a conspiracy against "American" ideals and customs, particularly in their attempts to restrict the use of Christian prayers, Christmas carols, and similar ceremonies in the public schools. Little new information on the Rosenbluth case is presented, except for the fact that the *Jewish Tribune* was responsible for publishing the libelous assertion—a reflection of the "malignity of the 'Yiddish' mind"—that Major Cronkhite's tombstone bears the ignominious label S.I.W., self-inflicted wound.

The sixth feature (February 3, 1923), "Producing Jewish 'Martyrs' by Propaganda," attempts to show that those behind Rosenbluth were prominent Jews and struggles to discount the support of those who were not Jewish. The support of Herbert Hoover is difficult to explain, and the writer is clearly reluctant to attack him directly. Thus indirection is necessary to discredit Hoover's interest in Russia. The article explains that Rosenbluth was reporting to Hoover in Washington only a few days before his arrest, and continues:

> Exactly what he was reporting to the Secretary of Commerce he does not state. However, Mr. Hoover, for many years previous, had been a partner in the mine operating firm of Bewick, Moreing & Company, of London, during which time he had become a director in the Russo-Asiatic Corporation, Ltd., and other mining properties in Russia and the Far East. It may be quite natural that Mr. Hoover wished to gain some information concerning the condition of such properties from a person who had been traveling through those countries for so long a time.

This innocent-sounding explanation is less harmless than it appears. In his *Memoirs,* Hoover explained that after the American Relief Administration had succeeded in preventing the worst ravages of famine in Russia during the winter of 1921–1922, the Soviets tried to discredit American efforts. ". . . a notice appeared in the Moscow papers that I had carried on the relief hoping that 'his mines in the Urals would be returned to him.' As this appeared in some of the American papers, I had to explain that I had not even the remotest interest in these mines, and that if they were restored to their rightful owners, it would not benefit me one dime."[18]

The *Independent,* then, took advantage of published reports that Hoover had a commercial interest in Russian mining property to hint that Rosenbluth's visit to that country was arranged by private interests. Following this indirect suggestion, which is combined with the statement that the Jewish committee was powerful enough to play off "one member of President Harding's cabinet against the other," Hoover's subordinate, Julius Barnes—head of the United States Grain Corporation—is directly attacked. Barnes was the chairman of the Institute of Public Service, here described as a "publicity and propagandist bureau." Since Rosenbluth had worked for this institute before the war, the writer can move neatly from an attack on Barnes to the fact that Barnes' pamphlet, "Teachable Facts about Bolshevism and Sovietism," had quoted one of Rosenbluth's reports on Russian conditions. "Just what Rosenbluth was doing in Kharkov at the time [July 27, 1919], Mr. Barnes does not say."

The letter Hoover wrote in Rosenbluth's behalf is printed without indication that an important paragraph has been omitted. The letter appears in the *Independent* in this form:

> It just happens that practically all the time since the war, Rosenbluth has been employed by relief organizations in Europe with which I am associated, first in south Russia and later in Siberia.
> I fear there is a great miscarriage of justice in the whole process.

The writer then comments: "It is scarcely possible that Mr. Hoover meant thereby to stand sponsor for all the activities of Robert Rosenbluth in Eastern Europe and Asia, but his letter gives that unfortunate impression." The omitted paragraph, however, makes it even clearer that Hoover did indeed intend to sponsor Rosenbluth. Between the two paragraphs printed above, are these statements in the original letter:

> One of the charges brought against him is that he has been a refugee from justice. This is absolutely untrue as his connection has been a perfectly open and public matter. I know the young man and it seems to me incredible that such a charge should be made.

Most of the article, however, is devoted to a parallel between the Rosenbluth case and that of Leo Frank. Marshall's efforts in Frank's behalf are contemptuously described in a paragraph headed "Oh Yes! Louis Was There." The depths of the writer's prejudice can be gauged by the description of Frank's lynching. Outraged, he asserts, by the efforts of Jewish lawyers in Frank's behalf, a mob of "sensitive southern people" dragged him from prison and took justice into their own hands.

Several months later (April 7, 1923) another story appeared, "Federal Court Flouted in Cronkhite Case." The text prints in parallel columns the hearings and decision handed down on Rosenbluth and Pothier, concluding "the Jew walks free, while the non-Jew [is] held in jail." Later in the month (April 21) a chapter with the intriguing title "His Son Was Probably Murdered—Pershing" was printed. This section demonstrates the flat contradiction of earlier statements, made many months before. In the December article it was stated:

Neither the comrades of Major Cronkhite, nor the heads of the Department of Justice, had been satisfied with the explanation given of the young officer's death, as being due to "accidental shooting." For two years, agents of the department worked in accumulating evidence bearing on the major's death, in tireless investigations.

Five months later we are told, ". . . the aggrieved father set about the task confronting him, alone, unaided in his effort to find the truth." As the quotation implies, this article sketches General Cronkhite's efforts to investigate his son's death and sharply criticizes the War Department for its lack of cooperation, being careful to assure its readers that officials like Pershing and Weeks are in no way responsible.

A subsequent article (April 29, 1923), "Cabinet Dragged into Cronkhite Case Through Intrigues of Racial Clique," endeavors with small success to justify the actions of everyone favored by the *Independent* and to condemn the actions of those they wish to discredit. Again, portions of Hoover's letter are reproduced, and Collman comments on the extreme oddity of his agreeing to write in behalf of an accused murderer. Then a letter from Senator Calder to Daugherty is printed, apparently in full; the letter urges the Attorney General to release the accused from their bail, since the government has denied jurisdiction. Since Calder refers to Hoover in his letter, it is judged to be a "studied attempt of a United States Senator, quoting the co-operation of a United States Secretary of Commerce, to bring influence to bear upon a United States Attorney General for an abandonment of all established methods of legal procedure. . . ." Hoover's support is "odd," Calder's is an attempt to thwart justice.

The writer then attempts to show that Daugherty and his staff, "unaware of the unscrupulousness of the 'oriental minds' that were pitted against them," were persuaded to look into the matter. Unable to exonerate Rosenbluth, Daugherty was forced to bring the matter before a grand jury. Once the men were indicted, "all pretense was thrown aside, and from Rosenbluth, his counsel's law partner Samuel Untermyer, and the leaders of the propaganda came loud outcries: 'Daugherty must be impeached!' " Here the writer deliberately misrepresents the actual chronology. Representative Keller's motion to impeach Daugherty was made on September 11, 1922, a few days after the Wilkerson injunction. Rosenbluth and Pothier were not indicted until October 13. But the effort was made, nonetheless, to show that the increasing criticism of Daugherty in Congress was inspired by Jewish forces.

A further essay (May 26, 1923)—"Shall Rosenbluth Be 'an

American Dreyfus'?"—calls Rosenbluth's support by the Yale Alumni Association into question. First, Collman asserts that Rosenbluth was not in fact a graduate of Yale, but "sixteen years ago, he merely took a two-year course in the Forest School," one of the "minor branches" of Yale. Rosenbluth did attend Yale for the last two years of college only, but the implication that he had taken a sort of "short course" in a minor skill is totally false; he was graduated with a degree of Master of Forestry. Second, the writer reports an interview with Professor Chapman, the secretary of the Alumni Association, the general drift of which was to suggest that he and his fellow faculty members had kind hearts, but really knew little about the case.

A year passed before the final article appeared: "Cronkhite Case to Trial: Highest Court Order" (May 10, 1924). The *Independent* saw in the Supreme Court decision a complete vindication of its entire campaign:

> The decision is a rebuke to the Wall Street bankers who advanced their protection to one of the accused; it renders impotent the intrigue of the New York *World* . . . it discredits the instigators of the extensive publicity campaign conducted to create an "atmosphere" on behalf of one of the accused . . . it is a reproach to those who expended such large sums of money in an attempt to defeat justice. . . .

The series concludes carefully with an expression of sympathy for the accused, "these two unfortunate men, whose misfortune it has been that they were deliberately entangled by misguided partisans into a racial and political intrigue."

"Racial and political intrigue" is an accurate description of the series in question, for Henry Ford's political ambitions can be seen clearly in the background. His growing support as a rival for Harding in 1924 was no doubt a factor in promoting these articles. They are uniformly careful to avoid any criticism of the administration; highly placed government officials are always given the benefit of the doubt, or their actions excused. Daugherty, Weeks, Hoover, and Pershing were the victims of "oriental minds," and in no way worthy of rebuke. Yet at the same time the articles implant in the mind of the reader a strong suggestion that the administration, however basically fair and honest, was unable to cope with the threat of organized Jewish pressure groups. The implication is clear: If Harding and his chosen staff are not capable of handling this pressure, why not choose a man known to be a champion of Christians against Semitic forces?

Ford's entrance into the case was very important for two reasons. First, he probably threw financial support behind the forces of the prosecution for political and ideological reasons, enabling General Cronkhite, who like Rosenbluth was not a wealthy man, to continue his campaign. He was apparently prepared to assist further. After the case came to an end with Pothier's acquittal, it was reported to the Justice Department that General Cronkhite was planning a full-scale congressional investigation of the entire case, allegedly subsidized by Ford.[19] Second, the articles achieved enormous publicity for the case. The *Dearborn Independent* reached people who never would have heard of the matter from any other source. Those inclined to anti-Semitism found these articles completely convincing, and the increasing protests that the government was yielding to Jewish pressure finally made it impossible for the Justice Department to do anything but continue the case to the bitter end.

For example, a resident of Salem, New Mexico, wrote to the Department of Justice in January 1923 to convey the interesting information that he had, with the assistance of the *Independent*'s photograph of Rosenbluth, spotted that suspected person camping on his land. He concluded his letter:

Ford's paper intimates the Jewish organizations are protecting him. I fear them financially and am in debt and they have a hold on finances in this community. So I would not want my name used in any connection if you should find this party to be your man.[20]

In February, the ex-naval commander who had earlier congratulated the department for its courage in continuing the case, sent a second communication:

Please advise me whether there is a Federal statute which makes it a criminal offense to start a salesman out upon the road with little funds, and to subsequently abandon him, leaving him penniless far from his home. The practice is one for which the international Jew exploiter may justly claim the odium.

As a World War volunteer in middle life I am curious to know why one "Rosenbluth," indicted, I understand, for "premeditated murder," was in New York admitted to bail. Is there any record of a Christian so indicted having been admitted to bail?[21]

The seriousness of the situation was demonstrated by the *Yale Forest School News,* which in April 1923 published a special issue devoted to Mr. Rosenbluth's defense. The magazine made it clear that it was totally uninfluenced by Jewish groups; the board members were "American citizens, of colonial ancestry, without Semitic blood." Only 12 of the 539 graduates of the Forest College were Jewish, and none had offered their opinions. The publication also denied that Rosenbluth had raised this issue or that they had received any money or documents from Jewish sources.[22] That the alumni association members of a respected university should feel the need to demonstrate they were not Jews in order to print a reasonable defense of an accused man shows, I believe, that the articles in the *Independent* had enjoyed a considerable success.

III

ROSENBLUTH'S RELEASE from federal jurisdiction following Hitchcock's ruling produced a predictably strong response from General Cronkhite. On February 14 he wired Crim:

> Press today contains announcement of the astounding action of the United States Commissioner in releasing from custody for the second time Capt. Rosenbluth who is under indictment for the murder of my son. In face of this appalling action I must request of you as head of the criminal branch Dept. of Justice that I be given full explanation as to this most extraordinary procedure.[23]

The general's agitation was understandable, particularly in view of his personal position at the time. On February 3 the *Times* carried the following announcement: "Major General Adelbert Cronkhite . . . went on the retired list today, making way for the promotion of Brigadier General Hanson E. Ely to be a Major General." Cronkhite had reached the age of 62 in January and had been at once retired "by order of the President."[24] In the background here are the frequent protests from the War Department that Cronkhite's refusal to return to duty or to retire was blocking the promotion of deserving younger officers. It is probable that Ely, an outspoken man, had encouraged the retirement arrangements. He was reported to have been greatly indignant during the war at being only a colonel. "He could name four colonels who got the star of a brigadier general, and who could not hold a candle to Hanson E. Ely. It was a lousy oversight."[25]

General Cronkhite, however, was outraged by this enforced resignation and exploded two weeks later in the *Times*. He charged he had been railroaded because of his efforts to solve the mystery of his son's death, "hampered by both War Department and Justice Department." He had been ordered, he maintained, by the President and the War Department to continue his investigations, then was penalized for this by being retired against his wishes.

Two former lieutenant colonels from the Eightieth Division, Jennings Wise and Ashby Williams, prepared and published an anonymous pamphlet titled "The Case of Major-General Adelbert Cronkhite, Privately Printed for the Information of His Friends." Colonel Wise had acted as the general's legal adviser throughout the case, and as a personal friend of Cronkhite was convinced the general's opinion of the case was correct.[26] This pamphlet has proved impossible to trace, but its contents were adequately summarized in the *Chicago Tribune* on February 15, 1923. The general charged that his retirement and his assignment to Panama were both reprisals for his efforts on behalf of his son and his son's murderers were being protected. He protested the procedures followed at Camp Lewis and described the missing evidence as well as the confusion in the official records. He charged that Daugherty had agreed to delay the case and finally had dropped it altogether because of pressure brought to bear by Senator Calder and Herbert Hoover. He attacked the War Department, saying his honor had been impugned, he had been denied the usual court of inquiry to defend himself, and he had been retired against his wishes despite his service and good health.

The article continued by reporting Secretary of War Weeks' comments on the matter:

> The secretary declared that he had personally arranged two conferences for the general with Attorney-General Daugherty and that the attorney general had finally been persuaded to take up the case, although the shooting occurred in a public highway and was not properly a case for the department of justice.
> "General Cronkhite," Weeks said, "had persuaded the attorney-general to pursue the case, though the department of justice was convinced that there was not sufficient proof to convict and that the necessary expense of time and money was not justified."[27]

There was considerable feeling expressed that the general had been unfairly treated. An editorial in the *New York Times* raised the point that this abrupt dismissal placed a blot on the record of a distinguished officer.[28] Men and officers of Cronkhite's regiment and the Veterans of Foreign Wars demanded a court of inquiry into the matter or, failing that, a full Senate investigation of the entire case. Louis Marshall wired Senator Calder to indicate Rosenbluth's desire to cooperate in a Senate investigation. As a result two senators, Carter Glass of Virginia—who had served as Secretary of the Treasury under Wilson and whose son had served in Cronkhite's division—and David Reed of Pennsylvania, indicated they would seek such an investigation. They were joined tentatively by Senator Caraway of Arkansas, always interested in anything that could be used as ammunition against Attorney General Daugherty and the Republican administration.[29]

Cronkhite continued to explain his position in the press. He was quoted as saying, "He resisted the suggestion of General Pershing and Secretary Weeks that he should apply for retirement, and 'found himself,' he says, 'subjected to the increasing disfavor of his military superiors.' "[30] In another interview, he asserted: "The facts in this whole unfortunate affair when they come to light will shock the conscience of the country, and unless something happens to me they will surely come to light. They are known to the Department of Justice, and all I ask is that those facts be presented to an American jury."[31] In response to these charges, the Secretary of War finally agreed to investigate the records and inquired into the general's charges that they were confused, tampered with, or missing. The senators agreed to delay the proposed request for an investigation until Weeks had completed his research. This arrangement delayed the matter until April, after Congress had recessed. Weeks reported that the records of Major Cronkhite's death were intact insofar as the War Department could ascertain. He also made clear that the retirement was a closed issue and would not be reconsidered.[32]

The newspaper coverage of the general's retirement, however, did result in a brief examination of the case on the floor of the Senate. An article in the *New York Herald* on February 19 charged that Senator Calder had used political pressure to have the case dropped by the government back in 1921. The article asserted that the "new, confidential, and thorough investigation" of the case promised by Daugherty in April 1921 was not carried out and that after Rosenbluth's hearing in June, Calder managed to persuade the Attorney General to abandon the case.[33] It is not unlikely that there was some truth to this allegation. After the hearing in June, Herron had recommended to Daugherty that the case be dropped by the Justice Department because of the "peculiar circumstances and the embarrassing position in which the Department finds itself." Part of the embarrassment may have been political; Calder was an important senator from a key state, New York.

In any event, Senator Calder requested in the Senate that the editorial and a series of affidavits in Rosenbluth's defense be entered in the *Congressional Record,* as well as his denial of the use of any unfair or unethical means to influence Daugherty to drop the case. After this statement Senator McKellar, a Democrat from Tennessee, asked some questions about the death of Major Cronkhite, revealing his personal impression that the death had been suicide. When Calder denied this, McKellar reported he had also been told that the family had clear evidence he had been shot in the back, where he could not possibly have shot himself. McKellar also questioned the board of inquiry and was clearly surprised to hear that the findings of that board had been confirmed by the War Department. The arrival of Senator Glass ended this dialogue; Glass protested, and Calder agreed, that it was improper to discuss a matter informally which was to be made the object of an investigation.[34]

The only other reference to the case in the Senate occurred a few days later. Senator Caraway was engaged in a protest over the arbitrary firing of a number of persons from the Bureau of Printing and Engraving, who had been, in defiance of the rules of Civil Service, abruptly dismissed in a manner which implied they had been dishonest. The motion to investigate the matter had been killed in the Appropriations Committee, of which Senator Calder was the chairman. Caraway attacked Calder by means of the Rosenbluth case:

> the Senator from New York . . . was named the other day by General Cronkhite, who says he helped smother an investigation into the charges against Captain Rosenbluth, whom he thinks killed his son; and when that charge was made, Senator Calder said last night that he was willing that there should be an investigation so that all might know he was innocent of this charge, but he smothers an investigation where 28 men and women are laboring under a charge and denies them a forum in which they may be heard. . . . He is quick to say, "I am willing to have an investigation of the killing of Major Cronkhite, when they say I induced the Attorney General to desist in the probe to determine who was guilty of the murder. I am willing that there should be a thorough investigation. . . .

Obviously political motives are involved here. Caraway, a Democrat, was interested in any issue, large or small, that could be used as a weapon against the Republican administration. Not at all interested in the Rosenbluth affair but outraged by the case he was investigating, he used Cronkhite's charges in a way that tended to reinforce the general's assertion of Calder's unethical behavior. The generalized political implications of Caraway's speech were made obvious by its conclusion:

> Why, who ever suspected that the Attorney General was appointed because he was a lawyer? You could not prove by the court records of Ohio that he tried a lawsuit there in 15 years. He not only has no knowledge of the law, but has no curiosity

about it. . . . He is going to quit before the Sixty-eighth Congress can have anything to say about his whitewash, and we know it; and there is another member of the Cabinet "fixing" to quit also, Mr. President. Whenever the lid on the Teapot Dome blows off—and it is already stewing—another who was a party to giving away all the naval-reserve fuel this country had, and one man for nothing got a hundred million dollars worth of it, is going to quit. Fall is not going to have to carry the entire responsibility for giving away all of the national wealth.

He is entitled to only his part of it. The President also "whitewashed" him. He said, "All this thing that Mr. Fall has done I sanctioned." I rather imagine they promised to divide the spoils, including the naval-reserve oils, before he was in a position to appoint a Cabinet. Anyway there will be but two or three of the master minds when we get back here in December next. The Secretary of State will possibly still be sitting on his iron safe, keeping anybody from finding out what the foreign policy of this country is. He will not even get off it long enough to get a shave. Doctor Sawyer will still be rattling his spurs around, just 2 inches beneath his ears.* But all the other master minds will have gone the way of all the earth.[35]

The Rosenbluth case, then, was worked into the remote fringes of far greater scandals. It was for Caraway and others a tiny affair, a most minor indication that Daugherty was susceptible to external pressures. And Caraway's speech implies the reason why Cronkhite's and Rosenbluth's repeated requests for a Senate investigation went unheard. There were simply too many scandals to investigate, many of which seemed far more serious to the nation.

One last attempt was made in February to have Daugherty reconsider his decision not to dismiss the charges. On February 1 Marshall received a reply from his letter to Albert Lasker quoted earlier. Lasker explained he was ill and unable to act in person. But he had done what he could:

The Attorney General, I am informed, is ill at home, and cannot be reached. I am instructing my assistant, Mr. Sollitt, to get in touch with the Attorney General's close friend and chum, Mr. Jess Smith, to show your letter and the briefs enclosed, to Mr. Smith (Mr. Smith and the Attorney General live together),

---

* The Secretary of State was the impressively bearded Charles Evans Hughes. Sawyer was Mrs. Harding's personal physician who was lured to Washington by a commission as brigadier general in the Army Medical Corps. Although he was an honest man who was instrumental in uncovering the corruption in the Veterans Bureau under Charles Forbes, he was also a comic character. "One of the perquisites of his office was a large cavalry horse, 'Turco'; and to see the wispy doctor-general in his high-collared uniform with its starred shoulder straps, a Sam Browne belt slapping against his hollow chest, his little pointed beard bobbing in the wind, as he cantered through the park, soon became one of the sights of Washington." (Frances Russell, *The Shadow of Blooming Grove* [New York, 1968] pp. 438–39.)

and ask Mr. Smith if he cannot burden the Attorney General
with it, won't he at least take it up with Mr. Beck.

I do this in this way because it is the only manner in which
we can get it to anyone's attention in the hope of any immediate
action.[36]

Smith apparently did not show the materials to Daugherty but
simply turned the letters over to the Justice Department. That
a distinguished attorney and the Chairman of the Shipping
Board were forced to approach the Attorney General through
Jess Smith is eloquent testimony to the truth of many complaints about this man. Smith was an amiable scatterbrain, a
former clothing store owner, who had joined his friend Daugherty in Washington and shared an apartment with him at the
Wardman Park Hotel. Mrs. Daugherty, who was in poor health,
spent much of her time in Florida. Smith had an office at the
Justice Department, regularly used the secretaries and facilities,
and had access to confidential files. He was generally considered second in command to Daugherty himself, although he was
not an employee of the department and had never taken an
oath of office. After his death in the summer of 1923—he was
officially considered a suicide—he was proved to have taken
bribes for his assistance in several questionable transactions.

Additional publicity was given to the Rosenbluth case in
a series of articles published in the *Chicago Tribune* April 1–8,
1923. These articles were written by Donald Ewing who unlike
Ford's writer tried to present a reasonably fair statement of the
facts of the case. He traveled all over the United States, securing interviews with people who had not previously been questioned. He interviewed Selden in Tacoma, and made it clear
that Selden was perfectly willing to try the case and would have
done so in 1921 had he been given any evidence by the Justice
Department. He interviewed Dr. Sommer, who had performed
the first autopsy upon the body of Major Cronkhite, printed
Rosenbluth's comments on the way in which his testimony had
been altered without his consent, and analyzed the defense and
prosecution cases. He also aired the jurisdictional problem for
the first time in an article headed, "Dilatory Moves Jumble
Quiz in Cronkhite Case. Government Record One of Indeci-
sion." He makes it quite clear that the government handling
of the case was exceedingly strange; he lays particular stress on
the government's failure to announce it had resumed jurisdiction. Ewing is careful to distinguish between fact and inference,
and I discovered only one factual mistake. He reported that
the Selden exoneration was published in November 1922 and
the indictment of the federal grand jury followed closely in

answer to it. The exoneration was in fact published in December 1921 in the *Tacoma Ledger* and subsequently issued in pamphlet form by the defense. Ewing can hardly be blamed for this mistake, however; the pamphlet is erroneously dated 1922—apparently a printer's error.

Nevertheless, despite their essential fairness Ewing's eight articles produced an effect harmful to the defense. The clash in testimony between the case as seen by Rosenbluth and as seen by Cronkhite produce in the reader a solid conviction there is *something* here that needs further explanation. This is essentially the position taken by the grand jury. As Revelle's letter made clear, the jury agreed it would not convict on the evidence it had heard but was so puzzled by the conflicts in testimony that it insisted further investigation was necessary.

Ewing's final chapter reached no conclusions. It ended with this comment: "Prosecuted murderer? Persecuted martyr? Accident? Willful murder? The answers to all of these questions, the government insists, can come only through a trial of Rosenbluth and Pothier—a trial now only a remote possibility so far as the immediate future is concerned."[37] This presentation of the case probably helped in some degree to encourage the department's decision later in the year not to abandon the extended struggle.

There continued to be signs, however, within the government that everyone was becoming tired of the case. Attorney Hayward wrote to Crim after Rosenbluth had been released by Commissioner Hitchcock:

> I have announced to the papers simply that I would await instructions from the Department, that the Government could not appeal but could re-arrest for hearing before a judge. The case was thoroughly prepared and presented by this office, and there would be many a dry eye hereabouts if no further proceedings eventuated.[38]

But apparently no way existed for matters to be dropped gracefully. By the spring of 1923 the department could not abandon the case without appearing to yield to the pressure of Jewish groups. A factor here in all probability was the growing popularity of Henry Ford as a candidate for president, which in the spring of 1923 was "causing deep concern to Democrats and anxiety to Republicans." A poll in *Colliers* gave Ford an 8 to 5 lead over Harding, and the *New York Times* considered him "a powerful and enigmatic figure on the political horizon."[39] The emergence of Ford as a rival for Harding interlocked with the Rosenbluth case. Ford's allegations in the

Dearborn Independent would be "proved" for many Americans if the Justice Department failed to press its case.

The decision of Federal Judge Brown to hold Pothier for removal to Tacoma was appealed, and after a series of delays greatly acerbating to General Cronkhite, the U.S. circuit court of appeals sitting in Boston reversed Brown's decision and ordered Pothier released. Agreeing with Marshall and others, the court held that the federal government had no jurisdiction over the alleged offense. Once again, it appeared that the matter would be dropped. Crim sidetracked the increasingly hysterical General Cronkhite by suggesting he take up the problem with Solicitor General James Beck, who had no knowledge of the case and was about to leave for Europe; the resultant exchange of letters kept the general occupied for nearly a month before he was passed back to Crim for information.

In the meantime a decision was necessary on whether or not to appeal the circuit court's decision to the Supreme Court. The initial reaction was negative. Replying to an inquiry from Attorney Case in Providence, Crim said, "I do not contemplate taking a writ of *certiorari* in this matter." Another letter of inquiry from Attorney Hayward in New York received a similar reply: "I do not believe the Government will seek a review of this case in the Supreme Court."[40] Some news of this attitude leaked to the press, and the *Baltimore Sun* published a statement that the government intended to drop the case. Crim wrote at once to Case, making it clear that his earlier letter had expressed his personal opinion only and the Solicitor General might well decide to ask for a review of the decision upon his return from Europe.

This uncertainty in July 1923 greatly alarmed General Cronkhite and his friends; his lawyer, Colonel Wise, wrote to Crim, strongly urging that the case be reviewed. This step, Wise argued, was the only way to prove that the government's interest in the case was more than lukewarm:

> You are, no doubt, aware that heretofore you have been charged with being arbitrary and vindictive in your pursuit of the accused. As I told you upon hearing it the absurd statement was made to me that you had actually directed the verdict of the Grand Jury. It is apparent, of course, from what source such absurdity emanated. . . . But it is not the truth but what comes to be believed that must be guarded against, and at present the conviction is being cultivated in the public mind that you are responsible for the dropping of the case in order to make it appear that the most partisan supporter of the Government's case against the accused has accepted their alleged innocence as a fact.

Wise concluded by mentioning the threatened congressional investigation being urged by Democratic Senator Carter Glass. The political implications are clear. If the department did not seek a Supreme Court review, the impression would be created that it had yielded to pressure, thus giving an exceedingly useful weapon to the opposition party—already too well supplied with ammunition—or to an alternate Republican candidate.[41]

Crim's reply assured Wise that he would await the return of the Solicitor General for a final decision. He also expressed very great indignation at General Cronkhite's behavior:

> Your client, General Cronkhite, has been advised of this re-peatedly. However, he insisted on calling me on the telephone every few days and repeating silly gossip as to what the Government was doing, or would not do in the case, and when I told him there was no truth to such gossip, he undertook to argue with me that he was being advised by people who knew just as much law as I, and who knew just as much about the facts as I. Now, I have a great deal of sympathy for General Cronkhite, but I cannot permit my sympathy for General Cronkhite to allow him to run my office, to call me on the telephone at any time he desires from his hotel in Baltimore, and insult me. The last time he did it I had him cut off, and I do not want him to call me on the telephone again under any circumstances. I do not want him to see me again about this case.[42]

Crim concluded by a flat statement that the case was now in the hands of the Solicitor General, but if that official wanted his views, he would give them regardless of others' opinions. He seems to be implying that he was not in favor of asking for a review of the case. Despite the fact that Crim was personally responsible for pushing the case and appeared to be convinced that the accused men were guilty, the general was becoming increasingly certain that the case was being deliberately stalled. He was particularly outraged to discover in August that Major Zajicek had been ordered to the Philippines after several years of delay.

In August Solicitor General Beck returned from Europe and began at once to inquire into the Rosenbluth case. A memorandum prepared for him on August 20 by Attorney George Hull sketched the various stages of the case and concluded that the federal government did not have jurisdiction. He suggested, however, that the Supreme Court should be asked to rule; a murder appeared to have been committed and no guilty parties had been brought to trial. Since the matter was in the federal courts, it should be finally decided there. Hull's reference to the state courts displayed the misunderstanding within the Justice Department about the case and implied that the files were incomplete:

> It appears from the file that two years ago this Department expressed the opinion that the defendant should be tried in the State courts and the facts were laid before the Prosecuting Attorney of the proper district court in the state of Washington. For reasons not appearing, he declined to act.[43]

This last statement misrepresents the situation rather seriously, since it implies that Selden had been given all the available evidence and further shows that the files did not contain any readily available material explaining why he had declined to act. Hull, who up to this time had no recorded connection with the case, was unable to explain the attorney's failure to prosecute.

Efforts were made by Rosenbluth's friends to challenge the published impression that the state of Washington denied jurisdiction and had declined to prosecute. Professor Chapman of the Yale Forest School Alumni Association corresponded with Selden on the matter and wrote to the Solicitor General, enclosing Selden's letters. Although admittedly not speaking as a lawyer, Chapman argued that Selden's letters showed he did not have all the evidence at his disposal and had not refused to try the case. Chapman also expressed concern over the proceedings against Pothier, feeling that to consider the jurisdictional issue in his case rather than in Rosenbluth's helped to suggest that Ford's allegations about Jewish pressure groups were true. In a second letter Chapman protested that the failure to take Rosenbluth before a district court judge (in contrast to the hearings accorded Pothier) left him unrepresented in a legal decision which affected him seriously. Beck's reply assured Chapman that the government was anxious to have the case fully argued and would be happy to permit Louis Marshall to appear in Rosenbluth's behalf.[44]

As the year of 1923 drew to a close, preparations had been made to argue the case before the Supreme Court. Pothier's attorney, Davis Arnold, was attempting to abandon what was for him an increasingly tiresome and unrewarding case and wished to turn the matter over to Louis Marshall. Marshall declined "the embarrassment of appearing on the record as counsel for Pothier," and asked for permission to enter the case as "a friend of the court" and to submit an oral argument. General Cronkhite, still certain that the case had never been properly argued, entered Attorney Jesse Adkins as a "friend of the court" also. The hearing was delayed several times to permit the various attorneys to construct their briefs.

Before the Supreme Court met, however, an event took place which appeared to alter the total situation sharply. President Harding had died in August of 1923, and Coolidge had become his successor. He was at once besieged by requests that Attorney General Daugherty be asked to resign. By this time Republicans as well as Democrats were concerned at the growing rumors of scandal. Republican senators Lodge and Pepper visited the President to ask that he dismiss Daugherty and Secretary of the Navy Denby; when they did not succeed, the Senate passed a formal motion requesting their removal. However, Coolidge remained indifferent to this pressure and took no immediate action. In his topical novel, *Revelry,* a very thinly disguised picture of the years of normalcy, Samuel Hopkins Adams has created a character, Senator Thorne (Lodge), who describes what will happen now that the president is dead:

> Vice-President Elliott, [Coolidge], who has about as much sentiment as a cucumber, but understands well the political value of the sympathetic sob, will announce that any Cabinet good enough for his martyred predecessor is good enough for him. That saves the Cabinet situation. The Welling [Wheeler] investigation will go on, but whenever and wherever it approaches Willis Markham [Harding], it will sheer off, leaving loose ends which nobody will be brutal enough to take up. Lurcock's [Daugherty] activities will be forgiven because he was a friend of the martyr. Gandy's [Fall] graft will be forgotten for the same reason. Free pardons for all the Crow's Nest Crowd. Their graft is over, but their skins are safe. The Party is rescued on the brink of the worst scandal since Grant.[45]

This is essentially what did occur, although some commentators speak more symphathetically of Coolidge's reasons for delay. Coolidge did not pursue investigation of party scandals nor did he ask for the resignations of Denby and Daugherty until the end of March 1924. By this time, Daugherty was under investigation at last by a Senate committee. The motion to inquire into the scandals of the Justice Department was initiated by Burton Wheeler, junior senator from Montana; the resulting committee was chaired by Smith Brookhart of Iowa. Before Daugherty resigned, however, he moved against the man who had attacked him. Wheeler found himself indicted by a federal grand jury in Montana on charges of having used his senatorial position illegally in behalf of private clients. In a speech made in Wheeler's defense, Senator Heflin of Alabama described Daugherty's tactics:

> I imagine I can hear Daugherty telephoning the district attorney, whom he had appointed, and saying, "I want this man Wheeler indicted; I do not know whether you can convict him or not; I do not care; but I want to besmirch him; I want to hang an indictment over his head; I want to hamper him in this

investigation; I want to hurt him; and I want to destroy him, if I can!"[46]

That the charges were designed to embarrass the Wheeler committee and had no basis in fact was convincingly demonstrated later. Senator Wheeler was proved overwhelmingly innocent at his subsequent trial, the only witness brought against him being proved a perjurer.

Rosenbluth believes that his case and Senator Wheeler's are essentially parallel: The decision to reverse the jurisdictional ruling and to take the case before a federal grand jury was made in reprisal for his demand for a formal exoneration from the Justice Department. From my study of the files on the affair, I am inclined to believe something more was involved, since the decision to resume jurisdiction was being made in October–November 1921, before the Selden exoneration appeared. But I completely agree that Rosenbluth's persistence and his refusal to slip back into private life quietly had a decided effect upon the department's attitude. Certainly this kept the case alive and eventually produced a situation from which the government literally could not afford to back down without appearing in a most unfavorable light.

In any event, Coolidge used the Wheeler investigation as an excuse for asking for Daugherty's resignation. His letter in no way cast doubt on Daugherty's integrity or actions, but argued that he could not function as Attorney General while actually under investigation. To replace him, Coolidge appointed the dean of the Columbia Law School, Harlan Fiske Stone. Stone, a man of high reputation and unquestioned character, did not remain Attorney General long, but during his term of office he vastly improved the functioning of the Justice Department. Among other major changes, he removed William Burns as head of the Bureau of Investigation and appointed J. Edgar Hoover to replace him. In addition, Stone asked "through channels" (I am told by Rosenbluth) what they wanted done with the Rosenbluth case. The defense lawyers replied that they wanted the case brought to a speedy trial. Whether or not that request had any influence upon the Supreme Court decision is impossible to judge. But the fact remains that the decision handed down made a trial necessary.

On April 7, 1924, the Supreme Court ruled that the question of jurisdiction would have to be determined in the court appointed to try the case, the United States District Court of the Western District of Washington. This court held that a decision of this kind could not be made as a result of a "habeas corpus" action, since this made the court a substitute for a trial jury. The case, as a result, was handed back to the district court, and Rosenbluth and Pothier were ordered to Tacoma for trial.

CHAPTER NINE
TRIAL
APRIL 1924-
OCTOBER 1924

As soon as the Supreme Court decision was announced, the Justice Department was busy with plans for an immediate trial. The question of jurisdiction was still an issue since the court had ruled on procedure only. Solicitor General Beck, in a memorandum on the case written April 19, expressed the opinion that he expected the defendants to demur to the indictment and raise the question of jurisdiction. "Indeed, as the question of jurisdiction is not free from doubt, this would seem to me desirable."[1] He was anxious that the lawyer given the case be both competent and confident and had been told that attorney Revelle had expressed doubts about the case.

Writing to the Justice Department on April 15, Revelle again stated his objections as he had after the grand jury decision:

> This case has given me a great deal of concern. Everyone who has had anything to do with the case except my former assistant and myself feel that these men are guilty of the crime alleged. I, personally, examined approximately eighty witnesses before the Grand Jury. I was forced, from the evidence, to have grave doubts as to the entire matter.

After describing his doubts and the great difficulty of presenting a convincing case to the jury, notwithstanding the opinion of many department officials that the two were guilty, he raised the problem of unfortunate publicity: "However, I have been concerned about the reflection upon the Department of Justice and also the reflection it might have had upon the former Attorney General."[2] In a second letter about a week later Revelle regretfully admitted he would prefer to have another attorney assigned to the case and urged that the man chosen be skilled in criminal cases involving homicide. He also suggested that Special Agent Chastain be assigned to the case again for the trial.[3]

While the department was arranging for a special attorney, the friends of Rosenbluth were urging that he also be tried *in forma pauperis,* since his financial position did not permit him to go to the heavy expense of calling witnesses on his own behalf. This arrangement was agreed to, and the government assumed responsibility for the entire expense of the trial. Simultaneously, General Cronkhite was bombarding the new Attorney General with special delivery letters, demanding personal interviews, and protesting that his letters to the Attorney General marked "personal" had been opened and answered by persons other than the addressee. In May he also sent the department a clipping from a Seattle paper, which stated that Pothier's attorney, Maurice Langhorne, and Revelle had met to discuss the jurisdictional question and were planning to raise it at once. Revelle denied any such arrangement, but the story did suggest that his doubts about the case were known outside his office, and this aspect of the case continued to annoy the general.

Jonah Goldstein continued his attempts to force an examination into the conduct of certain officials in the case, particularly agents Lee and Chastain. Assistant Attorney General Earl Davis asked for an investigation in May, and received a brief and unhelpful letter from J. Edgar Hoover. He explained that the bureau files containing reports from Lee and Chastain were not there, having been charged to Crim in 1923. Hoover quoted Herron's opinion on the hearing given Rosenbluth in June 1921, indicating that the charges against the department had not been proved. "From such information as I have been able to obtain it appears that this investigation was directed and handled exclusively by Mr. Herron up to the time of his death and the Agents working on this case worked directly under his instructions." Hoover expressed his opinion that Chastain, now U.S. assistant attorney in Atlanta, was considered an able and efficient employee. In regard to Lee, Hoover said only that he had left the bureau on October 27, 1921. Agent Billups Harris is not mentioned at all in Hoover's letter.[4]

It is perhaps significant that the file containing the agents' reports went to Crim's office in 1923. Crim may have ascertained the actual background of the case at this time. In 1923 Crim was warned by Cronkhite's lawyer that failure to ask for a Supreme Court review would lead to charges that he—once a strong supporter of the case—had developed doubts about it. Crim's reply and other letters on the matter reveal his personal lack of interest in carrying the case to the Supreme Court; he passed the matter on to the Solicitor General for a decision. Crim's sudden loss of interest may imply his discovery that there was no case against Rosenbluth. But if Crim did indeed realize that the government's handling of the affair had been gravely in error, he did not comment publicly on it. He resigned from the department without making any criticism, and he testified very vigorously in support of Daugherty's personal honesty before the Brookhart-Wheeler committee in 1924. Perhaps his personal loyalty to his chief prevented him from exposing the construction of the case.

Whatever the truth of the matter, obviously no clear answer was going to emerge. The files were not in the Bureau of Investigation, and the bureau claimed to have little information of any other kind. Almost all the persons closely associated with the earlier stages of the case were unavailable. Herron was dead; Burns, Lee, and Chastain were no longer employees of the bureau; Crim had resigned from the department; the personnel of the Providence office no longer included Cannon and Richards; and Billups Harris had vanished. While there is little doubt that the whole chain of circumstance was begun by the free-wheeling researches of Agent Lee and the complete lack of control exercised over his investigations and procedures, it was far too late to alter them, nor could Lee be penalized as a private citizen.

Rosenbluth made one last effort in June 1924 to reveal the conspiracy that had produced the case against him. In a lengthy affidavit he listed the witnesses he considered necessary for his defense: Sixty-five men and officers familiar with the details of Major Cronkhite's death or with Rosenbluth's military reputation, and forty-one other persons who could testify either to Rosenbluth's character or to the government's handling of the case. His list included most of the Bureau of Investigation agents who had worked on the case, as well as more famous names: John Weeks; W. J. Burns; Harry Daugherty; John Crim; Dr. Katherine Bement Davis, Herbert Hoover; Norman Thomas; Julius Barnes; Henry Ford; Gifford Pinchot, governor of Pennsylvania; and Lewis Lawes, subsequently warden of Sing Sing Prison.[5]

A later affidavit, however, modified this request:

> I am advised by my attorney and I believe that it will be unnecessary to summon those witnesses to establish a conspiracy to obtain my indictment and conviction, because I believe and hope that with the change of administration in the Department of Justice all efforts heretofore made to manufacture a case against me will no longer continue; if the methods and conspiracy inaugurated prior to my indictment should continue during the trial, I will then make further application to this Court for subpoenaing witnesses enumerated under Group 5 for the purpose of establishing such unlawful conspiracy to obtain the indictment against me.[6]

At the end of May, Earl Davis, Crim's successor as head of the criminal division, appointed James Osborne—a government attorney then engaged with cases in Oklahoma and special assistant to the Attorney General—to act as prosecutor at the trial. It is perhaps noteworthy that the attorneys originally suggested for this post had not agreed to take it. Earlier in the month, Davis had suggested to Assistant Attorney General Holland that either Hiram C. Todd or Arthur H. Sager, both special assistants to the Attorney General, be asked to conduct the Pothier-Rosenbluth trial. Davis laid considerable stress upon the need for an outstanding prosecutor and seemed anxious that Todd be selected.[7] Todd, however, declined to act; his reasons for refusing cannot be ascertained, since his reply is not in the file. But it seems possible that attorneys attached to the department in Washington were reluctant to handle a case which they knew was weak.

On July 8 he wired Attorney General Stone that Judge Cushman had set September 30 as the date for Pothier's trial and had granted a severance of the two cases "after argument." Thus the two defendants—arrested, charged, and indicted together—were to be tried separately. Another series of telegrams inquiring about the arrival time of Chastain suggest Osborne's growing concern about the weakness of the government's case. On July 17 four separate requests went to Washington: for the loan of pistols similar to ones allegedly used in the crime, for a copy of Adkins's (Cronkhite's attorney) brief, for all the records from the Providence office so that he might find the documents he needed, and for a written report from Agent Navarro concerning an alleged conversation with Pothier in which he voluntarily confessed.[9]

Osborne, however, was unaware of what was in store and expressed his hearty pleasure in the assignment, thanking Davis for the opportunity to try a case that he had heard of "for some five or six or more years."[8] As soon as Osborne arrived in Tacoma and began to study the evidence, he asked at once that Chastain be sent west to assist him. The deluge of wires that followed suggest that Osborne was rapidly becoming doubtful about the case he had been so eager to begin. In addition to the bulky files of documents forwarded to him from the attorneys in New York and Providence, he requested an increasingly large amount of particular information: the briefs of all of the lawyers who studied the jurisdictional question, the reports of Agent Navarro, and other materials.

On July 22 Osborne wrote to Assistant Attorney General Ridgeley in Washington, explaining in a postscript that he was using a pen because he did not wish "to have my stenographer know that I have anything but the utmost faith in the government's case." The body of the letter does not attack the case directly, although Osborne's doubts of it are clearly implied; he was concerned with the jurisdiction question. He explained he had expressed the opinion in Washington that the government had jurisdiction but this was based on "facts" given him by Revelle, which had proved untrue. Osborne feared that Judge Cushman would dismiss the case at once, and thus "the thought of expending for witnesses the thousands of dollars necessary seems little short of criminal." He believed that the defense could raise the question in September, before the witnesses had begun to travel, and such a question should not be opposed by the government. ". . . my conscience worries me about putting the government to the seemingly unnecessary expense." On August 26 he explained his position further. He had been under the impression that Pierce County had had a deed drawn up but the War Department had refused it, preferring to wait until all the land was available. But he discovered in Tacoma that no deed had been drawn or offered; the War Department had suggested it be postponed until after the entire transaction was completed. In Osborne's opinion the lack of an actual deed until a year after the major's death made it impossible for the government to claim exclusive jurisdiction.

The same day Osborne reported that Pothier's attorney had filed a petition asking for a bill of particulars of the place of death, a move which would lead to a demurrer and the raising of the jurisdictional question before the trial began. Osborne requested that the attorney's petition be unopposed, and the opportunity taken to settle the question before all the witnesses had begun to travel. Langhorne, however, withdrew his request a week later, and Osborne regretfully informed Washington that a way to prevent the trial no longer existed.

Once again the department was faced with the enormous expense of bringing Captain Jones and Dr. Schultze from New York to Tacoma and back, their total charges at $100 and $250 per day vastly increased by the fact that the accused would be tried separately and the span of time covered could not be less than two weeks. The expense sheet was passed to a subordinate for investigation, accompanied by an anguished handwritten note: "Have we ever paid any such fees to anybody?" But once again, it was clear that the two experts had the government backed against a wall; without their testimony the case had no chance.

Meanwhile frantic efforts were being made to find the wandering tobacco can or cans and the four empty shells allegedly found at the scene. After considerable expenditure in telegrams they were located in Seattle, where they had been sent two years before. Great pressure was put on the War Department to produce the written statements taken at the base hospital; Osborne's telegrams make it clear he believed the department was simply not trying very hard, but in spite of all efforts the statements were not located.

On September 9 Attorney General Stone wired Osborne to ask the reason for the severance, and to ascertain why he had not been in touch with General Cronkhite as planned. Osborne's reply was a revealing one:

> without Pothier as witness Government has absolutely no case against Rosenbluth and were both tried together impossible to escape direction of verdict in favor Rosenbluth and endanger chance of success as to Pothier. . . . was under impression Cronkhite was to communicate with me as to time of conference have heard nothing from him. Do not believe General Cronkhite has additional information as for past three years he has been constantly urged by Department to furnish all information. . . .

By this stage, however, General Cronkhite was clearly beyond reasonable behavior. His confusion is illustrated by correspondence with Assistant Attorney General Donovan. The general had demanded a list of witnesses subpoenaed for the trial so that he could be sure all essential ones had been called. He was provided with a list, delivered by telegram from Tacoma, and immediately expostulated angrily that the list was incomplete—many names he had wanted called were not included. Donovan politely reminded him that the list had been sent to him so that he could add names to it. The general, however, was unable to comprehend the situation and continued to protest about the handling of the case. Despite repeated reminders he did not submit a list of additional witnesses but continued to express his conviction that Osborne was secretly working to secure an acquittal.

As late as September 30, the day the trial began, Donovan wrote once more to the general in Baltimore, asking him to submit the names of any needed witnesses. He added:

> Mrs. Cronkhite talked with me over the telephone today and made some very serious charges against Osborne. When I questioned her on these, she was unable to be definite. As the Attorney General told you, if you have definite charges to make against Mr. Osborne, they should be submitted.[10]

Donovan then warned the general to leave for Tacoma to appear at the trial. The general promptly sent a lengthy wire to the Attorney General, reminding him of his assurance that if positive evidence could be presented that the case was being mishandled and Osborne was not prepared to give the case a full and fair hearing, Stone would at once remove him and appoint a new attorney. The general's position was simple: he had already presented the department with this evidence and naturally expected that the trial would be delayed while Osborne was being replaced!

Meanwhile, Osborne was becoming alarmed at the general's failure to appear. He was essential to the case in one way: Only he could testify to the fact that his son's body was the one examined by Dr. Schultze in the second autopsy. Osborne inquired, "Shall I have attachment issued for him resulting inevitably in wide publicity of his idiosyncrasies and attitude toward prosecution?" On October 4 Stone wired Osborne that the general was leaving for Tacoma, having been delayed by his wife's illness. The same day, Cronkhite sent a three-page telegram to Stone, still determined that Stone act to halt the trial and remove Osborne. He could not understand his own errors and omissions and did not, in fact, appear at the trial. The necessary identification of his son's body was handled through a written affidavit. His only "assistance" during the trial itself was another angry letter demanding that the government force Rosenbluth to plead guilty; the published "not guilty" plea outraged the general, who was by this time clearly beyond rational judgment.

While the combined efforts of the officials of the Department of Justice in Washington were being employed in a futile struggle to have General Cronkhite and his wife appear at the trial, the forces of the defense and the prosecution began to assemble in Tacoma. Rosenbluth and Goldstein arrived on September 23 and gave a brief interview to the press, praising their fairness and expressing conviction that a verdict of innocent would be reached. Excitement in Tacoma was high as the trial date drew near. Not only had the original accident occurred nearby, but the case had received national attention for almost four years and was probably the most exciting affair the courts had handled there in many years.

Newspapers in Seattle and Tacoma speculated excitedly about the probable legal tangles the trial would produce. It was predicted that it would take days to select a jury, and 200 extra veniremen were called to meet the expected demand for alternates. Space problems in the courtroom were dealt with to take care of the more than eighty witnesses and the expected crowds of spectators and reporters who were attracted by what the *New York Times* called "one of the most remarkable criminal cases in American jurisprudence." Testimony from the principals—Pothier, Rosenbluth, and General Cronkhite—was eagerly awaited by the press and public, while legal authorities anticipated a battle to determine the jurisdiction question once and for all. More than anything else, perhaps, those interested in the long-drawn-out struggle hoped that at last all doubts and questions would finally be resolved. The reality, however, turned out to be somewhat disappointing.

"Rosenbluth Reaches City
To Fight Charge of Murder"
headlines this 1924 picture
in the **Tacoma Ledger.**

II

IN A TRIAL held six years after the death in question, it was natural for the defense to attempt to avoid underlining conflicts of memory and honest mistakes and for the prosecution to attempt to exaggerate them; each side was concerned to win, not to uncover a "truth" already overshadowed by time and the frailty of human memory. In addition to the time problem, Pothier was tried first. This meant that in effect Rosenbluth was on trial with him, since any testimony in the first trial might be useful in the second, and there were obvious dangers in undue openness at Pothier's trial. This is not to suggest there was anything serious to conceal; but the many muddles and conflicts of the case were capable of producing the effect that *someone* had done *something* wrong. Juries are notoriously unpredictable; innocent men have been found guilty of crimes they did not commit because of the prejudices of the judge or jury or careless handling of the defense.

Pothier's trial began on September 30. The case for the prosecution was handled by James Osborne and Thomas Revelle and for the defense by Maurice Langhorne, assisted by L. L. Thompson, a former attorney general in the state of Washington. Thompson also expected to represent Rosenbluth at the second trial. Contrary to excited press reports on the length of time needed to select a jury, the attorneys agreed to a panel on the first day. Langhorne questioned jurors about their racial and religious prejudices, and Osborne objected to the inclusion of World War I veterans. Osborne also asked the jurors one by one if they would ask for the death penalty on circumstantial evidence. Attorney Langhorne inquired if the prosecution's evidence was indeed entirely circumstantial and was told it was; Osborne was prepared to consider Pothier's confessions as circumstantial evidence.

The opening speeches of the two attorneys hinted at the probable direction of the trial. Osborne stressed the impossibility of a self-inflicted wound and offered as a motive a quarrel between Rosenbluth and Cronkhite. The jury then was taken to the scene of the major's death, a spot marked by a small monument, and ate lunch at Camp Lewis—for which the Justice Department was later presented with a bill. In the afternoon, Attorney Langhorne opened for the defense, stressing the total lack of motive or real proof that the men had been unfriendly. The attention paid by both attorneys to relationships between Rosenbluth and Cronkhite showed how difficult the severance was going to make the case. Since no one had ever suggested that Pothier might have shot the major for reasons of his own, obviously murder could be proved only if it could be shown that Pothier had fired at the command of Rosenbluth.

The first witness called by the prosecution was Captain Will R. White of the Camp Lewis Quartermaster Corps, who testified about the exact location and position of the death scene. He was followed by the sergeants whose testimony before the grand jury has already been examined—George Root, Jr., of Seattle, and Charles Wuthenow of New York City. The newspapers whose reports of the trial have been examined give heavy coverage to Root's testimony, since it produced the first excitement of the trial. Again the issue was the puzzling matter of the condition of the weapon and the dropped shells. "From the lips of an unwilling witness, a former army buddy of Roland R. Pothier, came the first bit of sensational testimony against the defendant yesterday in federal court. . . ." Root's apparent unwillingness to testify is difficult to explain. His testimony before the grand jury had shown he was not a "buddy" of Pothier's but had strongly disliked and distrusted him. Root had believed from the beginning that Pothier had actually shot the major—he was the sergeant who reported his suspicions to Lieutenant Miller and Major Tucker at the time of the accident. Root believed that Pothier's shot was accidental, and may have been reluctant to testify in a way that might result in Pothier's or Rosenbluth's conviction for murder.

After Root's examination by the prosecution, Attorney Langhorne asked him directly, "Why is it that you can so distinctly remember picking up two exploded shells near the body of Major Cronkhite and one or two more near where Pothier was standing, and yet you cannot remember whether or not the gun of Major Cronkhite contained any exploded shells?" Root replied, "If I were you I would not ask that question, but if you really want to know I will tell you." Langhorne, warned off by this reply, shifted his line of attack to the question of Root's exact duties in the Intelligence Section. Finally, unable to avoid the question indefinitely, Root declared that to the best of his recollection there were no exploded shells in the Cronkhite gun. After Langhorne had finished, Osborne again attacked the witness, demanding to know why he had warned the defense attorney about asking certain questions.

> Visibly agitated by the insistent questions of both attorneys, Root whirled in his chair and created a sensation. "Well, I'll explain it this way. I want to get out of this case as quickly as I can and give as little information as possible because I am afraid my testimony might be damaging to the defendant and I don't wish it to be."

The *Tacoma Ledger* printed a long section of Root's examination, and several points are of interest. In his description of the attempts to assist the major, he said he had helped the doctor prepare the strychnine solution, and the injection was given before the bullet wound was discovered. He also stated that Wuthenow discovered the wound only after he removed the major's shirt in order to move his arms more freely while giving him artificial respiration. This detail suggests that the wound was genuinely inconspicuous and the failure of Rosenbluth or Seaburg to notice it at once was not surprising.

In response to a question about Rosenbluth's tone of voice—the defense had to establish that the conversation could have been heard by Pothier—Root replied, "He used the tone of a man much grieved at the loss of a friend." Pressed about the condition of the gun, he replied, "I have been trying to remember that for the last six years, but my memory is hazy on that point. I would prefer not to answer the question because I am not sure." He also admitted in cross-examination that the gun used was his, had been fired, and had an easy action, although he denied that the trigger had been filed or tampered with.[11]

No explanation was ever made about the dropped shells

Root alleged he had picked up at the scene. No other witness, at least in any recorded form, testified to having seen Root hunting for the shells or discovering them, nor was any attempt made to explain how or why they had been ejected from the revolver.

Wuthenow had earlier called amused attention to himself by asking that the windows be closed, since he was wearing silk socks and did not wish to risk a cold. He testified more briefly, mentioning that he had been shown a scratch on the gatepost and was told it was a bullet mark.[12]

On Thursday, October 2, the officers were examined. Colonel Robert Thomas created a mild sensation by stating that the grand jury record of his testimony had been altered. He was particularly insistent that he had been shown two tobacco cans at that time and had been asked to choose between them. Both Revelle and Chastain, who had conducted the grand jury hearing, denied that more than one can had been in use. The Colonel was correct here; the grand jury transcript makes clear that he was shown two cans. Thomas also insisted that the major's coat was withheld from Mrs. Cronkhite at his order. Doctor Tucker and Lieutenant Colonel Howard repeated their previous conflicting statements about the powder marks, Tucker standing by his statement to the board of inquiry and Howard denying that marks of any kind were visible.

The base hospital autopsy physician, Dr. E. A. Sommer, was also questioned. Osborne's handling of this witness was clearly designed to cast doubt on his accuracy and intelligence, as an examination of the exchange shows:

> In response to Osborne's questions as to where the bullet entered, Dr. Sommer, like several others, indicated a spot slightly above his right breast. "Describe it," Osborne insisted. "Three inches from the right breast on a line drawn from the point of the breast to the greater tuberosity of the right humorus," replied the physician. "I asked you to tell us where the bullet entered," Osborne retorted icily. "I just told you, Between the right breast and the greater tuberosity of the right humorus," Sommer replied. "Spell it," the attorney insisted. The physician hesitated and it became apparent that the attorney had scored. The court reporter helped the doctor out, however. . . .

A little later Osborne rejected the term "sternum," and had the doctor substitute "breastbone" in his remarks. At another point of the examination, Osborne handed Sommer two documents, apparently autopsy reports, and asked him to read them to refresh his memory. After reading them, Sommer began to say that it seemed to him there was something left out, but the attorney interrupted him with: "I am not in the least concerned about that. Does it refresh your memory?"[13]

It is obvious from this exchange that Osborne was trying in every possible way to make Sommer appear pompous and unreliable—not a difficult task for an attorney skilled in cross-examination. For example, his demand that Sommer "spell it" naturally produced hesitation, since the doctor could not be sure which of the two medical terms, tuberosity or humerus, he was being asked to spell. The business of the two reports and the questions about the doctor's memory appear designed to cast doubt on his accuracy. Osborne appeared from his letters and telegrams to be a hard-working and intelligent man who was good at his job. His descent into this sort of trick would seem to suggest his desperation, his recognition of the fact that the government was almost certain to lose its case.

Following Sommer's testimony Dr. George Kreutz of Saint Louis testified that he had loaned his gun, a .45 Smith and Wesson, to Pothier and the ammunition for it had been in a saddlebag over his bunk. He did not recall whether he had procured the gun himself or whether Pothier had gone to the barracks for it. Dr. Seaburg, the physician who had assisted Major Cronkhite at the death scene, was handicapped in his testimony because of his inability to recall Pothier's whereabouts during most of the episode. Since testimony about conversations unheard by Pothier could not be admitted as evidence, most of the doctor's testimony was thrown out as inadmissible.

The confusion about the can and shells was testified to by a variety of officers. The regimental adjutant, Captain H. M. Whiting who had not been at Camp Lewis at the time of the major's death, testified that he could not recall what had been done with the can and shells or with the various records concerning the major's death. As a result of this and other testimony the court finally directed the jury not to consider any of the various exhibits—can, shells, revolvers—as authentic. Other exhibits were demonstrated as having been lost: Dr. Sommer did not remember what had become of the bullet taken from the body; the major's uniform had been destroyed.

Also called that day was ex-sergeant James Crook, who contradicted the previous testimony of Root and Wuthenow. Crook maintained that Rosenbluth was in plain sight when the shots began but was disappearing into the brush by the time of the second shot. The earlier witnesses said, as they had before the grand jury, that Rosenbluth was out of sight ahead of the column before the shooting started.

This day's testimony was not seriously damaging to either defendant; the mixups of the exhibits and the brevity of the board of inquiry could not be blamed on either Pothier or Rosenbluth. Unless the government attempted to prove the existence of a deliberate attempt to cover up a crime, presumably to protect either one or both of the defendants or to conceal a plot, the testimony about the missing exhibits really led nowhere. All the prosecution could do, since it could not show a full-scale plot, was to mystify the jury, to arouse suspicions, and to hope that this jury, like the previous one, would move from mystery to an actual verdict of guilty.

On Friday, October 3, the prosecution began to call the government officials who had worked with Pothier in Providence following his initial arrest. Agent in Charge Thomas J. Callaghan of the Bureau of Investigation there provided some dramatic moments during his cross-examination by defense attorney Langhorne:

Q. Do you believe the shooting of the major accidental?
A. Yes.
Q. You don't believe he was killed intentionally?
A. No.
Q. You believe then that Pothier accidentally killed the Major?
A. Yes.
Q. Do you believe that now?
A. Yes.
Q. And you don't believe that Rosenbluth put him up to it, do you?
A. No.[14]

Callaghan, with Lee and Captain Jones, worked with Pothier to produce his first confession of accidental shooting. His statement was important, since it came from an official on the government side of the case and because the statute of limitations prevents a verdict of manslaughter or accidental homicide more than three years after the accident in question. Since six years had passed, Pothier could not be convicted on this count.

Callaghan's testimony also shows something else. If he is truthful in his statement that he never had believed the death was anything but an accident, then the further confessions obtained from Pothier by Lee were considered untrue by the agent in charge at the time of Rosenbluth's arrest. That Callaghan did not at the time interfere strongly suggests that he, like U.S. Attorney Cannon, was reluctant to do so. He had no authority over Lee, who took his orders from Washington; the local authorities were in a position to know what was going on and to judge it but were so placed that interference was difficult.

Callaghan's opinion of the matter was given some support from the testimony of another of Pothier's interrogators, William Conley, a railroad detective. Conley visited Pothier three times, pretending to be an insurance agent interested in proving the suicide story true so as to cancel a policy. Pothier stuck to his original story in the first two interviews, but at the third Conley managed to make him a trifle nervous:

> "I told him," Conley continued, "that it was a matter of bread and butter with me and I would make a nice piece of money if I could get the truth." He replied that the only split he would get would be a trip to jail. I said this seemed to show that there was something wrong and if there was why couldn't he be a good fellow and tell me about it. He replied suddenly, "No matter how it was, it was all an accident, and they can't hang a man for an accident."[15]

After Pothier's various confessions were entered as evidence by the government, former U.S. attorney at Providence Peter C. Cannon was questioned. His replies were very similar to those for the grand jury; he repeatedly made it clear he had made every effort to shake Pothier in his story, that Pothier was not subjected to any harrassment or abuse under Cannon's questioning, and that he was urged to get a lawyer and permitted visits from his priest and family. Cannon's testimony was important since it affected the eventual decision of Judge Cushman about the validity of the confessions.

On Saturday, October 4, Brigadier General John J. Richards, formerly marshal at Providence, contradicted the previous testimony of Callaghan that Pothier had fired accidentally. He repeated the explanation he had made to the grand jury, explaining in detail why Pothier's story could not be true. He also reported that Pothier had stated the board of inquiry did not really want to inquire into the matter and they were all "in on it." Both he and Cannon repeated Pothier's statement about the major's campaign hat "clearing up everything," but they were not permitted to go on to explain their personal theories of what he had meant by his statement, as they did before the grand jury.

Cannon was recalled after Richards testified, and examined by Thompson, who worked hard at trying to show that Cannon had been unfair and had acted illegally in holding Pothier. Cannon grew visibly irritated by questions which seemed to challenge his judgment and motives. He replied to one such query, "He was at least guilty of gross carelessness in the handling of his gun after giving him the benefit of every possible doubt." When the defense asked him to substantiate the charge of careless handling and to show why the first confession, disbelieved by those who took it, had resulted in the holding of Pothier, Cannon said, "There were two outstanding reasons in his statement which justified such action. First he had borrowed the gun and obtained ammunition on the morning of the march. Second, that he did not load the gun until he entered the clearing where Major Cronkhite was." Pressed further to justify his decision, Cannon snapped, "A man with an innocent purpose does not borrow a gun and steal ammunition for it."[16]

It can be deduced that Cannon was a trifle uneasy about his part in the whole affair. His statements to the grand jury had previously clarified his strong suspicions about the way Pothier's later confessions had been obtained. He did not trust Agent Lee and appeared in no way anxious to involve Rosenbluth in the matter. It can be suspected, at least, that Cannon felt a degree of guilt for refusing to interfere at the time. His motive for refusing is perhaps implied in Richards' statement that the order to take Pothier to New York came directly from the Attorney General. Cannon was in the unhappy position of choosing between annoying his superiors or letting Pothier take his chances.

After a weekend break, court was resumed on Tuesday, October 7, with another series of government witnesses. Dr. Schultze and Captain Jones repeated their earlier testimony that the wound could not have been self-inflicted. James Lee told the prosecuting attorney that Pothier had said Rosenbluth "was like a snake and everyone thought he was a spy."[17] His cross-examination by Langhorne was very stormy, with a fight threatening to break out at any moment. Lee grew angry when Langhorne asked if it were true that he had "called Rosenbluth a ——— ——— liar,"[18] and later grew almost violent when asked if he had told Callaghan, "I'm being made the goat, and I may tell who ordered us to get Rosenbluth."[19] Lee, naturally enough, strenuously denied having said anything of the sort. One can only wish that he had been angry enough to identify the person meant.

Agents Hoeckley and Navarro of the Bureau of Investigation testified Pothier had stated before them and Deputy Marshal Jordan that he had killed the major at Rosenbluth's order. Jordan later contradicted this flatly, insisting he had never heard Pothier say anything of the kind, in the presence of the two agents or elsewhere. He also reported that Pothier once asked him if you could kill a man without murdering him—another bit of evidence to suggest that Pothier at least thought he had accidentally killed the Major.[20]

After a lengthy examination of J. T. S. Lyle, former president of the Tacoma Chamber of Commerce, concerning the details of the sale of Camp Lewis to the government, the prosecution concluded its case. Defense Attorney Langhorne promptly moved that the charges against the accused be dismissed and the confessions be stricken from the record. Langhorne based his motion to dismiss on the argument that no

Ready For Final Probe Into Major's Death

This **Tacoma Ledger** photo carries the following caption: "Principals in the great legal battles which will be fought out in Federal court here to determine responsibility for the death of Maj. Alexander Cronkhite. 1. Roland Pothier who goes on trial Monday for the murder of Maj. Cronkhite. 2. Monument erected on the site where Maj. Cronkhite died. 3. Robert Rosenbluth, whose trial for Maj. Cronkhite's murder is set for October 22. 4. Maj. Cronkhite. 5. Maurice Langhorne, attorney for Pothier. 6. L. L. Thompson, attorney for Rosenbluth. 7. James H. Osborne, named special prosecutor by the government. 8. Judge Edward E. Cushman, who will preside."

evidence had been introduced to corroborate any of the alleged confessions. He argued that the confessions themselves were inadmissible because they had been obtained through undue influence without caution or warning to the prisoner. He added that the defense challenge to the government's jurisdiction would be held until after the case was concluded.

Judge Cushman's ruling on these motions came as a surprise to the prosecution, as Osborne later admitted in a letter to the Attorney General. Cushman ruled to exclude only one of the confessions obtained by Agent Lee, but retained three others: the original confession of accidental shooting (which the defense had not attacked), the confession in which Pothier alleged that Rosenbluth had told him the morning of the hike to shoot the major, and the last one, in which he claimed that Rosenbluth had approached him several days earlier and planned the killing with him.* The judge's ruling was based primarily upon the testimony of Cannon and Richards. After remarking that Pothier had been repeatedly urged to alter his statements and the advantages of doing so had been pointed out to him, the judge explained

> that to exclude all confessions made subject to a first one would establish a dangerous precedent as cases might arise where an over-zealous questioner would violate the law in obtaining an original confession which would react against subsequent ones regardless of how careful those who obtained them were.

In reply to the second defense motion to dismiss charges on the ground that no evidence had been presented concerning the truth of these confessions, the judge allowed the prosecution to reopen its case and to recall Cannon and Richards to testify. Again, the judge ruled that their testimony proved Pothier had had ample opportunity to change his story when he was interviewed by Cannon and Richards and since he had not done so, the confessions were admissible evidence.[21]

On Thursday, October 10, the defense called Prosecuting Attorney Osborne as a witness and inquired if he had in his possession a photograph of Major Cronkhite which showed him in a contorted or unusual position. Osborne admitted he had a copy of the West Point yearbook snapshot showing Cronkhite "twisted up in knots" and turned this over to the defense. The star witness for the defense, however, was Captain Eugene Caffey, who had been brought from duty in the Canal

---

* There is some confusion in the record concerning the number of separate confessions. Selden's exoneration prints the three listed above. Apparently the second confession was preceded by an original one obtained by Lee which was not forwarded to Selden. This version, taken by Lee in a private interview with Pothier, is apparently the one the judge ruled to exclude.

ALEXANDER PENNINGTON CRONKHITE

CANAL ZONE, PANAMA

Appointed from Fifteenth District, New York

"Buddy"

Corporal, Sergeant; A.B., B.A.; Marksman; Hundredth Night (4).

*"Can wisely tell what hour o' day
The clock doth strike, by algebra"—Butler*

THIS hivey Dutchman traces his descent right back to that band which lured old Rip Van Winkle off into the mountains to bowl, and those early settlers from Holland had nothing on Bud when it comes to rolling the ball along. What he does, he does with all there is in him, whether it's keeping himself in the first section, pulling a goat through six exams, or twisting himself up into knots over in the wrestling room.

For several months after we entered, Buddy seemed to be among us in body only. His spirit was forever deserting him and journeying off to unknown spheres but whether to the realms of Cupid or to the Land of the Fourth Dimension we have never been able to discover. Probably both. It used to be the chief delight of the "D" Co. runts to watch for Bud to come down to parade in a full dress hat and white gloves when the formation was in overcoats.

Dutch's great hobby is argumentation. He will argufy on either side of any question that ever was propounded and will attempt with the same confidence to convince you of the superiority of Grant over Lee or to give you indisputable proof that a man can get out of step with himself.

"Once your friend, always your friend" is Buddy's motto and he's a friend worth while. The surest thing that we know about him is that if he sets out to do anything with his whole heart he will surely come across with the goods.

Major Cronkhite's page from **The Howitzer**, yearbook of the U.S. Military Academy at West Point, 1915, carries the contorted snapshot which became an important exhibit for the defense.

Zone to testify. Caffey and his friend Major Zajicek did not appear in a particularly favorable light at the grand jury session because of the elaborate inquiry into the possibility that they had interfered with witnesses. At the trial, however, this issue was not in question, and they were able to assist the defense dramatically.

Caffey's main contribution was his personal demonstration of the possibility of firing a revolver placed in his hand in the position necessary to duplicate the wound Major Cronkhite had received. He first explained the West Point style of target practice in which the shooter stands at a right angle to the target, extending his arm and sighting down it, then bringing the weapon up sharply after the shot. He also testified to the fact that it was usually the man most accustomed to guns who was the most careless with them. "Instead of elevating the muzzle of the revolver at the safe angle prescribed, . . . I have also been guilty of such carelessness in pointing my weapon too far back and once shot away a lock of my own hair." Following this explanation, Attorney Osborne, assisted by Captain Jones, carefully placed the revolver in Caffey's hand, to duplicate the alleged position in the major's, and ordered, "Now, pull the trigger!"

Caffey snapped the trigger with no apparent effort, and excited laughter broke out in the crowded courtroom.[22] Major Zajicek later tried and failed to duplicate this feat, but the effect was nevertheless tremendously important. Caffey clearly made a very favorable impression on the jury; he was a very handsome man—never a handicap in such circumstances—and an able one, since he later became Adjutant General of the United States. His testimony gained force also since it contradicted the absolute certainty of the "expert" witnesses. Juries as a rule show a slight prejudice against the testimony of experts, at least to the extent of feeling more "at home" with testimony from someone like themselves. Also, word had leaked out earlier of the enormous fees that Dr. Schultze and Jones were receiving. There is a certain humor in proving a man allegedly worth $250 a day could be in error.

Other witnesses continued the defense case. The base hospital physician, Dr. Lupton, agreed that according to the records Cronkhite had been released from the hospital on October 21, with his release marked "Duty." This testimony challenged the claim of the defense that the major was released the day before the hike, which took place on October 25. However, other witnesses, Caffey and Zajicek, canceled the effect of this testimony by their certainty that the major had not decided to go on the hike until the last minute and had not intended to take command even if he did. Zajicek insisted also that Rosenbluth had not known he would be in command of the battalion until the night before—a circumstance which would have made advance planning of the shooting impossible. These two officers also confirmed that the major had been responsible for Rosenbluth's being included in the Camp Lewis contingent. Zajicek recalled being asked by Cronkhite for his opinion of Rosenbluth, and Caffey remembered that Rosenbluth was included partly because he spoke some Russian and the regiment expected to see service in that country.

The examination of ex-sergeant Elmer Kieffer was the one bright spot, the attorney for the prosecution later admitted, in an otherwise dismal case. Kieffer's testimony in court did not match the earlier affidavit he said he had made after he talked with Rosenbluth in New York. In this first statement, Kieffer alleged he had heard an occasional shot from the direction where the major and his orderly were and considered it unusual for an officer to be firing. In the courtroom, however, he could not recall these shots at all. The important aspect of his testimony concerned his claim to have seen Major Cronkhite shoot at a target and then walk toward it. Kieffer had stepped across the road and into some bushes to urinate, and from that position he was able to see into the clearing where the major and Pothier were standing. He denied that Pothier was holding a weapon; he insisted that Rosenbluth had passed from behind him going forward toward the shots and had not been with the major when they began. Attorney Osborne subjected Kieffer to what the defense attorney later called "the most relentless cross-examination" of his experience, trying to break down this crucial testimony. He did succeed in getting Kieffer's admission that he no longer recalled exactly where Captain Rosenbluth had been standing. Kieffer lost his temper at Osborne's attacks on his veracity, and his annoyance may have helped to weaken his testimony for the jury. He stuck to his story, however, that he had seen the major in the act of firing at a target.[23]

Other witnesses called by the defense included ex-lieutenant Haag, who stated that no quarrel of any kind occurred on the hike. Ex-sergeants Little and Turner insisted that Rosenbluth was in plain sight when the shooting began, in contradiction to statements of prosecution witnesses Root and Wuthenow. With this the defense suddenly concluded its case, to the considerable confusion of the prosecution. Since this was done without calling Rosenbluth, Osborne lost his chance to bring forth several witnesses for the prosecution he had held in reserve.

The defense had demonstrated that Major Cronkhite was unusually flexible, that at least some people could fire a revolver held in the correct position to produce the death wound, that the accident could not have been planned in advance, that no quarrel had taken place, and that Rosenbluth had been in sight when the shooting began. No more, in fact, was needed.

Before the attorneys gave their closing speeches to the jury, the defense raised the question of jurisdiction as it had promised, arguing that the land on which Major Cronkhite had died had not been shown to be in the exclusive jurisdiction of the federal government. The expected debate on this vexing question failed to occur. Both sides waived their right to argue the question, and Judge Cushman ruled abruptly that the government had jurisdiction over the alleged offense. The ruling was not challenged by the defense, presumably because there was very little doubt that Pothier would be acquitted, and to challenge the ruling would simply drag the case on indefinitely. The decision of the defense to raise this question after both sides concluded their cases was probably a matter of legal tactics. If the prosecution case had been stronger, the defense would have undoubtedly insisted upon argument and upon appealing the ruling to a higher court. But as the case was extremely weak, the defense stood to gain nothing except delay. Probably the judge was concerned also with the practical problem of concluding the case. If he had ruled against government jurisdiction, the two accused would have had to begin all over again in the state courts or, since the state probably would not try the case, remain under a cloud for the rest of their lives. The judge handed down a decision based upon an arguable position which he knew was unlikely to be challenged.

Revelle and Osborne for the government and Langhorne and Thompson for the defense made lengthy closing speeches on Friday and Saturday to conclude the trial. Revelle, as well as Osborne, made considerable use of the fact that Rosenbluth had failed to testify. He stated scathingly, "a man will often lay down his life for a friend, but not a conscience-stricken cringing coward. There are times when men wrap about themselves the great cloak of their constitutional rights to escape the consequences of their acts." When we recall that Revelle had insisted from the beginning that he did not believe in Rosenbluth's guilt, we can imagine his probable feelings during this speech. Revelle also insisted that the wound could not have been self-inflicted and the powder mark on the sleeve described by Dr. Tucker and Lieutenant Hannaman was impossible. His main effort, however, was directed toward underlining the point that Pothier had never denied shooting the major:

However Pothier may have changed his story and whatever new details he may have supplied, the one fact he never contradicted and which runs through every statement and confession he made is "I shot him." How was he shot? He couldn't have killed himself that way. But the defendant says, "I shot him at the command of the man who was with me."[24]

Defense Attorney Thompson followed Revelle and delivered a scathing indictment of the government case. He protested the manner in which Pothier's confessions had been obtained and said he was prepared to take full responsibility for Rosenbluth's failure to testify. Undoubtedly, his nonappearance gave the prosecution an advantage in their closing speeches, since it was easy to charge that he must have had serious reasons for refusing to take the stand. The defense, however, believed that the risk of submitting Rosenbluth to cross-examination in advance of his own trial was more dangerous than the prosecution's charges.

Thompson also gave significant stress to an important flaw in the government's case:

> From the number of department of justice agents who have been working on the case it is fair to assume that they have combed the field to find any cause of enmity between the principals in this case at Camp Forrest. There is no evidence of any disagreement between them. There is no evidence that during the trip to Camp Lewis anything occurred to mar the amicable relations that existed between Major Cronkhite and Captain Rosenbluth. They had had nothing to do with each other in a military way at Camp Lewis and if there was any disagreement between them it must have come through social intercourse. But there is no evidence of any such differences and no motive at all for the crime which is alleged to have been committed. Rosenbluth didn't even know Pothier by name at the time that Lee extracted his statement from Pothier implicating Rosenbluth.

He also sketched the story of the hike and alluded to the government attorneys' failure to shake Kieffer on essentials, even though they were able to confuse him about "some minor details of things which had happened six years before."

The attorney also criticized the government for not taking evidence from the medical orderlies who had been present as the Major died. "Where are these two orderlies?" he demanded. "Why are these two important witnesses who reached the scene as soon as anyone after the shooting not called to tell what they know? Why is it that their testimony is not wanted by the government?" Here Thompson was perhaps taking advantage of an omission that the defense itself had caused. Medical Orderly Croy had been summoned to Tacoma, but he may have been one of the witnesses held back by Osborne, who wanted to use certain ones in an effort to refute expected parts of Rosenbluth's testimony. Thompson concluded his speech with a bitter attack on Agent Lee, "an ambitious professional detective out to make a record," and upon the government for its handling of the case.[25]

Langhorne followed for the defense and covered much of the same ground as Thompson. He stressed the fact that Pothier could not be convicted of manslaughter, not only because of the statute of limitations but because no evidence had been submitted to show criminal neglect on his part. He stressed the total lack of motive in either Pothier or Rosenbluth and summarized the weakness of the prosecution case:

> So far as the defense is concerned, you can cast this reasonable doubt to the four winds of heaven and decide this case solely on any evidence which, distort it as you will, shows that Rosenbluth knew anything of this hike until the night before. Nor is there any evidence of a conversation between Pothier and Rosenbluth on reaching the road leading to the abandoned farm where the Major was shot.
>
> Experience has taught us that weak minded men may be forced to confess crimes they never committed by over-zealous and sometimes brutal agents of the state.
>
> In the days of the rack, even strong minded men and men with brilliant minds could be forced to make such admissions. This was the reason for the humane law that a prisoner must make a confession freely and without duress if it is to be used against him.[26]

The final argument in the case was given by Osborne, who bitterly attacked Rosenbluth for not taking the stand. "You know," he told the jury, "and I know, and everyone in this courtroom knows that he didn't testify because he didn't dare."[27] He charged that some of the defense evidence was perjured and false and attacked the board of inquiry severely—a strong point since carelessness of the board could easily be shown, a weak one since there was no way to connect either Pothier or Rosenbluth with the board's behavior.

> This was the most slipshod, careless investigation ever made by a military board of inquiry into the death under mysterious circumstances of a brilliant young officer. Not a single exhibit has been preserved in this case. Even the shells which we have are not known to be the ones picked up at the scene of the shooting immediately afterwards. Examination would have shown whether they were fired in two guns or one. The major's coat with the bullet hole in it has been destroyed. We cannot examine it to point out the absence of powder burns. Everything has disappeared or been destroyed.[28]

Judge Cushman directed the members of the jury that if they believed Pothier had accidentally shot the major, they must return a verdict of not guilty, and they retired at 2:45 in the afternoon to consider their verdict. The *Seattle Daily Times* sketched the scene in some detail:

> While the jury deliberated, Pothier was kept locked up in a cell a short distance away. Captain Rosenbluth and his friends from New York and his aged father paced back and forth along a third floor of the Postoffice Building. A bailiff sat on a tilted chair outside the jury room. A group of former Army officers who came from all parts of the world to testify gathered in a room and for a half an hour sang in lusty voices. As the strains of "It Ain't Goin' to Rain No More" and "Hinky Dinky Parlez-vous" drifted back to Pothier's cell, he threw away a half-smoked cigarette impatiently.[29]

Pothier was indeed the forgotten man in the case. Although the trial was his, most of the evidence and the speeches of the attorneys were directed at proving Rosenbluth guilty or innocent. But the man on trial and the man yet to be tried did not have long to wait. The jury took only one ballot and returned to the courtroom at 4:15. The foreman presented the verdict, "Not guilty."

> There was no demonstration as the words "not guilty" fell from his lips. Pothier smiled, Captain Rosenbluth sighed.
> As the jurors filed past Pothier, he thanked them and shook their hands. Captain Rosenbluth and his friends hurried about greatly excited. Many persons shook Rosenbluth's hand.[30]

The long struggle was over.

III

A SERIES OF STATEMENTS were made almost at once by various principals in the case. Attorney Revelle announced that the charges against Rosenbluth would almost certainly be dismissed. He also admitted that the government was aware its case was not a strong one. He explained the decision to go to court after the grand jury indictment by saying Attorney General Daugherty had ruled that since the men had been indicted, they were entitled to have their names cleared by a jury. In the background here we can see Revelle's expressed concern for the reputation of the Justice Department and for the former Attorney General. As we have seen, the reason for Daugherty's decision to go to court with the case—a decision which reversed a telegram sent only hours before—is not known. But it is

The Tacoma Sunday Ledger

State Edition

FIND POTHIER NOT GUILTY

SHENANDOAH WILL START BY TUESDAY

BABE RUTH EN ROUTE TO TACOMA; TO PLAY IN GAME HERE, OCT. 18

SMALLEST STATE FOR PRESIDENT

Pothier, Who Is Freed From Cronkhite Murder Charge

VERDICT OF JURY REACHED ON FIRST VOTE OF MEMBERS

CHIEF BENEFIT AT GENEVA HOPE OF REAL PEACE

MAP SHOWING WAY TO SHENANDOAH'S BIG MOORING MAST

ZR-3 WILL START FOR U.S. TODAY

FURNISHING OF HOTEL BIG TASK

The picture caption reads: Photo of Roland Pothier standing by the monument which marks the place where Maj. Alexander Cronkhite was killed in 1918, and for whose death Pothier has been facing a charge of murder in Federal court. The trial closed Saturday afternoon with the jury bringing in a verdict of "not guilty."

highly unlikely that concern for the reputations of the defendants was his primary motive. Certainly this explanation for the decision to go to trial was not made until long after the decision itself, in an obvious attempt to justify it.

Pothier had little to say after his acquittal. He submitted to being photographed standing beside Major Cronkhite's monument, but his main concern was getting back to Providence. He insisted that the government would have to pay his expenses: "They brought me out here. Now they have got to take me back."[31] The government, however, had no funds for this purpose, and Pothier stayed for several days at the home of his friend, Mrs. Herman Watson, before the Tacoma American Legion volunteered to pay his train fare. Pothier left at once, refusing an offer to sing in a local movie theater, and vanished from history, rejoining his wife and three-year-old son in Central Falls.

Rosenbluth's father also made a statement to the press:

> This is the first time that I have felt free to say a word of heart-felt condolence to the parents of Major Cronkhite, and I do so. I lost my oldest son by sudden death. I feel with them. I know they will feel better knowing that an American jury has removed any stigma from the circumstances surrounding the untimely death of the brilliant and beloved son. I thank God and the good people of Pierce County for this further evidence of American justice. My heart is too full for me to say more. I thank God for sparing me to see my son and our beloved family name cleared.[32]

The elder Rosenbluth's entrance into the case at its conclusion reminds us that the sufferings of the accused were shared by others. Rosenbluth had worked steadily with his son to assist him in any way he could. Mrs. Pothier had supported her infant son by working as a telephone operator while her husband spent the better part of three years in prison.

Robert Rosenbluth also made a press statement as he left the courtroom:

> The truth will set me free, just as it set Pothier free. If people would only take the lesson of this case to heart, the world we live in would be better. Lies imprison, truth frees. I offered my life to my country in the World War, and in my struggle to reestablish confidence in the administration and justice—both sacrifices worthwhile.
>
> I was trained as a forester, I want to return to forests—far away from spying agents. I hope my government will help undo the wrong done me, though I realize as never before that in all wars innocent bystanders may be hurt.[33]

While the witnesses enjoyed their vacations in Tacoma or began to leave for their homes, the officials continued working to close the case. On October 12, Osborne wired Attorney General Stone that Pothier would not testify against Rosenbluth and it was useless to attempt to try him without this testimony. Osborne requested permission to dismiss the charges against Rosenbluth, remarking bitterly that he had more important business to attend to in Arizona and would be glad to leave the west coast. Two days later the charges were formally dismissed, and Robert Rosenbluth was free at last.

He left Tacoma with his father for a brief vacation in California before returning to the east coast to resume his long-interrupted career. The eighty witnesses called to participate in both trials were free to go; only twenty-nine of the group were actually called to testify. General and Mrs. Cronkhite stayed in Seattle until after the trial was over, and then descended in fury on Prosecutor Osborne.

Both Revelle and Osborne wrote long letters to the Attorney General describing the case and evaluating it. Revelle's letter repeated his earlier protests about the weakness of the case, and enclosed a carbon of his letter written after the grand jury indictment to replace the "lost" original. He praised Osborne for his efforts, saying he "put into it everything and got out of it everything that any human being could get." He concluded with sharp criticism for General Cronkhite's refusal to assist and protested the enormous expense to the government the trial had produced. Revelle's letter was filed with a comment attached: "He's written to say 'I told you so'—no reply necessary."

The letter from Osborne on October 20, however, is worth printing in full, for it contains an acute analysis of the weaknesses of the case and of the personalities involved.

> As I telegraphed you on October 11th, Pothier was acquitted. I have delayed writing you concerning the trial until I had the opportunity of seeing General and Mrs. Adelbert Cronkhite. They came in to see me Thursday, October 16th, and expressed their opinion as to the trial and its results. If there is any reflection upon my integrity and intelligence that they failed to make, I did not make a note of it.
>
> However, the acquittal was inevitable. The confessions obtained from Pothier by the Department Agent James J. Lee were obtained under circumstances which I believe were unparalleled. I was amazed that the court admitted them in evidence. He did exclude the first of a series of three, stating that it was manifest that it was incompetent and that Lee had brought undue influence to bear upon Pothier. The literal falsity of the confessions was proved at the trial in too many respects. Scarcely a line in them coincided with the testimony coming from witnesses, in a great many instances.
>
> I tried this case as well as I believe it was possible to try it. Of course, if I had it to do over, there are some things that I would change, but looking at it from the point of view that I had at the time I started the trial, I think I would do it practically the same way.
>
> Some witnesses were not called that were available, for the reason that I saved them to contradict Captain Rosenbluth when he took the stand. These witnesses tended to show some disputes between Rosenbluth and Cronkhite.
>
> The trial proceeded upon the theory that Rosenbluth was going to be called by the defendant and the fact is that until the last day no one had any idea but that he would be called, and this statement including both counsel for Pothier and Rosenbluth. The defendant's decision not to put him on the stand was not made until the very last minute.
>
> The strain of the trial was terrific. I do not think that I ever have gone through a trial at higher nervous tension.

Wednesday and Thursday night I spent in preparing to cross-examine Rosenbluth. Friday night I spent in preparing my speech to the jury, which I delivered Saturday. The only things I had in my favor was the fact that the defense failed to call Rosenbluth, and the fact that a witness named Kieffer, called by the defendant, had filed an obviously false affidavit with the Department, tending to exonerate Rosenbluth.

When I started to speak Saturday morning I had such a heavy cold that I could hardly make myself heard and was in considerable physical distress. However, after the noon recess I felt a good deal better, and to a certain extent recovered my voice and got along much better.

I do not believe that it was possible to win this case for the Government. However, I can truthfully state, and do, that I worked as hard on this case as it was possible to do, and as conscientiously as I ever worked on any case, and tried it to the best of my ability.

I am enclosing a newspaper clipping of the acquittal that gives a rather fair report of the trial.

/s/ James W. Osborne

Two final documents from the affair were yet to come. On October 21 Assistant Attorney General Donovan received a letter from J. Edgar Hoover, reporting a conversation between Agent Navarro and James Lee in Tacoma:

It appears that Lee received a telephone message from Seattle from General Cronkhite and Lee proceeded to Seattle and had quite an interview with the General in reference to the case.

When the writer commented on the fact that General Cronkhite had not appeared at any time during the trial although he was so nearby, Lee stated that Cronkhite had a feeling or information that this case was going to be handled in such a way that there was not a possible chance for any conviction, etc. Lee further stated that after election General Cronkhite had arranged with certain Senators to have a Senatorial investigation made on the way the case was handled in the War Department, the Department of Justice and certain incidents connected with the trial, and management of the case by the Special Prosecutor James Osborne.

It was also intimated by Special Employee Lee that the finances of Henry Ford were to be used in case any further investigation had to be made in connection with this possible Senatorial investigation.

In the *New York Times* on October 17 an editorial written by Louis Marshall summarized the history of the case in some detail, describing the Selden exoneration and the various court decisions. The trial itself he labeled an utter fiasco, unknowingly echoing Attorney Revelle, who had warned the government in 1922 that an attempt to try Rosenbluth would result in "a fiasco of a most shameful nature." The "star prosecution witness" [Callaghan] testified he never believed Pothier guilty of murder. The trial, Marshall asserted, cost the government $200,000 and wrecked Rosenbluth's career. "United States Senators did not, however, hesitate, for political ends, to arraign him at the bar of public opinion, evincing entire willingness that a man, though totally free from a fault, should die upon the scaffold in order that they might gain a petty political advantage." He began his final paragraph, "There lives in Michigan one Henry Ford . . ." and strongly protested the blackening of the names of Rosenbluth and his supporters, Jewish or not, the labeling of men like Hoover, Calder, Chapman, Warburg, and Lehman as "malefactors . . . tools of a Jewish conspiracy."[34]

Despite Rosenbluth's vindication, the *Dearborn Independent* continued its attacks by attempting to cast doubt upon the verdict. The *American Jewish Year Book* for 1925–1926 contains a report on the matter, sharply criticizing Ford for the harm he had done and was continuing to do. The *Year Book* quotes the *Independent*'s assertion: "The shameful interference of racial organizations and the hysterical efforts to make of Captain Rosenbluth an American Dreyfus were amply illustrative of the length to which an alien type of mind will go to neutralize the safeguards which have been set up for the people in our laws and courts." The *Year Book* then comments:

> Even now Ford is attempting to minimize Rosenbluth's judicial exoneration by saying that the trial has not "cleared up the mystery of Major Cronkhite's death." There never was the slightest mystery concerning it. The Court of Inquiry held immediately after his death, consisting of brother officers of high rank, found that his death was due to an accidentally self-inflicted wound. The State authorities, after careful investigation, reached the same conclusion, as did the jury in the Federal Court. Again, with the characteristic suggestion of a falsehood, Ford declares that "the confession of Pothier implicating Rosenbluth is still unexplained."
>
> That the prosecution of Captain Rosenbluth did not have a shred of evidence to support it, is established by the fact that the special counsel employed by the Government . . . of his own motion and in the absence of Rosenbluth and his counsel, moved for a dismissal of the indictment. . . . There never was a more complete admission of the utter absence of probable cause than that thus made by the prosecution.

The *Year Book* concludes its remarks with a warning of the far-reaching harm that was being done by these and similar articles in the *Independent:*

> And yet Ford, the intellectual brother of the Ku Klux Klan, the inspirer of Hitler and Ludendorf, whose textbook is "The

International Jew," which is distributed throughout the world by this irresponsible disseminator of libels, instead of making reparation, persists, as one would expect a man of his low mentality to do, in his crusade against him upon whom he has inflicted so terrible a wrong. There is not a decent man who would not rather stand in the shoes of Captain Rosenbluth than in those of Ford, even though he be the richest man in all the world.[35]

In fact after the trial was over, Rosenbluth intended to sue Ford for libel, but he decided against this after being told that such a suit might take more than four years, would cost a great deal, and might result in nothing more than the traditional token payment of six cents in damages. Louis Marshall was eventually successful in halting Ford's attacks upon American Jews. When legal suits were threatened, Ford expressed surprise at Jewish concern, denied knowing about the nature of the articles, and refrained thereafter from such attacks.

Marshall's reference in his editorial to senators who were willing to hang a man to gain a petty political advantage ties in nicely with Hoover's letter warning of an expected Senate investigation after the presidential election, and with the *Independent*'s continuation of its campaign against Rosenbluth. This investigation was genuinely feared; the somewhat unusual expense of printing the prosecuting attorney's closing speech was defended by explaining that in case of such an investigation, it would be important to have a complete record of the trial. But the investigation never in fact occurred. It is not known, therefore, which senators were meant or exactly what advantages would accrue from a further pursuit of the case. The files of the Department of Justice do not contain letters from any political figures urging continued prosecution, although statements made by Crim assert that many congressmen were eager for the government to continue its efforts to convict. The only senators known to have interested themselves in the affair were Carter Glass of Virginia and David Reed of Pennsylvania. Glass's support of General Cronkhite did not diminish after the trial. In a rather superficial article on the case which appeared in *Liberty* magazine in May 1930, the writer asserts, "In March 1925 Carter Glass said in the United States Senate that it was all a case of murder and that he would have had it investigated at the time had not the War Department held up its reports until it was too late."*

---

* It will be recalled that in February 1923 Glass and Reed agreed to delay asking for a Senate investigation of the case in order to allow Secretary of War Weeks to examine the records in his files. Weeks did not report his findings until April, a month after the Senate had recessed. By the time it reconvened in December, the jurisdictional question had been referred to the Supreme Court.

It is possible that the general's friends hoped for a Democratic victory in November. The Teapot Dome scandal, which erupted in 1924, and other associated revelations of official misconduct made it appear for a time that the Republican party was unlikely to win. A Democratic victory, however, was made impossible by party opposition to Catholic Al Smith and the nomination of the comparatively colorless John Davis, former ambassador to Great Britain. The Democrats were further handicapped by the formation of the Progressive party, headed by LaFollette and Wheeler. The personal probity of President Coolidge and a slight rise in farm prices completed the picture. Coolidge and Dawes won easily in 1924, and whatever plans the general had for carrying on his fight for "justice" never materialized.

The article in *Liberty* concludes: "General Cronkhite and his ailing wife, lonely and bereaved and bitter, sit in their Baltimore home." One can imagine a rather pathetic retirement period—the general and his wife going over and over the evidence of their case, certain of the rightness of their cause and of a tragic miscarriage of justice. But the name of Cronkhite vanishes from the press, and no mention is made in the *New York Times* of his death in 1937.

Rosenbluth, however, went on to overcome the handicap of his four-year delay and eventually established himself in a long and worthy career in social work. He served for many years as assistant commissioner of social welfare for the state of New York and was the chief aide to Victor Ridder, who headed the W.P.A. there. After a period of serving in an advisory capacity to the Chicago public welfare board, he accepted a permanent position in that city, as assistant commissioner of public aid for Cook County. His move to Chicago was made because the county had no formal policy of retirement age. Thus he was able to remain at work as long as he desired. He married after the trial, raised two sons, and retired at the age of 80, after a distinguished career of social service. In 1967 he received the John Howard Award for his outstanding work in pioneering various approaches to rehabilitating juvenile offenders. He was able to overcome the natural bitterness produced by his years of struggle, and ends his unpublished autobiography: "I enjoy life; I love people; and I deeply love my country."

CHAPTER TEN
EPILOGUE

WHAT, after all, did happen at Camp Lewis? The itch to construct a final explanation that ties together all the conflicting testimony into a coherent and orderly picture is very strong. My suggestions follow, with the clear understanding that it is my interpretation only. It has proved rather difficult to discuss alternate possibilities with Robert Rosenbluth; his memory of his painful struggle has not dimmed with time, but I suspect he does not remember with complete clarity exactly what did happen during those confused moments more than fifty years ago. It seems to me possible that the events on the hike occurred like this: After the shots began, Captain Rosenbluth ran forward, exchanged a word or two with Major Cronkhite, and turned back to the road to rejoin his battalion. He was paying no attention to Pothier, who was not close by but had drifted off to a slight distance. When the fatal shot was fired immediately after the call," I got it that time, Rosie," Rosenbluth turned and rushed back through the bushes to the fallen major. He did not, I think, actually see the accident, although he was very near. As he reached Cronkhite, Pothier was standing nearby.

This analysis fits a good many otherwise confusing statements. Pothier, for example, testified on several occasions that he did not see the captain until after the major was shot and Rosenbluth came running in from the bushes. It may explain the variation in testimony concerning whether Rosenbluth was or was not "in sight" when the shooting began. It explains the uncertainty shown in Rosenbluth's and Pothier's statements about the whereabouts of the other. It explains the modification of Dr. Seaburg's affidavit, where in the second version he claims only that the captain as a matter of speculation discussed how the accident must have occurred. It explains, if more explanation is needed, Rosenbluth's failure to realize at first that the major had been shot. It agrees, moreover, with the memory of both Colonel Thomas and Lieutenant Colonel Howard that in their talks with Rosenbluth immediately after the tragedy he stated that he did not see the fatal shot. The testimony before the board of inquiry can be read to support this conclusion. After describing the major's turning or twisting to the left after his successful shot, Rosenbluth says, "I take it that the extra movement . . . twisted the pistol down . . . so the bullet fired." The phrase "I take it" seems to me somewhat ambiguous. He does not say that he *saw* the weapon twist in the major's hand, but that he believes the accident can be explained in that way. However, since he had stated a moment before that he was standing about two feet behind the major when he aimed at the can, the impression is certainly created that he was still there when the last and fatal shot was fired.

But the board of inquiry report is somewhat suspect in any case. It is true that Rosenbluth seemed to accept it as accurate when I supplied him with a copy and he was able for the first time to read this record. But he could not possibly, fifty years later, discern any small alterations made in it at the time. I, like General Cronkhite, cannot overcome my suspicion that the report was edited before it was filed. Lieutenant Colonel Howard's total inability to recall Major Tucker's testimony about the powder mark on the sleeve is inexplicable, unless we consider the possibility that some additions or changes were made. But unlike the general, I do not believe that the changes, if they were made, were done with any sinister intent. I do not for a moment believe that the major's death was the result of a plot involving several senior officers, nor do I believe that these men were covering up for Captain Rosenbluth.

General Cronkhite's suspicions of the board of inquiry report were based upon two things: The only copy the War Department could produce was marked "Duplicate," and the copy was not signed. My Xerox copy of this document, obtained from the office of the Adjutant General in Washington, D.C., has a cover sheet which contains the findings of the board, followed by the signatures of the three officers and the signature of the base commander, Major General Leitch. The page also contains five initialed date stamps indicating it was received in November 1918. In other words, my copy appears to be the original signed one; why it could not be found for inspection by the general or the Justice Department in 1920 is not known.

One suggestive possibility exists, however. If the War Department had come to realize that the report was inaccurate, a duplicate unsigned copy was less dangerous than a signed original. If the original copy could not be found, any questions raised about the accuracy of the report could be ignored. Parallel with this speculation is the loss of the written statements taken at the base hospital immediately after Cronkhite's death. What Lieutenant Wallace could remember of these statements several years later was not damaging; the statements themselves may have conflicted with the board of inquiry testimony. Thus their loss was perhaps vital to the War Department's determination to conceal, if possible, that the record had been tampered with.

The board of inquiry testimony itself contains evidence that there is a certain confusion of copies. First, the testimony taken by the board is separate from the signed cover sheet; three and a quarter pages of question and answer interrogation follow. Obviously this testimony could have been altered at any time without affecting the signatures; Major Tucker's testimony about the powder mark appears at the end of the report, on an almost blank fourth page. In addition, my copy shows that the signed cover sheet and the testimony were typed on two different machines; the cover sheet is elite type, the testimony pica. Also in the files of the Justice Department are the final two pages of testimony containing the last few answers of Pothier, Dr. Seaburg's statements, and Dr. Tucker's testimony. The pagination is different from the original Xerox copy.

Obviously in pre-Xerox days any copies had to be made on the typewriter, and these variations in type and pagination do not necessarily mean anything. But it can be said fairly that it would have been perfectly simple to alter the actual testimony at any time, had anyone wished to do so. To make a possible suggestion, consider Rosenbluth's testimony about the fatal shot. In the report he is quoted as saying:

> He lifted his pistol again, well up and slightly back, and then turned or rather twisted to the left and rear and told me that he got it that time. I take it that the extra movement, swinging around to the left and rear, twisted the pistol down. . . .

But suppose we construct a hypothetical insertion: ". . . and told me that he got it that time, as I turned back to the road to rejoin the battalion. I take it that the extra movement . . ."*

I cannot help but believe that the board of inquiry was motivated by a strong desire to modify or ignore the directive to determine if the major died in the line of duty or if his death was the result of willful misconduct. The rumors of suicide may have had an effect also. It is impossible to determine the extent of these whispers, nor can we trust the various affidavits asserting that the witness never heard such rumors. In Lieutenant Reeves's affidavit, for example, he declares that he never suspected or heard of any other cause for the major's death except the official explanation. But through private conversation with Reeves—my father—I know that he personally

---

* In a conversation in July 1969 Rosenbluth indicated to me that he thought this hypothesis was a fair and probable one. He also confirmed that the officers concerned were strongly motivated to avoid any blot on Major Cronkhite's memory.

believed that the major had taken his own life in a state of depression resulting from his illness. But this private suspicion does not appear in his official affidavit. In other words, if the board had even the faintest reason to suspect suicide, or even to fear that it would be suspected by others, they would have been exceedingly anxious to take testimony which convincingly demonstrated that the major's death was simply a tragic accident.

The testimony taken at the board of inquiry contains a highly significant omission, one that is difficult to account for except by the hypothesis that material was removed after the testimony was taken. Although all three witnesses describe the medical treatment (the injection of strychnine and the artificial respiration) there is no mention whatever of the reason for this treatment: that those in charge supposed at first that the major had had a heart attack. Only one explanation exists, I believe, for this. If Rosenbluth was to be placed in position as an eyewitness of the accident, standing only two feet behind the major, it was clearly impossible to admit he had been at first unaware that the major was shot.

Although the board was much criticized later for its failure to call other witnesses—the two sergeants, the medical orderlies, and others who were on the scene—I think it probable they were not called because they could not have been prevented from describing the scene as it actually occurred. Desirous of taking testimony which convincingly supported the verdict of accident, and unwilling to include in an official document statements which might imply the possibility of suicide, those in charge apparently decided that partial secrecy was preferable to complete openness.*

No definite conclusion can be reached. But we must allow for the fact that the board of inquiry testimony is not precisely accurate and there was more concern to stifle discussion than to encourage it. Pothier's various assertions that he was not allowed to speak openly, the feeling of many of the enlisted men that things had been hushed up, and the failure to call more witnesses may reflect the strong wish of the board to settle the matter promptly and definitely. It is ridiculous to suppose that anyone wished to cover up for Pothier; if testimony tending to implicate him was ignored, some larger issue must have been in question—the reputation of Major Cronkhite and, as Major Zajicek put it, "the honor of the regiment."

Needless to say, none of this speculative material reflects in any way upon Rosenbluth. There is no reason to suppose he was in any way involved or had any reason to believe lack of

---

* For the full text of the testimony, see the Appendix.

openness existed at the time. A distinction is usually made between regular and draft army officers. It seems to me quite plausible that the private concern of the board and Colonel Thomas for the affair to be ended without scandal or rumor made them perhaps overwilling to accept Captain Rosenbluth's view of the accident. Granting the probability that he was not actually looking at the major when the fatal shot was fired, his analysis of what happened is, as Dr. Seaburg's second affidavit stated, "a matter of speculation." But given the circumstances—a sudden death in a concealed spot with the only other witness a sergeant of highly doubtful honesty and reliability— the temptation to accept Captain Rosenbluth's analysis was strong.

All the records of the case combine to deny that any of the senior officers had any reason at the time to fear investigation on their own behalf. But given the elaborate newspaper coverage of the case and the interest aroused in it later, it was natural that the War Department would attempt to prevent an investigation which would have unquestionably reflected upon several regular army officers and their superiors who had accepted the findings without question. General Cronkhite's belief in an army plot had no real basis in fact and never came to anything. But an actual investigation into the affair would have smeared many officers nonetheless.

It seems to me that two alternate explanations of the death of Major Cronkhite still remain: First, that he shot himself by accident in the manner Rosenbluth described and believed. There is nothing factual in the evidence of the case to prohibit acceptance of this explanation. But the fact that an accident *could* have occurred in a particular way is not in itself evidence that it *did* so occur. Second, that Pothier, *unknown to Rosenbluth or anyone else,* was fooling with his borrowed revolver and accidentally discharged it in some fashion. In a telephone conversation with Rosenbluth I raised the question of this possibility, unable to understand why everyone dismissed it so casually. Rosenbluth seemed a bit annoyed at this line of inquiry, insisting that theories on the accident were irrelevant and the important aspect of the case was the behavior of the Justice Department. Realizing that he perhaps misinterpreted my questions, I remarked that this possibility in no way reflected upon him or upon the other officers, since apparently no one had any idea that Pothier was carrying a gun. He replied instantly, "That's right; we didn't know he had a gun."

Guns had been issued to only a few of the men, and Pothier borrowed a weapon the day of the hike, not having one of his own to use. As a noncommissioned officer he had the right to wear a sidearm if he wished, but there is evidence he did not carry the gun in a holster. This question unfortunately was not asked at the grand jury investigation, but one witness, ex-sergeant James Crook, testified twice that he was sure Pothier was not wearing a gun on the hike. Crook said he had walked beside Pothier and chatted with him and was certain he had no weapon.[1] Pothier's revolver must have been carried in his pack rather than in a holster. Thus, unless he was actually observed holding the gun or firing it—and absolutely no one claimed to have seen him do so—it was probably taken for granted, quite naturally, that he was not carrying a gun at all. This makes explicable, I think, the failure of the board of inquiry to raise the question of which gun had been in use, to check the bullets against the major's revolver, or to record officially the make of gun. It also explains, in part at least, Major Tucker's failure to attach importance to Sergeant Root's theory that Pothier had fired the shot accidentally. If the camp records showed that Pothier had not been issued a revolver and no one recalled his carrying one on the hike, then Root's ideas naturally appeared "one of the many theories" being discussed, not a possible or realistic explanation.

I think it possible that Pothier borrowed the gun from Kreutz at the suggestion of Major Cronkhite himself. This is admittedly highly speculative and depends upon a fragment of Pothier's final confession. He stated Rosenbluth told him the morning of the hike to borrow a gun and ammunition for it and "the person from whom you borrow the gun must not be told what you want it for." This statement, allegedly made by a man plotting a murder, is ridiculous. No man engaged in such a matter would feel it necessary to warn his accomplice not to mention casually that he needed a gun to shoot his major! Where then did the sentence originate? Perhaps it was suggested by Agent Lee, but it seems possible to me that it might have been made by Cronkhite. If he asked Pothier to accompany him as he prepared to follow after the column and he himself had just borrowed a gun and ammunition, perhaps he suggested to his companion that he also borrow a gun in case some informal shooting were possible. The warning, "Don't say what you want it for," is explicable if a minor breach of regulations were being planned. Considerable evidence indicates that Major Cronkhite was an informal and somewhat impetuous young man; his friendship with Pothier may have made such a suggestion natural.

In addition, there is considerable evidence that Pothier had had little experience with handguns and was on record as being careless with them. He himself said in one of his confessions that he had only shot a pistol a few times. Further evidence of his inexperience was offered to the Department of Justice at the very beginning of the case. On April 20, 1921, a Major Jones filed a report with the Attorney General in which he described an episode from Pothier's early service career. While on duty in Panama in 1914, Jones had given Pothier his pistol for cleaning. A few moments later, a shot rang out and a bullet crashed through the room, narrowly missing Jones and a bunk upon which a soldier was lying. Jones rushed into the room where Pothier was:

> I found Pothier with my pistol in his hand and a sort of silly grin on his face. He said he didn't know it was loaded. As a matter of fact . . . all firearms were carried loaded and there was no excuse for the accident. However, there being apparently no motive for the shooting and owing to the neglect on my own part in failing to remove the cartridges the matter was dropped without further comment.[2]

We can assume his inexperience and that none of the officers concerned knew that Pothier had a revolver with him. Given these facts, it seems to me possible that Pothier discharged his gun accidentally and managed to replace it in his pack unseen. Rosenbluth, who ran forward to assist the major, would not have paid any attention to Pothier in those first hurried moments in any case; he examined the major briefly, then ran back to the road at once to call for help. No one, then or later, paid any attention at all to Pothier; no one, regardless of his theories about the matter, reported having seen Pothier with a gun.

This second solution seems to me somewhat more likely than the official one for the following reasons:

1. The oddness of the angle of the wound, and the fact that the heavy-caliber bullet did not leave the body.
2. Pothier's reported change in manner after the Major's death.
3. Sergeant Root's otherwise confusing statements about the shells are allowed for. If Cronkhite fired three times, hitting the can on the last shot, and unloaded the exploded shells before Pothier's gun accidentally discharged, then we have the findings Root reported—that the major's gun contained three unexploded shells, and that Root picked up four exploded shells (three from the major's gun, one from Pothier's).
4. The quickness with which Lee and Callaghan produced the accident confession ("about an hour") and Pothier's reported state of emotional distress at that time.

5. The fact that, although his first confession was almost immediately forthcoming, it took Lee five days to persuade
Pothier to implicate Rosenbluth.
6. Pothier's continued failure to retract the accident confession.
7. His attorney's apparent belief that Pothier had fired the
fatal shot.
8. Pothier's various remarks that express or imply his own
belief that he had fired the shot by accident.

But the real solution remains, in Dr. Seaburg's phrase, "a matter of speculation," teasing the mind without the possibility
of any final decision. Nor is it, of course, the most significant
aspect of the affair.

Regardless of possible solutions, the larger issue concerns
the War and the Justice Departments and their handling of
the case. It appears unmistakably clear from the record that
the War Department was concealing something and was trying
to impede the investigation in various ways. Its repeated efforts
to transfer General Cronkhite to an overseas command, its refusal to permit Rosenbluth to consult the board of inquiry
report, its failure to produce the signed original of that document at the time, its loss of the written statements taken at
Camp Lewis, and the confusion over the various exhibits in
the case, all point in the same direction. Crim's repeated complaints and Osborne's certain conviction that the War Department was not cooperating express the same thing. Although
this must remain conjecture, it seems highly probable that the
War Department was protecting high ranking officers who had
accepted the original investigation without question.

In this sense, then, the Rosenbluth affair perhaps deserves
the title "the American Dreyfus case." Dreyfus was made the
scapegoat to protect the real culprits; his Jewishness was a con-
venience, not a necessary condition. Similarly, Rosenbluth was
left entangled in the investigation of his case in part because
the War Department would not admit it had been in any way
at fault. This position is to be the more condemned as there
appears to have been little to conceal beyond carelessness and
a concern for Major Cronkhite's reputation. But forced to
choose between embarrassment and rescuing Rosenbluth, the
department chose to save itself.

Criticisms of the Justice Department cover many facets of
the case. The opening stages of the affair can be condemned.
The personal investigations of Agent Lee were accepted as evidence without question or inquiry by his superiors in Washington, while the local authorities were unable or unwilling to

interfere. The premature arrest of Rosenbluth, which followed
Pothier's initial and clearly inaccurate confession, placed the
Justice Department and the Bureau of Investigation in the
position of having to create a case to conceal their own ineptitude. The damaging press releases concerning Rosenbluth's
character, reputation, and alleged spy activities were never corrected, despite their obvious foolishness. These faults concern
a fairly low level of department responsibility; although some
of the newspaper stories were quoted as coming from Chief
Baley, it is likely that most of them were unofficially released
by employees who overheard gossip about the case. But they
were nonetheless damaging.

Next, the nonconciliatory behavior of William Herron
can be criticized. Herron was not an underling, but an assistant attorney general and certainly in a position to examine
the records of the case in detail. He must have known, although
he denied it, how Pothier's confessions had been obtained and
that they had been retracted. Herron's total lack of regard for
Rosenbluth's position, his flat refusal to correct the damaging
newspaper stories, and his lack of concern for the massive evidence of Rosenbluth's good and even distinguished reputation
can be explained in one of three ways. Either he was personally
antagonistic to the accused; he sought some private advantage
in the case; or he was prevented from interfering by his superior, Attorney General Daugherty. From the record of correspondence, the first explanation appears the most likely.

A third and major criticism of the Justice Department's
behavior is also of high-level responsibility: its failure to notify
the accused that the department had resumed jurisdiction of
the case in the final months of 1921. Again, this was not a decision made by minor officials, but one which must have been
decided upon at the highest level. Associated here is John
Crim's neglect in his analysis of the public announcement made
in July 1921 that the government was dropping the case. His
assertion that no formal instructions had been given to turn the
case over to the state authorities is not true. It is unlikely that
Crim was deliberately falsifying his statement; he seems to be
depending here upon the analysis of the case made earlier by
Guy Goff, who had argued similarly that what records James
Selden had been sent were given him by the Seattle Bureau of
Investigation, not by the department's legal division. Crim,
however, could not plead ignorance of the government's publicly expressed intention to turn the evidence over to Selden.
Crim had notified General Cronkhite on October 25, 1921, that
the papers would be sent to the state authorities within two or
three days. As we have seen, by 1924 Attorney Hull could not
find in the records any explanation for the state prosecutor's

refusal to try the case. There would seem to be evidence that the awkward decision to resume jurisdiction was deliberately concealed and the records were, if not actually falsified, carefully made unclear. It will be recalled in this connection that the file for November 1921 contains only one item; since the government decided to resume work on the case at this time, documents relating to this decision seem to have been removed. Another hint of this technique appears in Revelle's letter after the trial, in which he enclosed a carbon of the letter written in 1922 begging the government to dismiss the charges. He sent the carbon because he had been informed the original letter had been lost or mislaid.

Another count against the senior officials of the department is their failure to insist that General Cronkhite either stop bothering them or turn over his evidence for a full examination. Throughout the four years of struggle, the department depended largely upon the general's personal evaluation of evidence in his possession. As Revelle pointed out, neither he nor other attorneys in the department would pursue a private client's case under such restrictions. As a result, much of the supposed evidence evaporated when witnesses were actually examined; the general's obsessive suspicions distorted everything he touched. The department's failure was even more pronounced since it was fully aware that the general was not entirely normal mentally, as Crim's letter to Revelle makes clear. That the department would persist for four years in a struggle to validate "evidence" which it was not permitted to examine points to external pressure and to the growing determination to defend itself from criticism.

And finally, the failure to accept the recommendation of Herron to transfer the case to state authorities and of Revelle to dismiss charges completes the picture. Here again, a decision was reached on the very highest level, undoubtedly by Harry Daugherty personally. What forces operated to prevent his acceptance of these recommendations cannot be determined, yet they obviously existed and were unrelated to any real consideration of Rosenbluth's probable guilt or innocence.

Thus these many mistakes of a specific sort can be traced to personalities. General Cronkhite's obsession, Agent Lee's idiotic preoccupation with spies and plots, Chief Baley's fondness for exciting press coverage, Herron's bad-tempered attitude, Crim's stubborn refusal to yield to what he believed was unethical pressure, and Daugherty's proven inability to think in any terms but those of personal and political advantage, all combined disastrously in the Rosenbluth case.

But since these men are no longer with the department and are not, for the most part, living, nothing significant is accomplished by a demonstration, however convincing, of their personal limitations. The basic criticisms of the department must be made in more general terms, which reveal that the conditions which permitted Rosenbluth's struggle have not, by and large, been overcome. Since we cannot hope, in the course of nature, for a large organization completely free from foolishness, bad temper, stubbornnesss, and doubtful ethical standards nor for one unaffected by personal dislikes, prejudices, and a desire to protect itself, improvement can be sought only through correction of a system that can permit free play to these human but unattractive tendencies.

As any citizen knows, often from personal experience, it is almost impossible to straighten out a mistake, however simple, when he confronts an impersonal and large department. Anyone who has engaged in correspondence with the Bureau of Internal Revenue, for example, has experienced the maddening feeling of helplessness as he is passed remorselessly from one secretary to another, each communication revealing a total lack of knowledge of previous letters. The problem is not restricted to government departments; a misunderstanding with any large organization such as a credit bureau or an insurance company can and does produce the same effects. We read increasingly often of persons who are unable to alter mistaken information which has somehow crept into their credit rating files, or who have been summarily dropped by an insurance company without explanation or recourse. Sheer size is a natural hazard to effective communication.

In addition to the problem created by the size of government agencies is the problem of unreasonable delay. The inordinate length of time involved in the Rosenbluth case was caused by a variety of factors, some of which were perhaps unavoidable. For example, after the grand jury indictment in October 1922, Revelle was told to come to Washington to confer about the case. But his responsibilities as attorney in Seattle made it impossible for him to leave until the following April. The same thing had occurred when the grand jury hearing was being considered; the department's tentative decision to reopen the case was made in November 1921, but the conference on the matter did not take place until April 1922. Similarly, Rosenbluth's hearing on the removal proceedings was scheduled for October 1922 but delayed until the following February, the defense believing, with reason, that this delay was deliberate.

Conferences among busy officials, particularly before air travel existed, perhaps involved necessary delay. But many time lags in the case have no such excuse. For example, the hearing granted to Rosenbluth was held in June 1921; almost a month passed before the Attorney General announced that the charges were being dropped. After this announcement, the department spent July, August, September, and October "assembling" the papers for transmittal to Tacoma. Lengthy delays of this sort obviously were a serious matter to the accused.

The conduct of apparently responsible officials in the case provides a dramatic illustration of a point made in the introduction. Once the prosecution is organized and apparent evidence of guilt acquired, it is almost impossible to introduce contrary evidence or gain a hearing for the accused. Once a case has been constructed, those who have worked on it grow more convinced of its accuracy each time it is challenged. Revelle and Falknor, previously uninvolved in the case, were certain of Rosenbluth's innocence after the grand jury hearing. Chastain, the agent responsible for constructing the case, remained certain that Rosenbluth was guilty. Similarly, Crim's analysis of the case reveals considerable unfairness to the accused. Both Chastain and Crim were respected by their associates and were generally considered honest and reliable officials. Unless this reputation is totally undeserved and mistaken, we must assume that their continued belief in Rosenbluth's guilt stemmed from psychological motivations, a blind spot produced by their strenuous efforts to construct a case and unwillingness to face the fact that their efforts had done irremediable harm to an innocent man.

And finally, it is overwhelmingly obvious that the Rosenbluth affair was in a large part produced by political pressures which unfairly but inevitably influenced the decisions of the Department of Justice. The defense pleaded on several occasions for the entire matter to be given to some official previously unconnected with the case for an impartial examination; William Allen made this suggestion in his final letter to George Christian, asking that William Burns be allowed to study the case. But even if this had been done, the obvious problem still existed, that Burns (or any other official of the department) was necessarily involved in politics. Burns's job depended upon Daugherty's position as Attorney General, which in turn depended upon a continuing Republican administration with Harding as president. Or to put it another way, Rosenbluth actually did receive an impartial study of the case from Thomas Revelle during the grand jury hearing. This man was convinced the whole affair was a mare's nest and strongly recommended that it be dropped. But the recommendation was ignored, as we have seen. The opinion of a remote attorney from Seattle was not as important as the political situation in Washington.

It is perhaps a truism that a natural clash exists between

the political world and the more rarified world of justice. Perhaps the fundamental problem in this and similar cases is that the Department of Justice, as well as the state courts, must function in a political arena, and decisions are necessarily controlled in some degree by political considerations. Insofar as its officials depend upon their party and ultimately upon the electorate for their positions, a Department of Justice cannot always be guided by abstract considerations of truth and fairness, in spite of the personal honesty of individuals. While this remains the condition, the ordeal of a Rosenbluth always remains possible.

APPENDIX

IT HAS BEEN ARGUED here that the testimony taken by the board of inquiry shortly after Major Cronkhite's death appears to have been altered, and some of the reasons for this hypothesis have been discussed. A direct analysis of the testimony tends to confirm this argument. It can be shown that some of the statements attributed to Rosenbluth and Seaburg could not actually have been made by them. This assertion rests on the following assumptions:

1. There is no evidence of any kind to suggest that Rosenbluth and Seaburg were more than casually acquainted or were in league. Even granting for the sake of argument that Rosenbluth lied to protect himself, it is highly improbable that Seaburg would have confirmed his statements. If their stories match and are inaccurate, then they must have been altered after the testimony was taken.
2. The account given by both men concerning the medical treatment is both inaccurate and unbelievable. One cannot imagine any set of circumstances that would produce such a damning story except subsequent tampering with the testimony. Intelligent men do not tell incredible lies reflecting on themselves.
3. Although the testimony in this case is confused and considerable variation in memory exists, the grand jury testimony, the affidavits, personal letters, and other documents show that the testimony taken by the board of inquiry is in many ways inaccurate and contains significant omissions. It is a likely hypothesis that the testimony was reworded later in an attempt to create an unambiguous and definite accident.

The proceedings of the board of inquiry, October 30, 1918, appear below in full, with the major confusions analyzed.

A cover sheet separate from the testimony contains the findings of the board:

1. Death occurred, October 25th 1918 in woods on reservation at Camp Lewis, Washington; caused by bullet wound in right upper chest, passing through both lungs and severing the aorta.
2. That deceased was shooting at a target with his revolver and while turning to speak to another officer, his revolver accidentally discharged causing wound above named.

232

3. That death was in line of duty.
4. That death was not the result of the deceased's own willful misconduct.

Below these findings appear the signatures of the board members: Lieutenant Colonel William J. Howard, Major Henry Tucker, and Major John F. Zajicek, and the base commander, Major General J. D. Leitch. Five initialed date stamps indicate that it was received by the War Department in Washington, D.C., in mid-November 1918.

Testimony of Captain Robert Rosenbluth

Q. You were present when the Major shot himself?

A. Yes, sir.

Q. Will you state to the Court, as nearly as you can, what took place.

A. This was on last Friday, October 25th. We were out on a march with the Regiment, and had been having some advance guard problems on the march, Major Cronkhite was with us, although not acting as Commander, as he wished to give problems and look around a bit. A few times he had taken out his revolver and just pointed it without shooting. I believe he had no bullets in the gun at that time, because he snapped the trigger a few times without the gun discharging. He picked out a place for lunch, and had reached that destination; and I was with the Regiment, about fifty yards behind the Major. I called to the Major and told him I thought that was the place to lunch, so he signalled to hold it. He pulled out his revolver and this time one of the shots went off.

> *Here Rosenbluth seems to say that he could see the Major while standing back with the men. Not only is this contradicted by the testimony of everyone else, but is also contradicted by his last answer, in which he says that the Regiment could not have seen the accident.*

I thought there had been an accident, because there had been no shots before; and I ran to him. I asked what he shot at, and he said he was shooting at a tin can on a post. I told him he made a clean miss. So he shot again. The first shot he missed, then raised his pistol and turned around. I was about two feet behind him, on his left.

Q. You said before that you heard a shot and you were some distance from him then?

A. Yes, sir, I was about fifty yards from him, and ran up to where he was, because I thought something had happened.

On the second shot after I had reached him, I was standing about two feet behind him, to his left. He came down with his pistol and shot a second time, and that time the can dropped off the post. He lifted his pistol again, well up and slightly back, and then turned, or rather twisted to the left and rear and told me that he got it that time. I take it that the extra movement, swinging around to the left and rear, twisted the pistol down, and also that he had a lighter pistol squeeze than he calculated, so the bullet fired. He immediately staggered, and I was right there within arm's reach and grabbed him. He exclaimed, "My God, I'm shot." About the same instant that the shot went off, and while reaching for him, I hollered at the column that was about fifty yards away, to send up Dr. Seaburg and the medical men. I opened his shirt to see around the heart if there was any shot-wound, and then the neck, and then opened his pants, while the Sergeant Bugler took off his puttees. I also told them to send the fastest runner that they had back to the machine gun company for an ambulance.

Told who? No one is yet present except Pothier. A minor point, but suggests that material has been rearranged or omitted. It is also suggestive that he makes no mention of Pothier until the accident has occurred.

The Doctor came up, and it wasn't over two minutes after the shot was fired. When he came I told him I thought the Major was dying, and that I couldn't find the wound, and to get some ammonia or strychnine right away.

The request for a stimulant is ludicrous if Rosenbluth believed the Major had been shot. There is no doubt from the testimony of the orderlies and the sergeants that both Rosenbluth and the doctor believed at first that the Major's heart had failed. Since this misjudgment is not recorded, it produces the unbelievable statement that Rosenbluth, unable to find the wound, does not suggest that the doctor look for the injury, but give an injection! In one explanation, Rosenbluth said that when he could not see any sign of a wound or bleeding, he supposed that the bullet had passed very close to the Major's head, and that the shock of the report had caused his collapse. Later, when the wound was found, it was a natural development of this theory to suppose that the same shot had fatally wounded him.

The Doctor immediately got out the strychnine, and he was injecting it, he took a glance at the Major and said he also thought he (the Major) was dying. We waited a couple of minutes. I thought death had come already, as I had seen men die before, and the Doctor, as a professional man, pronounced him dead. He said to try artificial respiration, and we tried it for about twenty minutes. It was clear then that the Major was dead. Right after injecting the strychnine we found the bullet wound in his right breast.

According to the testimony of the sergeants and medical orderlies, the wound was found during the efforts to give artificial respiration.

There was nothing else that could be done, so we picked up the can that was used as a target, and the empty shell cases, which I gave to the Sergeant Bugler to bring in, and covered the body up and waited around there. I had also sent in word, as soon as we came to the point of trying artificial respiration, to the Regimental Headquarters, as we weren't sure the machine gunners had an ambulance. So we sent Lieutenant Morrison and another runner in to report the facts to the Colonel. They did so. About 11:30 or 11:40 an English Major and two machine gun officers came up, one Lieutenant and one Captain or Major of the machine gunners; and shortly after that the stretcher-bearers came running ahead of the ambulance, and then the ambulance. We immediately brought the body of the Major to the Headquarters of the Regiment, and delivered it to the Officer of the Day at the Base Hospital, reported the case to him; and Lieut. Seaburg, Sergeant Bugler Pothier and myself each wrote out separate statements of the occurrence; and I told the Officer of the Day to take from the Major's clothing his watch and other personal effects, which he did, and I came back and reported personally to the Colonel.

Q. Did you note the exact time that the shot was fired?
A. It was somewhere between 11:00 and 11:15, but I am quite sure it was nearer 11:00 o'clock.
Q. Was there anyone near when this accident took place, besides yourself?
A. The Sergeant Bugler was nearby—he was acting as the Major's messenger, and he was also there—possibly four to six paces away.

It is noteworthy that no previous mention is made of Pothier's position. In Rosenbluth's extended description of the accident and immediate aftermath, he does not seem to be aware of Pothier's presence.

Q. You three were the only ones there when he shot himself?
A. Yes. The Regiment was about fifty yards away, as was also

the rest of the men. I don't think they could have seen the accident or how it happened.

Testimony of Roland R. Pothier

Q. Were you present with Major Cronkhite at the time of the accident?

A. Yes, sir.

Q. State to the Court what transpired.

A. We were walking down through a path in the field, and he and I were keeping about fifty yards in front of the company. The major picked up an empty Piper Heidsieck tobacco can, and said he thought he would try his shot. He put the can on a fence-post and shot and missed it. I turned around and looked for the company. The next shot he said to Capt. Rosenbluth that he got it that time. I turned to see if Capt. Rosenbluth was nearby and then I heard another shot, and heard the Major say he was shot.

Q. About how near to him were you?

A. About six paces.

Q. Where was Captain Rosenbluth?

A. I didn't see him until the Major was shot. The Captain ran up and took the Major's pack and coat off.

Consider here my hypothesis that Rosenbluth "arrived" twice, once to exchange a few words with the Major, and again after the cry for help. Although Pothier later changes his statement, his first answer suggests that he had not been nearby during the brief conversation just before the accident. This matches Rosenbluth's description of the scene; prior to the accident, he does not seem to be aware of Pothier.

Q. Did you say you heard the Major say he was shot?

A. Yes, sir.

[Here a damaged original prevented a clear Xerox, but Pothier describes calling for the doctor and for men to give artificial respiration.]

Q. Did you know what time it was when the accident took place?

A. No, sir.

Q. How many shots did he fire, altogether?

A. Three, I think. I don't know for sure how many he fired.

Q. You didn't see him when he shot himself?

A. No, sir; but before I turned around, I heard him say he was shot, and saw him fall.

Q. Did you see the Doctor when he came up?

A. I saw the Doctor running toward us with the Medics.

Q. They came right up then?

A. Yes, sir.

Q. He fired three shots before he shot himself?

A. Yes, sir, I think so.

Q. Was the shot very loud?

A. Yes, sir.

Q. Did it sound just as loud as the other shots did?

A. Yes, sir.

Q. There was no one there but you and the Major when he started shooting?

A. Captain Rosenbluth came up just before he was shot.

Q. Did anyone else come up before he was shot?

A. No, sir.

Q. After he was shot, who came up besides the Doctor?

A. After Capt. Rosenbluth hollered asking who knew about that there air business, two men came up that Captain hollered for.

Q. Did Captain Rosenbluth come up while Major Cronkhite was shooting?

A. Yes, sir.

Testimony of Elmer W. Seaburg

Q. You were with the party that went out with Major Cronkhite the day he was killed?

A. Yes, sir.

Q. Will you state what transpired?

A. My position in the column on the march was midway, and we came to the place of halting. The shrubbery was pretty thick along the roadside. After halting the first shot was fired, and one or two of the line officers and I stepped up to the fence, but could not see the Major. While standing there I was informed that Major Cronkhite had shot himself.

The doctor nowhere else claims this. In his second affidavit, and testimony before the grand jury and at the trial, he says that he was first led to believe that the Major had had a heart attack. Asked at the grand jury investigation if the shots did not suggest an accident to him, he replied, "No, because we were hearing shots all the time. We would hear shots all the time here and there. I do remember hearing those shots. I made some remark to someone near me, 'Well, I wonder what that is.'" In any case, who could have told him this? The doctor and the orderlies were the first men to go forward to the scene of the accident.

I only recall hearing three shots. After the third shot, that is what I thought was the third shot—no doubt it was the fourth, I heard Captain Rosenbluth call for me. I immediately double timed up to the spot, which I should imagine was fifty yards. In the meantime, I called Croy and Bazell of the Medical Department, to follow me. As I neared the Captain I saw Major Cronkhite on the ground—that is, he was not completely on the ground—Captain Rosenbluth had his head. His shirt and drawers. . . [sic] Immediately I was convinced that he was almost dead. The first thing that attracted me, his dippnoea [dyspnoea] was nearly stopped; and at the same time, I tried to take his pulse. He was pulseless. To confirm this, I placed my ear over his heart area, and could not hear the heart-tones. Though realizing he was dead, I gave him a hypodermic of strychnine sulphate. While in the process of getting this ready, a couple of men were giving him artificial respiration. This is what the Sergeant Bugler referred to when testifying as "some kind of air business."

This is very hard to believe. Why would a doctor, even a young and rattled one, inject strychnine into the dead body of a man he believes has died from a gunshot wound, or permit artificial respiration to be tried? In his second affidavit Seaburg asserted: ". . . it was because this affiant had no suspicion that the major's condition was due to a bullet wound, that he resorted to artificial respiration and the hypodermic, which would not have been administered and resorted to had this affiant thought that he had been shot; that it was because of the foregoing that I refer to myself worrying about whether there were things which I might have done. . . ." In both affidavits he expresses his deep relief when the autopsy showed that no treatment could have saved the Major's life.

It can be argued that Seaburg deliberately omitted reference to his mistake in diagnosis, reluctant to admit he had been so careless, but it is hard to see why he preferred to state that he had given the treatment he did.

Also during this time there was no breathing, ears were cyanotic, eyes dilated. Almost instantly upon first noticing patient, eyelids retracted immediately. Then I looked for and found the wound in the right upper chest.

According to all other witnesses the wound was found by the men giving artificial respiration. The doctor is very shy about admitting this; in his first affidavit he makes no reference to it, and in his second one says that he found the wound. He avoided the admission before the grand jury until forced to do so by a direct question. In any case, this statement still leaves unanswered the question of why he did not look for a wound in the first place if he in fact had been told it was a shooting accident.

Upon stating that the patient was dead, he was straightened out, chin supported, eyes closed, hands placed and tied over his body, and body covered with raincoat, awaiting arrival of the ambulance.

Q. When you arrived did you ask Capt. Rosenbluth or anyone what had taken place?

A. I don't recall that I asked any questions. I believe Captain Rosenbluth told me the Major shot himself. I do not recall having asked any questions. Possibly I did.

Again, this seems unlikely. One would expect a doctor arriving at the scene of a serious accident to ask the obvious question: What has happened? As Seaburg tells the story in other places, Rosenbluth shouted as he approached that the Major had had a heart attack, and if no questions were asked, it was because the doctor accepted this diagnosis.

TESTIMONY OF MAJOR HENRY TUCKER

There was a powder burn on the inner surface of the right sleeve of the Major's coat, in line with where muzzle of gun would have been, or at entrance of bullet, which proves that gun was in his right hand when fired. It is absolutely confirmatory evidence of the position of the gun.

This concludes the testimony taken by the board of inquiry. Considering all these confusing statements together, it is hard to believe that Rosenbluth and Seaburg told such absurd falsehoods to protect themselves. The truth—the mistake in diagnosis—was less damning than the treatment described here. Working on the hypothesis that the testimony was reworded later, what has been left out? Apparently two things:

1. That Rosenbluth was not immediately present when the accident occurred, although very near to it.
2. That it was at first supposed that a heart attack explained the Major's collapse.

Associated with these omissions is the failure to name some of the other witnesses on the scene, or to call any of them to testify.

I can find no reason but the strong desire to produce a clear and unambiguous "accidental" death behind this reworking of the testimony. What was needed was a responsible *witness* of the accident. Of the two possibilities, Rosenbluth was clearly the better choice; he was respected, of excellent reputation and high character, and an officer. Pothier was disliked and generally distrusted. So Rosenbluth was selected—he had been for all practical purposes "present"; it was only a slight stretching of the truth to assert it.

This alteration, slight in itself, necessitated removing references to the heart attack. If Rosenbluth had been in truth two feet behind the Major when the gun twisted and discharged, he could not have been unaware of what had happened. All references to this mistake were removed. The other witnesses were not called; they could not have been prevented from explaining the reason for the treatment. A clearcut accident required the literal presence of Rosenbluth and the omission of the original reasons for the medical treatment.

One last question. Did Rosenbluth know that these changes were made, and was he directly involved in these revisions? The probabilities are heavily against either. His behavior in 1921 when the matter was reopened does not suggest that he had the slightest knowledge. He quite clearly did not know just at first that these puzzling confusions in the record existed. When he began to realize them, he could not straighten out the confusion since he was not permitted to examine the testimony taken before the board.

Confirming his ignorance of these alterations is his dependence upon the affidavits of Turner and Kieffer, both of which allege that he went forward after the shots ceased, and upon Seaburg's affidavit in which the treatment for the supposed heart attack is described. If Rosenbluth had been aware of alterations in the testimony, he would have realized that these affidavits contradicted it. The same applies to Dr. Seaburg. In spite of his obvious embarrassment over his handling of the emergency, he does not hesitate to describe the scene as it occurred in his other testimony, except for his natural reluctance to admit that it was not he who discovered the wound.

NOTES

INTRODUCTION
1. "The Department of Injustice," *The Nation* 114 (Jan. 4, 1922), 6.
2. Harry Golden, *A Little Girl Is Dead* (Avon ed.; New York, 1967), p. xiv.
3. For an acute analysis of the Dreyfus case, see Hannah Arendt, *The Origins of Totalitarianism* (Meridian ed.; New York, 1962), ch. 4.
4. Golden, *Little Girl.*
5. Francis Russell, *Tragedy in Dedham: The Story of the Sacco-Vanzetti Case* (New York, 1962), pp. 122–23.
6. H. L. Mencken, *On Politics: A Carnival of Buncombe,* Malcolm Moos, ed. (Vintage ed.; New York, 1960), pp. 24–25.
7. Ibid., p. 125.

CHAPTER 1
All materials cited below are contained, unless otherwise indicated, in Justice Department Straight Numerical File No. 211831. Following each entry, the section name or number will be indicated in parentheses.
1. New York *World,* May 23, 1921, p. 5.
2. Report of Testimony before United States Grand Jury at Tacoma, Washington, in the Matter of the Death of Major Alexander P. Cronkhite, I, 77–78 (Special Enclosure Sect.).
3. Ibid., II, 96.
4. Ibid., II, 36–37.
5. Exoneration of Captain Robert Rosenbluth, Official Report of Hon. J. W. Selden, Prosecuting Attorney, Pierce County, Washington, in the Matter of the Death of Major Cronkhite, p. 45 (Special Enclosure Sect.).
6. Grand Jury, I, 31.
7. *The Howitzer,* Yearbook of the U.S. Corps of Cadets, 1915, p. 68.
8. Grand Jury, I, 218.
9. Ibid., V, 122.
10. The sketch of Rosenbluth's life is drawn both from conversations with him, and from his unpublished autobiography, "The Many Lives of Robert Rosenbluth."
11. Exoneration, p. 59.
12. Ibid., p. 44.
13. Grand Jury, I, 218, 223.
14. Ibid., I, 6–7.
15. Ibid., I, 11.
16. Exoneration, p. 45.
17. Grand Jury, I, 121.
18. Ibid., I, 64.
19. Ibid., IV, 73.
20. Ibid., I, 195.
21. Ibid., II, 133.
22. Ibid., II, 351.
23. Exoneration, p. 57.
24. Proceedings of the Board of Inquiry, Oct. 30, 1918. (Office of the Adjutant General, Washington, D.C.).
25. Grand Jury, I, 66–69, 198–201, 350–56. Sergeant Root, who assisted the doctor in preparing the injection, commented on his trembling: "Lieutenant Seaburg was very nervous and was spilling the water" (I, 67).
26. Exoneration, pp. 5–6.
27. Grand Jury, II, 179, 188.
28. Ibid., III, 29, 36, 39.
29. Ibid., I, 312.
30. Ibid., I, 262–76.
31. Board of Inquiry.
32. *New York Times,* Oct. 26, 1918, p. 4; *Official History of the Thirteenth Division* (Tacoma, 1919), p. 27; *Biographical Register of the Officers and Graduates of the United States Military Academy,* suppl., vol. VI-B (1910–1920), 1726.
33. Exoneration, p. 52.

34. *New York Times,* Apr. 22, 1921, p. 5.
35. Statement of Lt. Col. William Howard at a Justice Dept. hearing, 1922. (Special Enclosure Sect.)
36. Exoneration, p. 6.
37. Grand Jury, I, 112.
38. Ibid., I, 18.
39. *Regimental History,* 213th Engineers (Tacoma, 1918), not paginated.
40. Grand Jury, II, 384.
41. *Chicago Tribune,* Apr. 6, 1923, p. 14.
42. Grand Jury, IV, 58.
43. Ibid., II, 378.
44. Ibid., I, 216.
45. Ibid., III, 49.

CHAPTER 2

1. *Chicago Tribune,* Apr. 2, 1923, p. 3.
2. Letter from Mrs. Cronkhite to Colonel Thomas, Aug. 22, 1919 (Special Enclosure Sect.).
3. Grand Jury, I, 40, 58, 110.
4. Ibid., IV, 56–57.
5. Ibid., II, 377 ff.
6. Analysis of case made in 1922 by General Cronkhite, p. 1 (Special Enclosure Sect. The analysis is not identified as being by Cronkhite, but references to Major Cronkhite as "my son" make the authorship clear.)
7. Grand Jury, V, 101–2.
8. Special Enclosure Sect.
9. Grand Jury, I, 24.
10. *Chicago Tribune,* Apr. 7, 1923, p. 16.
11. Sect. 1.
12. *New York Times,* Feb. 15, 1923, p. 8.
13. Exoneration, p. 46.
14. Grand Jury, II, 227.
15. Ibid., II, 380–81.
16. Special Enclosure Sect.
17. Ibid.
18. Ibid.
19. Grand Jury, I, 427–28, 451.
20. Statement of W. A. Jones and Autopsy Report before the Justice Department, April 1922 (Special Enclosure Sect.).
21. Lewis L. Strauss, *Men and Decisions* (New York, 1962), p. 74–76.
22. *New York Times,* Mar. 10, 1921, p. 3.
23. James M. Cox. *Journey through My Years* (New York, 1946), p. 302. (© 1946 by James M. Cox. Reprinted by permission of Simon & Schuster, Inc.)
24. Karl Schriftgiesser, *This Was Normalcy: An Account of Party Politics during Twelve Republican Years, 1920–1932* (Boston, 1948), pp. 28–29.
25. 62 *Congr. Rec.,* 7316 ff. (1922) (remarks of Senator Caraway).
26. Oswald Garrison Villard, *Fighting Years: Memoirs of a Liberal Editor* (New York, 1939), p. 475.
27. Schriftgiesser, *Normalcy,* p. 82.

CHAPTER 3

1. Francis Russell, *The Shadow of Blooming Grove* (New York, 1968), p. 516.
2. Don Whitehead, *The F.B.I. Story* (New York, 1956), p. 69.
3. Section 5.
4. Section 6.
5. New York *World,* May 23, 1921, p. 5.
6. Grand Jury, II, 84.
7. William Preston, Jr., *Aliens and Dissenters: Federal Suppression of Radicals, 1903–1933* (Cambridge, Mass., 1963), p. 13.
8. Max Lowenthal, *The Federal Bureau of Investigation* (New York, 1950), p. 211. (© 1950 by Max Lowenthal. Reprinted by permission of William Sloane Assoc., Inc.)
9. Ibid., p. 214.
10. Ibid., pp. 7–8.
11. Ibid., p. 365
12. Exoneration, p. 17.
13. Ibid., p. 18.
14. Grand Jury, II, 48, 57–58.
15. *Chicago Tribune,* Apr. 4, 1923, p. 6.

16. Grand Jury, I, 138–39; II, 343–44.
17. Ibid., II, 343–46.
18. Exoneration, pp. 18–19.
19. Ibid., p. 19.
20. *World,* May 23, 1921, p. 5.
21. Exoneration, pp. 19–20.
22. Ibid., p. 21.
23. Ibid., p. 22
24. Ibid., p. 20.
25. Ibid., pp. 33–34.
26. Grand Jury, II, 74.
27. Exoneration, pp. 30–31.
28. Grand Jury, II, 63.
29. *World,* May 23, 1921, p. 5.
30. Exoneration, pp. 23–26.
31. Ibid., p. 44.
32. Grand Jury, II, 66–67.
33. Ibid., II, 80.
34. *World,* May 23, 1921, p. 5.
35. Ibid.
36. Ibid.
37. *Chicago Tribune,* Apr. 3, 1923, p. 4.
38. Exoneration, p. 18.

CHAPTER 4

1. "A Study in Justice—The Rosenbluth Case," *The Nation* 113 (Oct. 19, 1921), 441. A galley proof of this article in the Archives file (Sect. 2) carries Norman Thomas's name; the published article is not signed.
2. Grand Jury, IV, 12.
3. *New York Times,* Mar. 24, 1921, p. 1.
4. Ibid., Mar. 25, 1921, p. 10.
5. Ibid., Mar. 29, 1921, p. 19.
6. Sidney Sutherland, "The Mystery of the Target Range," *Liberty* (May 10, 1930), p. 55.
7. *New York Times,* Mar. 26, 1921, p. 6.
8. Ibid., Mar. 30, 1921, p. 8.
9. Sect. 2.
10. Sect. 3.
11. Sect. 1.
12. Ibid.
13. *New York Times,* Mar. 28, 1921, p. 11.
14. Sect. 1.
15. Ibid. A lengthy document written by Rosenbluth asks that certain witnesses be reexamined about their testimony. He states that Agent Lee had reported their charges to him.
16. Ibid. This section contains a transcript of the Justice Department hearing of June 18, 1921, at which Rosenbluth and his lawyer made a series of criticisms of the department.
17. *New York Times,* Apr. 18, 1921, p. 7.
18. Exoneration, p. 47.
19. Rosenbluth Hearing (Sect. 1).
20. *New York Times,* Apr. 19, 1921, p. 3.
21. Sect. 1. New York *World,* Apr. 21, 1921, p. 1. The article is titled: "Mother Ran Down Cronkhite Murder in Tireless Chase."
22. Ibid.
23. Exoneration, pp. 12–13.
24. Ibid.
25. *New York Times,* Apr. 23, 1921, p. 8.
26. Ibid., Apr. 29, 1921, p. 14.
27. Sect. I.
28. *World,* May 23, 1921, p. 5.
29. Ibid., May 24, 1921, p. 1.
30. Letter from James Lee to Attorney General Stone, Aug. 29, 1924 (Sect. 5).
31. Harry Golden, *A Little Girl is Dead* (Avon ed.; *New York,* 1967), p. 255.
32. *New York Times,* May 30, 1921, p. 22.
33. Exoneration, p. 14.
34. Sect. 1.
35. *New York Times,* July 19, 1921, p. 9.

CHAPTER 5

1. Sect. 2.
2. *Chicago Tribune,* Apr. 5, 1923, p. 6.
3. Sect. 3.
4. Ibid.
5. *World's Work,* 37 (Jan. 1919), 288.
6. *Dearborn Independent* (Apr. 21, 1923), p. 6.
7. Sect. 2, July 21, 1921.
8. *Dearborn Independent* (Apr. 28, 1923), p. 13.
9. *Biographical Register,* suppl., vol. VII, 1920–1930, 189.
10. *Chicago Tribune,* Apr. 5, 1923, p. 6.
11. Ibid., Apr. 8, 1923, p. 10.
12. Special Enclosure Sect.
13. "A Study in Justice—The Rosenbluth Case," *The Nation* 113 (Oct. 19, 1921), 442.
14. *Literary Digest* (Jan. 28, 1922), p. 46.
15. *New York Times,* Oct. 17, 1924, p. 20.
16. Exoneration, pp. 52–55.
17. Ibid., pp. 56–58.
18. Grand Jury, III, 1–23.
19. The Rosenbluth letters that follow are in the Special Enclosure Sect., except for the two letters to Fred Reeves found in his papers.
20. Special Enclosure Sect.
21. "The Department of Injustice," *The Nation* 114 (Jan. 4, 1922), 5.
22. Sect. 2.
23. *Chicago Tribune,* Apr. 5, 1923, p. 6.
24. Sect. 2, Dec. 13, 1921.
25. Sect. 2.
26. Exoneration, p. 62.
27. Sect. 4.
28. *Chicago Tribune,* Apr. 6, 1923, p. 14.
29. Sect. 2.
30. "Department of Injustice," p. 6.
31. Sect. 2, Jan. 10, 1922.
32. Ibid., Jan. 11, 1922.
33. Ibid., Jan. 12, 1922.

CHAPTER 6

1. Information received in a personal letter from Rosenbluth.
2. Information received in a conversation with Rosenbluth.
3. 62 *Congr. Rec.,* 5293 (1922).
4. Ibid., 6605–6.
5. Ibid., 7712.
6. Ibid., 6364.
7. Max Lowenthal, *The Federal Bureau of Investigation* (New York, 1950), p. 294.
8. Ibid., p. 299.
9. Samuel Hopkins Adams, *Incredible Era: The Life and Times of Warren Gamaliel Harding* (Capricorn ed.; New York, 1964), p. 330. (© 1939 by Samuel Hopkins Adams. Copyright renewed 1967 by Hester H. Adams. Reprinted by permission of Brandt & Brandt.)
10. Sect. 2.
11. Ibid., Apr. 25, 1922.
12. Ibid., Apr. 1922.
13. Ibid., June 1922.
14. Ibid., Feb. 28, 1922.
15. Ibid.
16. Ibid., Mar. 3, 1922.
17. Ibid., Mar. 27, 1922.
18. The statements and analyses of the case presented at the April meeting are filed in the Special Enclosure Sect.
19. *Dearborn Independent* (Jan. 13, 1923), p. 7.
20. Sect. 3, Aug. 31, 1922.
21. Sect. 1.
22. Sect. 2.
23. Ibid., Aug. 17, 1922.
24. Sect. 3, Aug. 30, 1922.
25. Ibid., Aug. 31, 1922.
26. Ibid., Sept. 1, 1922.
27. Ibid., Sept. 6, 1922.
28. Ibid., Sept. 1922.

29. Ibid.
30. *New York Times,* Sept. 24, 1922, p. 7.
31. "More Daugherty," *The Nation* 115 (Oct. 4, 1922), 323.

CHAPTER 7
Because of the many references to the grand jury testimony, the abbreviation GJ will be used.
1. GJ, II, 134.
2. GJ, II, 143.
3. GJ, II, 163.
4. GJ, IV, 1–3.
5. GJ, I, 70–92.
6. GJ, I, 62.
7. GJ, II, 130.
8. GJ, II, 138.
9. GJ, I, 199.
10. GJ, I, 352.
11. GJ, I, 201.
12, GJ, I, 351.
13. GJ, I, 203.
14. On the subject of morgue conditions, see testimony of Terry, GJ, I, 147 ff.; Staniford, II, 1 ff.; Kelly, II, 204 ff.; Hirsch, II, 273 ff.; Shaw, II, 370 ff.
15. GJ, I, 48.
16. GJ, I, 24.
17. GJ, II, 373 ff.
18. GJ, II, 431–35.
19. GJ, V, 90 ff.
20. GJ, V, 113 ff.
21. GJ, II, 45 ff.; 69 ff.
22. GJ, II, 345–46.
23. *New York Times,* Oct. 17, 1924, p. 20.
24. Sect. 3.
25. GJ, I, 297.
26. GJ, I, 301.
27. GJ, I, 297.
28. GJ, IV, 82–87.
29. Sect. 3.
30. Ibid.
31. Sect. 7.
32. Sect. 3.
33. Ibid.

CHAPTER 8
1. *Dearborn Independent* (Apr. 23, 1923), p. 13.
2. *New York Times,* Oct. 17, 1924, p. 20.
3. Sect. 4, Jan. 22, 1923.
4. Exoneration, pp. 7–10.
5. Sect. 4.
6. Ibid., Apr. 1923.
7. *New York Times,* Oct. 22, 1922, p. 7.
8. Special Enclosure Sect.
9. Ibid.
10. Sect. 3.
11. Sect. 4, Dec. 8, 1922.
12. Special Enclosure Sect.
13. *New York Times,* Feb. 14, 1923, p. 18.
14. Ibid., Feb. 17, 1923, p. 5.
15. Allan Nevins and Frank Ernest Hill, *Ford: Expansion and Challenge, 1915–1933* (New York, 1957), p. 317.
16. Stephen Birmingham, *Our Crowd: The Great Jewish Families of New York* (Dell ed.; New York, 1967), pp. 18, 340.
17. *Dearborn Independent* (Jan. 27, 1923), p. 8.
18. Herbert Hoover, *The Cabinet and the Presidency, 1920–1933* (New York, 1952), p. 26.
19. Sect. 7, Oct. 24, 1924.
20. Sect. 4.
21. Ibid.
22. Ibid.
23. Ibid.
24. *New York Times,* Feb. 2, 1923, p. 14.

25. Lawrence Stallings, *The Doughboys: The Story of the A.E.F., 1917–1918* (New York, 1963), p. 58.

26. *New York Times,* Feb. 15, 1923, p. 1.

27. *Chicago Tribune,* Feb. 15, 1923, p. 3.

28. *New York Times,* Feb. 16, 1923, p. 12.

29. Ibid., p. 5.

30. Ibid., p. 12.

31. Ibid., Feb. 17, 1923, p. 5.

32. Ibid., Apr. 4, 1923, p. 3.

33. 64 *Congr. Rec.,* 3977–78 (1923).

34. Ibid., 3980.

35. Ibid., 4096–4100 (1923) (remarks of Senator Caraway).

36. Sect. 4.

37. Chicago Tribune, Apr. 8, 1923, p. 10.

38. Sect. 4, Feb. 15, 1923.

39. Francis Russell, *The Shadow of Blooming Grove* (New York, 1968), p. 564

40. Sect. 4, June 27, 28, 1923.

41. Ibid., July 16, 1923.

42. Ibid., July 17, 1923.

43. Ibid., Aug. 20, 1923.

44. Ibid., Dec. 18, 1923.

45. Samuel Hopkins Adams, *Revelry* (New York, 1926), pp. 311–12.

46. 65 *Congr. Rec.,* 5950 (1924) (remarks of Senator Heflin).

CHAPTER 9

1. Sect. 5.

2. Ibid.

3. Ibid., Apr. 23, 1924.

4. Ibid., May 14, 1924.

5. Motion filed in United States District Court, Western District of Washington, Southern Division, No. 3862, by Robert Rosenbluth, July 1, 1924.

6. Affidavit filed in United States District Court, Western District of Washington, Southern Division, No. 3862, by Robert Rosenbluth, July 11, 1924, pp. 6–7.

7. Sect. 5.

8. Ibid., May 25, 1924. All Justice Department communications up to July 11, 1924, are filed in Sect. 5.

9. Sect. 6. All Justice Department communications up to September 10 are filed here unless otherwise indicated.

10. Sect. 7. With a few exceptions, all communications of the Justice Department subsequent to September 10, 1924, are filed here.

11. *Tacoma Ledger,* Oct. 2, 1924, p. 1.

12. *Seattle Daily Times,* Oct. 2, 1924, p. 1.

13. *Tacoma Ledger,* Oct. 3, 1924, p. 2.

14. Ibid., Oct. 4, 1924, p. 3.

15. *New York Times,* Oct. 4, 1924, p. 1.

16. *Tacoma Ledger,* Oct. 5, 1924, p. 1.

17. Ibid., Oct. 8, 1924, p. 2.

18. *New York Times,* Oct. 9, 1924, p. 25.

19. *Seattle Daily Times,* Oct. 8, 1924, p. 3.

20. *New York Times,* Oct. 8, 1924, p. 19.

21. *Tacoma Ledger,* Oct. 10, 1924, p. 3.

22. Ibid., p. 1.

23. Ibid.

24. Ibid., Oct. 11, 1924, p. 3.

25. Ibid.

26. Ibid.

27. *Chicago Tribune,* Oct. 12, 1924, p. 1.

28. *Tacoma Ledger,* Oct. 12, 1924, p. 1.

29. *Seattle Daily Times,* Oct. 12, 1924, p. 15.

30. *Tacoma Ledger,* Oct. 12, 1924, p. 1.

31. Ibid.

32. Ibid.

33. Ibid.

34. *New York Times,* Oct. 17, 1924, p. 20.

35. "Report of the American Jewish Committee," *American Jewish Year Book* 27 (1925–1926), 450–59.

EPILOGUE

1. Grand Jury, IV, 23–48.

2. Sect. 1, Apr. 20, 1921.

BIBLIOGRAPHY

THE FOLLOWING MATERIALS, while not used directly in the text, are valuable sources of information on the history of the period.

Allen, Frederic Lewis. *Only Yesterday*. Bantam ed., New York, 1959.

——. *The Big Change, 1900–1950*. Bantam ed., New York, 1965.

Aspects of Jewish Power in the United States, Vol. 4 of *The International. Jew*. Dearborn, Mich., 1922.

Coben, Stanley. *A. Mitchell Palmer: Politician*. New York, 1963.

Daugherty, Harry M., in collaboration with Thomas Dixon. *The Inside Story of the Harding Tragedy*. New York, 1932.

Hays, Arthur Garfield. *Let Freedom Ring*. New York, 1937.

Hicks, John D. *Republican Ascendancy: 1921–1933*. New York, 1960.

Hoffman, Frederick J. *The Twenties: American Writing in the Postwar Decade*. Collier ed., New York, 1962.

Means, Gaston B., as told to May Dixon Thacker. *The Strange Death of President Harding*. New York, 1930.

Murry, Robert K. *Red Scare: A Study in National Hysteria, 1919–1920*. Minneapolis, 1955.

Myers, Gustavus. *History of Bigotry in the United States*. New York, 1943.

New Republic, The. 1922–1924.

Paxson, Frederic L. *Postwar Years: Normalcy, 1918–1923*. Vol. 3 of *American Democracy and the World War*. Berkeley, 1948.

Schlesinger, Jr., Arthur M. *The Crisis of the Old Order, 1919–1933*. Cambridge, Mass., 1957.

Sinclair, Andrew. *The Available Man: The Life behind the Masks of Warren Gamaliel Harding*. New York, 1965.

Stevenson, Elizabeth. *Babbitts and Bohemians: The American 1920's*. New York, 1967.

Sullivan, Mark. *Our Times: The Twenties*. New York, 1946.

Wheeler, Burton K., and Healy, Paul F. *Yankee from the West*. New York, 1962.

White, William Allen. *A Puritan in Babylon: The Story of Calvin Coolidge*. New York, 1958.

INDEX